Black Managers in
White Corporations

JOHN P. FERNANDEZ
Yale University

Black Managers in White Corporations

A WILEY-INTERSCIENCE PUBLICATION

JOHN WILEY & SONS
New York • London • Sydney • Toronto

This book is dedicated to
Carolee, Michele, Eleni, and Sevgi.

Copyright © 1975, by John Wiley & Sons, Inc.

All rights reserved. Published simultaneously in Canada.

No part of this book may be reproduced by any means, nor transmitted, nor translated into a machine language without the written permission of the publisher.

Library of Congress Cataloging in Publication Data:

Fernandez, John P   1941–
  Black managers in white corporations.

  "A Wiley-Interscience publication."
  Bibliography: p.
  Includes index.
    1. Executives—United States.   2. Negro executives—
United States.   3. Negroes—Employment—United States.
I. Title.

HF5500.3.U54F47   658.4   75-6820
ISBN 0-471-25764-8

Printed in the United States of America

10 9 8 7 6 5 4 3 2

Preface

Because of the lack of in-depth, comprehensive, and objective studies on the careers of black managers in white corporations, I decided as a graduate student to undertake a comprehensive study of black managers in the white corporate world. The bulk of my research was carried out in 1971–1972. In the years since, my continued research in the academic world and my employment at American Telephone and Telegraph Company in the area of management assessment, evaluation, and development substantiate my initial findings.

The main purpose of this book is to present to members of government and social institutions, the corporate world, social science and business students, as well as other concerned people, a realistic, objective analysis of the present situation of black managers in white corporations. I hope the reader with this analysis will be able to better understand and deal with an economic, social and moral problem that will be with us for a long time.

Government, corporate, and social organization leaders will gain in-depth knowledge about black and white managers' careers, attitudes, and opinions that will be of help in understanding and developing procedures to implement and maintain equal employment opportunities. They will also be offered some concrete suggestions as to what can and should be done to provide all employees equal opportunities.

College students from various fields will be given an intellectual understanding of an extremely crucial economic, social, and moral problem; they will also be assisted in understanding the roles they might play and the problems they might face as members of the corporate world.

Although the book focuses on black managers, it is basically a comparative analysis of the careers, attitudes, and opinions of black and white male and female managers of all levels from six large corporations and two small operations of large corporations in California.

The fact that this is a regional study does not make the findings inapplicable to the United States in general. A Labor Department study on black managers in white corporations throughout the United States supports many of the findings in this study. Therefore, these firms appear to be representative.

The following pages include comparisons of biographical data on the managers, their firms' Affirmative Action Programs, and the present situa-

tion of black managers in the participating firms. In addition, the managers'
views of their companies and the corporate worlds' employment policies
toward blacks, the racial attitudes existing in the companies, and the
managers' image of the most promotable executives are critically analyzed.
The managers' goals, aspirations, work environment, job satisfaction, and
the black managers' relationship to their community and their views on
assimilation and integration are dealt with in detail. Finally, an overview is
presented of the basic problem facing black managers and what can be done
to make the employment policies equal not only for blacks but for all
minorities and majorities, women and men.

JOHN P. FERNANDEZ

New Haven, Connecticut
December 1974

Acknowledgments

Sincerity needs no embellishment. Briefly:

I would like to thank the management of the eight firms for their cooperation, which made this study possible. To protect the anonymity of their firms, I cannot name those executives who advised me before, during, and after the study and gave me much more than compliance.

I must express my deep appreciations to the chairman of my dissertation committee, Professor Harold L. Wilensky and the other two members, Professor Dow Votaw and Professor Robert Blauner.

Professor Wilensky initially suggested the idea of this book. From that initial suggestion to the completion of this book, Professor Wilensky's constructive criticisms and strong support were invaluable. The numerous quotations from his works clearly demonstrate my intellectual debt.

I am deeply grateful to Professor Dow Votaw for patiently reading many drafts, for many valuable suggestions, and for solid moral support when I needed it.

Professor Blauner's comments resulted in some necessary chapter revisions and a reevaluation of some of my analysis; his help was prompt and valuable.

Due to the scope and time frame of this study, I needed assistance, both financially and professionally. Both kinds of support were provided by the Urban Institute. I am greatly indebted to Mike Garn of the Urban Institute, partially because he stretched his budget to the limits to give me financial assistance, but primarily for his faith that such a sensitive in-depth study could be successfully completed and be substantive in its conclusions.

I am also grateful for financial assistance from the Labor Department Manpower Administration.

Caroline Kerr and Gerald Bradshaw conducted half the interviews. I appreciate the excellent job they did under a very strenuous and demanding schedule.

Frank Many, Margaret Brown, and Professor David Nasatir helped me to understand the uses and misuses of the computer and statistical methods.

John Hislop of the Institute of Industrial Relations and coordinator of its management programs helped me to write a brief letter of introduction explaining the purposes of the study. He also gave me valuable advice regarding the general direction of this study.

Dean Sanford Elberg had the patience to listen to me complain about the difficulties in conducting this study; equally important he arranged financial assistance.

Also, I appreciate the assistance of Gene Kofke at A.T.&T. who gave me some financial aid to wrap the study up and for his critical comments on content.

I must also thank Douglas Bray and Donald Grant of A.T.&T. for their assistance in helping me find a publisher, and Pamela Steen of A.T.&T. for giving me numerous critical remarks on content and style.

A great deal of gratitude must be given to Dr. Noelle Sterne, who edited the manuscript.

Finally, my wife Caroline did more than her share in helping me complete this study, from interviewing, key punching, editing, and proofreading to giving endless moral support. I would also like to tell my daughters Michele, Eleni, and Sevgi, whose needs have been greatly neglected over the past few years because of this and other work, that I will now have more time for their needs.

J. P. F.

Contents

CHAPTER ONE

Main Concerns and Methods

A black manager in one of the companies participating in this study was so light skinned that, unless people had been told otherwise, they considered him white. His credentials were impeccable, and at work he was completely accepted. However, when his colleagues discovered that he was black, their behavior changed completely. They no longer asked him for advice. They no longer spoke to him freely or invited him to join them for lunch or a drink. In short, he was isolated and ignored. And this was not the first job on which he had experienced such reactions. This anecdote, a true one, reflects the situation of many blacks in the world of business.

Among the strongest values that pervade American society is the belief that every individual should have an equal right and opportunity in every aspect of life, without prejudicial treatment because of his or her personal characteristics and beliefs. But in the business world, especially at the management level, as seen above, this ethic may be believed, but it is little practiced. Recruitment and promotion have been heavily influenced by such irrelevant factors as social class; religious, organizational, and political affiliations; race; sex; and age.

The most notable characteristic of these factors is their irrelevance to job performance. They are generally conferred by an individual's social background, and most people use these factors as a basis for forming social relationships not related to work. Furthermore, these factors usually cannot be modified either by formal education or work-related experience (see Quinn et al., 1968, pp. 2-3).

It is true that in our decade more equitable practices are slowly taking hold, and potential managers are being hired for sounder reasons, such as experience, training, and general ability. But the situation is still far from truly equitable, and the extent to which progress has been made, and not made, has become a serious and heated issue.

Until recently, one of the most blatantly underplayed inequities in the business world has been the racial factor. One of the prinicpal purposes of this book is to show the immediate need for concrete, determined action by government, business, and society in general to improve the situation of black managers in the predominantly white business world. This book will present new and broader knowledge about black managers that will in turn aid in the understanding of their circumstances. It is hoped that the findings presented here will not only help accelerate the progress of firms and agencies already moving in the direction of full and effective utilization of blacks at all levels of management, but that it will also serve as a spur to those firms that have not yet begun to move.

Blacks suffer particularly from the psychology of group life, in which conformity in areas totally unrelated to ability is made the primary factor for acceptance. The experience of the black manager related at the beginning of this chapter is a dramatic example of this phenomenon. The sociologist Theodore Caplow describes the psychology of group life this way:

[T]he continuity of a group depends upon its ability to enforce its standards upon its members. At each hierarchical level certain secondary qualities determine which of a number of equally intelligent or equally efficient candidates . . . shall be favored. . . . The elders are inclined to select those who are like themselves in general appearance, and who, in addition, have demonstrated specific ability to conform to hierarchic expectations. . . . (Caplow, 1954, pp. 71–72).

The outcome of such organizational structuring "is to bring to the fore persons who have carefully shaped themselves to conform precisely to group norms imposed by authority . . ." (Caplow, 1954, pp. 71–72; for particular application to religion, see Wilensky and Ladinsky, 1967).

Blacks may be able to shape themselves to conform to the corporate "ingroup" in almost every way. They can, if they wish and if they must, change their style of dress, speech, social skills, and religious and political affiliations. But they cannot change their color. Even if they *look* white, like the black manager mentioned earlier, the negative stereotyped attitudes among many whites bar blacks from fully participating in many work activities and social functions directly and indirectly related to their work. In short, blacks are kept from rising in the corporate world, often in extremely insidious ways. One researcher in the area of equal employment opportunities has observed that the "subtle discrimination which may exist in a closely knit group is particularly difficult to overcome. A tacit agreement among certain key leaders in a unit can assure that a Negro never performs work above a minimum level of skill and responsibility" (Bullock, 1966, p. 103).

Although executive career patterns have been studied from the standpoint of personal characteristics and organizational, religious, and political affiliations, there have been few studies of the effects of race on the careers of business managers. This book attempts to fill this void. Thus the central question of this book is: What are the major determinants of the career patterns of black managers in white corporations?

A number of researchers have asked a similar question, but their concern has been primarily with white managers. They have found, for instance, that two-fifths of the American white business elite were educated at Harvard, Yale, or Princeton (Keller, 1953). Many factors besides ability have been found to be crucially important in promotional opportunities—national origin, family status, personal friendships, social and community activities, political and religious affiliation, personal lifestyle, and appearance (Dalton, 1951; Coates and Pellegrin, 1956; Bowman, 1962, 1964; Quinn et al., 1968). These scholars generally have concluded that the most promotable manager in the business world is a native-born white Protestant male with a college education who belongs to the "right" organizations.

The general employment situation of blacks has not been overlooked by researchers, but most of the studies are deficient in some respect. One of the better ones was a large study of 500 black managers sponsored by the Labor Department in 1971–1972. The findings concur with most of those in the present study, but the Labor Department work was much less comprehensive in a wide range of areas. In addition, it did not include the important comparative tool of data on white managers, which is an integral part of this book (Freeman and Fields, 1972; similar drawbacks are found in Morgan and Van Dyke, 1970).

Some studies make broad generalizations unsupported by any concrete evidence (for instance, Northrup, 1968, 1968a, 1970, 1970a). Others rely primarily on data collected from official company representatives, who may feel duty-bound to present the position of blacks in their company in the best possible light (Gourlay, 1965). The above studies plus others do not fully compare the black and white managers, their backgrounds, career patterns, and aspirations. Past studies also almost wholly neglect racial attitudes and possible conflicts between community and company loyalties. And finally, if the difficulties of black managers are discussed at all, they are typically treated as if in a vacuum, out of the social and political contexts, and with no mention of the civil rights movement and the riots of the 1960s. In short, existing studies to date are limited in context and incomplete and superficial in analyses. They do not present a clear, concise, and accurate picture of the black and white managers' views and attitudes toward their own companies and the larger corporate world.

One of the main reasons previous studies have been unsatisfactory is that only in the last 10 years have there been enough black managers in the business world to study, because the white corporate community's "closed-door policy" effectively kept blacks from reaching managerial ranks. There is another equally important reason, obviously connected to this. Exclusion of blacks from management was considered the norm in business, and so questions were rarely asked about the racial composition of managerial ranks. Thus both the interest and opportunity were lacking for such a study as the present one.

Furthermore, the subject is not only very complex; it is also very sensitive. I was often warned by academicians, researchers, and business people of the difficulties of such an undertaking. Primarily, they recognized the white business community's sensitivity and caution on the matter of equal employment opportunities for blacks. They saw little hope for the white business world's cooperation, which would be necessary to obtain needed data. Fortunately, although these warnings were well advised and appreciated, the obstacles proved to be less than expected.

In this book many of the gaps in comprehensiveness left by previous studies are filled. Each chapter deals with a different aspect of the major factors that determine black managers' career patterns in the white business world. Throughout, findings are discussed against the background of occupational mobility theories, especially those dealing with managerial mobility. Chapter 2 draws general profiles of the black and white managers, their personal backgrounds, political and religious beliefs, levels of education, and lifestyles, particularly in terms of contact with the other race. In Chapter 3 the managers' companies are examined from the standpoints of their special policies for the employment of blacks—their Affirmative Action Programs.* Two of the firms, the best and the worst, are compared to assess in general the strengths and weaknesses of the Affirmative Action Programs of the firms. Various explanations for the extreme differences in Affirmative Action Programs are presented and critically analyzed. A direct result of the success or failure of the Affirmative Action Program in a given firm is the number of black managers. Chapter 4 discusses black representation with regard to levels and types of jobs. In addition, the participating firms' efforts are compared with the federal government and the corporate world in general.

Chapters 5 and 6 deal with the same basic question: Why aren't there more blacks in business? In Chapter 5 the managers' views on the overall fairness of their companies' and the corporate world's employment policies toward blacks are explored. Furthermore, the managers explain their reasons for the low number of blacks in management, and these explanations are discussed. Chapter 6 looks more closely at the white managers' racial attitudes. In addition, the racial atmospheres in which blacks must work are discussed.

The managers have definite ideas on what type of person would make the best manager. In this way they influence company employment policies. Chapter 7 deals with their opinions and observations of the kind of person

---

* A written plan of steps to be taken, with definite timetables and goals to ensure the fair treatment of minority ethnic groups and women.

who is most promotable as a manager. Chapter 8 asks how satisfied the managers are with their work environment and specific duties, and what their aspirations in business are. Chapter 9 concentrates on the black managers, specifically in the context of their home communities. This chapter analyzes the effects of the black managers' relationships with their communities as a result of participating in white corporations. The black managers' conflicts are examined also, as well as the kinds of behavior and degree of assimilation they think is necessary or desirable for acceptance in the white business world.

Finally, in Chapter 10 I draw some conclusions as to the overall situation of black managers in white corporations and on the kinds of racism that hinder blacks from equal opportunities throughout the business world and our society in general. I suggest concrete step-by-step action in the form of a managerial program, already in operation in some firms, that would vastly improve the present racial inequities in the corporate world.

THE SELECTION PROCESS: FIRMS

To explore the areas just described, I approached a number of firms in California to request their participation in this study. Eight firms finally participated: two banks, two public utilities, and four manufacturing companies, two of which belong to the same parent company. The other two are smaller subsidiaries of large corporations with headquarters in the East. To ensure anonymity, each firm is given a fictitious name and is referred to by that name. The two public utilities are called Ace Public Utility and Deuce Public Utility; the two banks, Triple A Bank and Triple C Bank; the two manufacturing firms from the same parent company, Aunts Manufacturing Company and Cousins Manufacturing Company; and the two smaller manufacturing firms, Ajax Manufacturing Company and Century Manufacturing Company.

Several criteria were used to select these particular companies. Most important, these firms are all leaders within their industries. Six of the eight are listed in *Fortune 500*. The firms all have a heavy impact on the economy and on employment practices in California, if not the entire country. Four of the firms are among the top ten companies in California in dollar volume, and the six largest have a total employment force of approximately 210,000, of whom 85 percent are employed in California. All these firms are influential in molding both public and private opinion with regard to equal employment opportunities. Their positions within our society make them leading candidates for social change. If the business community is to initiate any great social changes, these companies, because of their size and influence, must be among the leaders.

Four secondary criteria were used to make the final selection of firms. First, it was desirable to have at least two sets of firms from the same industry so that a comparative analysis could be made between the firms—one set in banking and one in public utilities. There was, second, a desire to include two small operations of large corporations with headquarters located outside California (Ajax and Century Manufacturing Companies). This was done to see whether blacks fare better or worse in small, somewhat autonomous branches of large, nationally known corporations. The third aim was to include two firms that are part of the same parent company but relatively independent in policy making, except for general directions set forth by the chairman of the board (Aunts and Cousins Manufacturing Companies). These companies were chosen to discern local similarities and differences in their employment policies toward blacks (Affirmative Action Programs). And finally, it was felt important to obtain a distribution of firms between those subject to public (governmental) regulation and those that are not. By comparing such firms, I hoped to determine to what extent governmental regulation is effective in assisting blacks to gain meaningful equal employment opportunities.

THE SELECTION PROCESS: MANAGERS

The next step was to select managers from all the firms. For selection purposes, "manager" is defined here as including individuals generally designated managers, officials, and professionals. The exact difinitions as given by the Equal Employment Opportunity Commission in its reporting forms follow:

Managers and Officials—Occupations requiring administrative personnel who set broad policies, exercise overall responsibility for execution of these policies, and direct individual departments or special phases of a firm's operations. Includes: officials, executives, middle management, plant managers, department managers and superintendents, salaried foremen who are members of management, purchasing agents and buyers, and kindred workers.

Professionals—Occupations requiring either college graduation or experience of such kind and amount as to provide a comparable background. Includes: accountants and auditors, airplane pilots and navigators, architects, artists, chemists, lawyers, etc.

"Manager" is used in such a broad way because many firms expressed difficulty in distinguishing among managers, officials, and professionals within their companies. In addition, the more technically oriented firms have very few black managers and/or officials but relatively more black professionals.

The firms generally used a stratified, random sampling model, guided by me, to select the participating managers. When possible this model divided the managers by race (black and white), managerial level (lower, middle, and upper), and location (San Francisco/Los Angeles and other). After arriving at this basic breakdown, the firms selected the managers as follows. Each firm chose a random number and from its lists singled out each man or woman, such as every fifth person, whose name coincided with that number.

During the selection process, only two black and two white managers who were asked to participate refused. The two blacks said they did not want to "get involved in any study on race" and the two whites were not interested in participating in any type of study.

The final sample of managers was 272—156 whites and 116 blacks. At the upper level there were only whites—30 managers, including two women. At the middle level there were 34 blacks, including one woman, and 79 whites, including five women. And on the lower level there were 82 blacks, including 22 women, and 47 whites, including 16 women. The number of participating managers in each company by race and sex is shown in Table 1-1. Although the total number of women participating was 46, notice that Cousins, Ajax, and Century Manufacturing had no women participants at all. In fact, Ajax and Century Manufacturing did not have any women employed as managers.

The number of black managers interviewed is not far below that of the white managers. But there is a large difference in percentage. Of the entire

TABLE 1-1 PARTICIPATING BLACK AND WHITE MANAGERS: NUMBERS, RACE, AND SEX

Company	Black Men	Black Women	White Men	White Women
Ace Public Utility	14	12	17	10
Triple C Bank	21	4	25	5
Cousins Manufacturing	13	0	15	0
Aunts Manufacturing	17	2	20	2
Triple A Bank	13	1	13	4
Ajax Manufacturing	3	0	15	0
Century Manufacturing	1	0	15	0
Deuce Public Utility	11	4	13	2
Subtotal	93	23	133	23
Total	116		156	

white managerial work force in all the companies, a total of 0.4 percent was interviewed. This includes 10 percent of the senior policy makers in four of the large firms, excluding Cousins Manufacturing and Deuce Public Utility. There were no blacks in senior positions, as noted above, but of the black middle level managers, approximately 80 percent were interviewed. Table 1-2 shows the total percentages of blacks who participated from each firm.

The final total sample arrived at is not representative of any large population. This is because of the occasional relaxation of the random selection criteria, because of the desire to study special categories of personnel, especially women and blacks above the lower level, because of the companies' personnel restrictions, and in two cases, because of minor company inhibitions on upper-level participants. But the sample nevertheless does represent a wide range of variation in terms of race, sex, and managerial level. These variations will provide many insights into the differences between the career patterns of white managers and those of black managers in white-controlled corporations.

THE SURVEY INSTRUMENT

To understand the factors involved in the corporate situation, data were collected by means of an eight-part administered questionnaire.* Mailed

TABLE 1–2 PARTICIPATING BLACK MAN-
AGERS: PERCENTAGES

Company	Black Managers ($N = 116$)
Ace Public Utility	5
Triple C Bank	22
Cousins Manufacturing	37
Aunts Manufacturing	25
Triple A Bank	30
Ajax Manufacturing	100
Century Manufacturing	50
Deuce Public Utility	40

* For a detailed discussion of the reasons a personally administered questionnaire was used, its general structure, the steps taken to assure that the managers' responses would be as valid as possible, and the quality of the interviews, see Appendix A, pages 219–223.

questionnaires were decided against for a number of reasons, among which was the unlikelihood of a large return. The questionnaire included both closed-end and open-end questions and was divided into the major parts as follows (see Appendix B, pages 224–258, for the entire questionnaire):

1.   The managers' job histories, work environment, job satisfaction, promotional opportunities, and goals.

2.   The managers' relationships to their companies' employment policies in the areas of understanding, practice, agreement, and influence.

3.   The managers' views and attitudes about past and present opportunities for black managers in their firms and in the corporate world as a whole.

4.   For whites: their views and attitudes toward blacks. For blacks: their views and attitudes about their experiences in the corporate world and the effects on them of membership in the business community.

5.   The managers' image of the most promotable manager in business.

6. and 7.   Views and comments of the companies' official personnel representatives concerned with the implementation of corporate Affirmative Action Programs.

8.   The managers' biographical backgrounds: race, sex, family history, education, marital status, organizational affiliations.

Approximately half of the interviews with both black and white managers were conducted by me, a black, and the other half by two white interviewers, Gerald Bradshaw and Caroline Kerr. No significant differences were found in the aggregate responses of the managers with respect to candor and sincerity in relation to the race of the interviewer. Concerning the quality of the interviews, only 3 percent of the black interviews and 3 percent of the white were considered of questionable reliability, but 74 percent of the black and 51 percent of the white interviews were rated to be of high quality.

In retrospect, the decision to use an administered questionnaire seems to have been a wise one, because the managers supplied a rich body of data on which to draw.

CHAPTER TWO

General Profile of the Managers

What kinds of families do the managers come from, what kinds of education have they had, what are their families like now, and what are their major activities and beliefs? Can typical profiles be drawn along racial lines? These are some of the questions to be answered here.

GEOGRAPHICAL BACKGROUNDS

Although most of the participating firms are based in the San Francisco Bay and Los Angeles areas, the managers come from almost every state in the union. Of the white managers, 50 percent grew up in California and 27 percent in the Northeast or Midwest. Of the blacks, 22 percent grew up in California and 38 percent in the South. The remaining percentages represent managers' childhood and adolescent years in various states throughout the country. The managers' adult lives, because of the regional sample, have been spent primarily in California. This is true for the vast majority of the whites and a majority of the blacks.

AGES

As will be seen throughout this study, age is one of the factors that has a strong influence on many of the managers' attitudes and opinions. The black managers who participated are generally much younger than the white managers. This is shown in Table 2-1. The mean age of the black managers is 32 and of the white managers 41. This large difference in age may be accounted for by the fact that the firms have only recently (1967) begun to hire and promote more than a few token blacks into management positions. When the firms began to seek more black managers, only Ace Public Utility already had a large number of blacks in nonmanagerial positions whom the company could promote to managerial status; therefore, the other companies began to actively recruit young, college-educated blacks.

However, some of the firms have recently sought to hire older, college-educated blacks who have already had management experience in universities, government (the military), social agencies, or their own businesses. For instance, the Affirmative Action Program coordinator from

TABLE 2–1   THE MANAGERS' AGES (in %)

Age	Black Managers ($N = 116$)	Cumulative Frequencies	White Managers ($N = 156$)	Cumulative Frequencies
21–25 years	13	13	2	2
26–30 years	26	39	10	12
31–35 years	27	66	9	21
36–40 years	18	84	19	40
41–45 years	9	93	19	59
46–50 years	6	99	20	89
51–55 years	0	0	15	94
56–60 years	1	100	5	99
Over 60 years	0	—	1	100
Refuse to give	0	—	1	101
Total	100		101[a]	

$p \leq .05$

[a] The percentage is over 100 because of rounding errors.

Aunts Manufacturing says:

My firm is discovering that there are many blacks with technical and professional backgrounds in the government services who could bring valuable experience into our company. Also, we just hired a black in Public Relations who wanted to give the corporate world a chance after being in business for himself for five years.

This trend can be seen by the fact that of the blacks over 40 years of age, 47 percent have been with their firms four or fewer years, all have college degrees and lengthy experience in at least one of the work areas mentioned above, and all are middle level managers.

FAMILY BACKGROUNDS

Parents' Educational Levels

In many cases social scientists have noted that aspects of managers' family backgrounds can have a lot to do with the managers' later achievements. When the educational levels of the managers' mothers and fathers are examined, especially along racial lines, the results are significant. The group in which the highest percentage completed four years of college is the white managers' fathers, 21 percent. Next are the black managers' mothers, 19 percent, the black managers' fathers, 15 percent, and last the white managers' mothers, 13 percent. Although the white parents have been the more privileged, it is the black managers' mothers who are the most highly educated. Their mean educational level is 12 years and 1 month. The white parents are next with 11 years and 6 months for the fathers and 11 years and 5 months for the mothers. The black fathers have a mean level of 11 years and 2 months. (See Table D-1, Appendex D, page 279, for breakdowns by years of the parental educational levels.)

Fathers' Best Occupations

Although there were no great differences between the black and white fathers' educational levels, there were significant differences in their best occupations. Whereas two-thirds of the black managers' fathers were laborers, skilled and unskilled, two-thirds of the white managers' fathers were professionals, managers, or business owners (see Table D-2, Appendix D, page 280). The discrepancies in occupational achievement can be attributed to the lack of opportunities black people have had.

When the educational levels of the black fathers are correlated with their best jobs, it is found that the educated fathers generally found employment in the professional areas serving the black community. They realized that, primarily because of racial discrimination, their best chances for employment were within black communities rather than in white corporations.

A substantial majority of the white managers come from the middle or upper class.* Sixty-five percent of all the white managers' fathers and 80 percent of the upper level white managers' fathers are middle or upper class. This is not surprising in the light of larger studies in this area that have found that between 60 and 70 percent of the business elite come from middle and upper class family backgrounds. Many sociological studies have suggested that the reason for such a pattern is that children born to middle and upper class families have more advantages in the corporate world than those born to lower class families because the corporate system is still considerably status bound (Taussig and Joslyn, 1932; Miller, ed., 1952; Newcomer, 1955; Warner and Abeggelen, 1955; Bendix, 1956; Mills, 1963).

But two-thirds of the black managers who are now in the middle class come from working class backgrounds. This is a measure of an impressive degree of intergenerational mobility, and a sign that to a small extent discrimination against blacks has decreased. Over the past 10 years, more

---

* The classes are defined in this study as follows: working class includes families in which the father held a position such as skilled or unskilled laborer, service worker, small farmer, or porter. Middle and upper class include families in which the father held a position such as business owner, corporate manager, educator, or professional.

blacks have had an opportunity to obtain better educations and better jobs than had their parents.

EDUCATION

Relationship to Family Background

As one might expect, for both the black and white managers, there is a strong relationship between parental educational levels and those of the managers themselves. For example, 83 percent of the black parents and 63 percent of the white parents who have bachelor degrees had sons or daughters with at least bachelor degrees. The stronger relationship of the blacks probably results from parental pressure for the children to achieve, especially since the black parents able to obtain a college education achieved one under extremely oppressive conditions. As one black middle level manager at Cousins Manufacturing recalls: "Both my parents, who were pretty highly educated, were always encouraging my brothers and sisters and myself to go to school. Make something of yourself, they kept saying, you know you have to be better than the white man."

It is not only the middle class that has a strong desire for education. A recent study of welfare recipients revealed that welfare mothers are at least as concerned as the white middle class about their children obtaining the best education and training possible. The welfare children expressed a similar concern and desire (Goodwin, 1972). The participating managers further attest to this concern. Of those from working class families whose parents had fewer than twelve years of schooling, 55 percent of the black managers and 43 percent of the white managers received college degrees.

It is well known among social scientists that lack of money and other restrictions on obtaining higher education have limited the number of black and working class people obtaining a college education (see Sexton, 1961; Warner and Abeggelen, 1955, pp. 95–114; 1963, pp. 34–58). However, it has also been rightly noted: "If education is oftentimes taken for granted by the business class, it is no exaggeration to say that it evokes the fervor of a religion, a means of salvation, among a large section of the working class" (Lynd and Lynd, 1929, p. 187). The managers bear out this statement. On the one hand, although two out of three of the black managers come from working class backgrounds, nine out of ten of them had completed at least one year of college. On the other hand, two out of three of the white managers come from middle and upper class backgrounds and only three out of four had completed a year of college.

Recently many white middle class students have been questioning the necessity of a college degree. While these white men and women are questioning this need, they are being replaced by whites from the working class and large numbers of persons from minority groups who believe that a college education is the steppingstone to a better life (see Peterson, 1972). Table 2-2 shows the managers' education levels. Considering society's preferential treatment of men and the recent emphasis on high educational achievement for advancement in business, it is not unexpected to find that the men are more highly educated than the women, and the higher the managers are in the business organization the more likely they are to have college degrees. But what is especially striking is that cumulatively black men and women of all ages have completed more years of college than their white counterparts.

By managerial level, the blacks outstrip the whites both in high school and college achievement. Whereas 28 percent of the white middle level managers and 13 percent of the white upper level managers have only a high school education or less, only 3 percent of the black middle level managers have a high school education or less. Of the lower level managers, 32 percent of the whites have a maximum of a high school education, compared to only 11 percent of the blacks. As to college achievement, not only do 30 percent more of the black middle level managers than their white peers have at least a Bachelor degree, but also twice the percentage of the black middle level managers have done graduate work, 46 percent as compared to 23 percent of the whites.

These figures support a consistent claim made by the vast majority of the

TABLE 2-2   MANAGERS' EDUCATIONAL LEVELS (in %)

Educational Levels	Black Men ($N = 93$)	Black Women ($N = 23$)	White Men ($N = 133$)	White Women ($N = 23$)
Grade school	0	0	1	0
9th grade	0	0	1	0
10th grade	0	0	1	0
12th grade	8	13	20	52
One year of college	5	22	7	13
Two years of college	20	26	12	9
Three years of college	2	0	2	0
Bachelor degree	42	30	29	9
Graduate school	23	9	28	17
Total	100	100	101[a]	100

$p \leq .05$

[a] The percentage is over 100 because of rounding errors.

black managers and supported by many of the white managers in this study: Black managers must be much more qualified than whites in order to get equivalent positions. The figures also refute the opposite claim made by most whites in business, that blacks do *not* have to be more qualified to reach positions similar to those held by whites. (These views will be discussed in greater detail in Chapters 5 and 6.)

A typical example of this latter claim is found in the work of D. E. Kidder et al., in which their sample showed that more of their black respondents completed 16 or more years of school than their white respondents (52 percent to 46 percent). Yet the proportion of whites and blacks who attended college in their sample was virtually the same, 78 percent and 76 percent. They concluded: "These figures lend little support to speculation that blacks must overcompensate in educational attainment to reach an occupational level comparable with less-qualified whites" (Kidder et al., 1971, p. 20). But they based their conclusions on a sample of only 33 blacks who were selected in various nonrandom fashions such as "leads, . . . contacts and the like" (p. 16). Furthermore, only 50 white managers made up the white sample. The information the authors presented on the white managers' educational achievement was drawn from another study, and the selection procedure they used was not discussed. Therefore, their conclusions are quite dubious, although many whites persist in using such information to justify their positions.

Subject Areas of Managers' Degrees

The evidence in this study for the managers' educational achievements and what they signify contrasts greatly with the findings of Kidder et al. As Table 2-2 has shown, almost two-thirds of the black managers have achieved the bachelor degree. The white business community has often claimed that it is unable to find qualified black managers because most blacks have degrees in the social sciences and humanities rather than in business and science. But in our sample almost equal proportions of the black and white managers received degrees in the social sciences and humanities—38 percent of the blacks and 37 percent of the whites. Twenty-five percent of the managers of both races earned degrees in scientific fields, and 44 percent of the black and 59 percent of the white managers received degrees in the technical–professional fields—business administration, accounting, economics, and law. (See Appendix C, pages 259–278, for the frequency distributions of the degrees the managers received and the subject areas of their degrees.)

In a longitudinal study of over 400 managers in the Bell Telephone System, Bray et al. found similar areas of degree concentration, and this study included *only* white men (Bray et al., 1974, p. 41). Thus the contention that blacks are underqualified in the necessary specializations is false—the firms in this study have been able to find blacks with business and scientific backgrounds. Furthermore, these firms utilize managers with all types and levels of educational training, many of whom, mostly white men, are without college degrees.

Colleges and Universities the Managers Attended

The majority of black managers attended predominantly white colleges or universities, a fact similar to the findings of the Labor Department study of 500 black managers (Freeman and Fields, 1972, p. 12). But a relatively high proportion of the black managers, 35 percent, attended predominantly black southern colleges or universities. This high percentage of graduates from largely black colleges in these California-based participating firms is probably due to recruitment efforts to hire blacks with scientific backgrounds.

Most of the white managers whose degrees are from public universities and colleges attended the "select" public schools, especially the fine University of California system. Only a few of the managers attended high prestige private schools such as Harvard, Stanford, and MIT. (For the frequency distribution of the colleges and universities attended by the managers see Appendix C, pages 259–278).

Students of social stratification have often observed that the type of school attended is an important factor in determining success in business. For example, it has been found that graduates of Harvard, Yale, and Princeton go further and earn more money throughout their careers than graduates from any other group of colleges (Bendix and Lipset, 1953, p. 474; see also Haveman and West, 1952, pp. 179–181). Our data on the schools attended by the white managers tends to support this pattern. Of the white managers with college degrees, 61 percent of those managers at the upper level had attended either Ivy League colleges or prestigious public or private universities. This is almost three times the percentage of select school attendance of the lower level managers.

With the black managers, the pattern is somewhat different. Twenty-one percent of both the middle and lower level managers had attended Ivy League or predominantly white select schools. The black managers from the prestigious schools have all been with their firms less than four years. Thus, it remains to be seen if their educational backgrounds will have the same "payoff" effect it appears to have for the white managers.

In sum, although the educational levels of the black and white managers' parents are not significantly different, with regard to fathers' occupations as indications of class origins it can be said that two in three of the white managers come from middle and upper class backgrounds, whereas in sharp contrast two in three of the black managers come from working class back-grounds. Nevertheless, the black managers have achieved a higher level of education than the whites, and in the same subject areas.

There seems to be a shift downward in social origins: The black managers entering the business world in recent years are coming more from the work-ing class than the middle class. With white managers, regardless of length of service, approximately 33 percent come from working class backgrounds. With the black managers, generally those who have more years of corporate experience, approximately 66 percent come from the middle class, whereas of those blacks with fewer years of experience only 30 percent come from the middle class.

To give the reader an insight into the composite of family and educational differences between the black and the white managers, backgrounds of two typical managers are presented below.

Mr. B. is now a middle level manager. He is a 32-year-old black, born in Virginia. His father had an eighth-grade education and is a janitor; his mother completed two years of college and teaches school.

Mr. B. says he remembers that as a boy he heard his parents tell him often to get all the education he could and "make something of yourself." His father also emphasized the importance of a business education, "so that I could get a job in the business world or go into my own business." So he attended Hampton Institute, a top-grade all-black college in Virginia, where he majored in accounting.

He was recruited directly from college by his company. In California he enrolled in Golden Gate College and graduated with an M.B.A. in business administration while working full-time in the company.

The white manager, Mr. H., is a 45-year-old upper level manager. He comes from a professional family, his father a doctor and his mother a nurse. Tall and good-looking, Mr. H. attributes his rapid rise in part to his looks and outgoing personality. Although he reached business by a somewhat circuitous route, Mr. H. feels that a business career was almost inevitable "with my background."

He had majored in English at Stanford, following a long-standing desire to become a writer. After a short stint in this field, he went back to Stan-ford to study law but dropped out fairly soon. A friend who worked for the company told him about the potential opportunities there, and Mr. H. then joined the company, beginning a successful career.

THE MANAGERS' SPOUSES

As there are many striking differences between the black and white managers with regard to family backgrounds, so there are differences in the backgrounds and present status of their spouses. But before these areas are discussed, something needs to be said about marital status in general in the corporate world.

The managers were asked no specific questions dealing directly with marital status as a help or hindrance in promotions, but several of the managers of both sexes and both races indicate that there are definite disadvantages to being single, separated, or divorced. For instance, a white divorced woman from Ace Public Utility says: "My promotion was held up for six months. Why? My supervisor and his boss both believed divorce was a sign of immaturity, instability, and emotionalism in a woman—but not in a man." In another case, a middle-aged black woman believes that being divorced has not hindered her particular career to any great extent, but this is because of her unique training in chemistry and library services, a combination in great demand.

The reasons against being single may be quite different for men managers. As an upper level white manager from Triple A Bank says: "Single and divorced men are handicapped. At the upper levels, especially in banks and public-related industries, socializing is very important. A man needs a wife to help entertain all the way down the line, from the bosses to the customers and subordinates."

However, being single may be advantageous for one category of manager—the older woman. The male-dominated bureaucracy believes that single, older women are more likely to stay with the firms than married women whose family responsibilities may take precedence. It is striking that none of the white women in upper and middle management positions was ever married (see Appendix C, page 259, for the frequency distribution of the managers' marital statuses).

Over half of the managers believe that a helpful spouse should be an important factor in considering a potential manager. And over half also believe that both their firms and business in general take this into consideration. Again a sign of our male-dominated society, the men managers of both races feel this way more than the women.

The Spouses' Backgrounds and Educations

What kind of spouses do the managers marry? Our data show that the managers most often marry at their class level. As with the managers' own fathers, white spouses' fathers are more likely to be business managers or owners or professionals, and black spouses' fathers are more likely to be skilled or unskilled laborers or government workers. Also, the higher the educational level of the manager, the higher is his or her spouse's educational level (see Appendix C, pages 259–278, for the frequency distributions of the best occupations achieved by spouses' fathers and the educational levels of the managers' spouses).

Do the Spouses Work?

There are three answers to this question—one based on sex, one on managerial level, and one on race. Spouses of all of the women managers of both races work. Also, the higher the level of the manager, the less likely is the spouse to work, especially if the manager is a white male. And finally, of the white managers' spouses only 28 percent work, compared to more than twice this for the black managers' spouses—66 percent. One explanation for such a large difference in percentage is mentioned by some of the black managers: Because most of them are on the lower level, their pay is lower and their spouses work to supplement the family income. As one black manager says: "We couldn't make it if my wife didn't work too. I guess a lot of people at my level are in the same boat."

It is possible that if the male black managers are allowed to move up the occupational ladder, their spouses would cease to work—first because supplementary income would not be crucial, and second, because the wives would need to perform the social functions characteristic at the higher levels. But such a change may not occur at all. As the women's movement gains ground and new and equal opportunities for women become more widespread, women will increasingly take their place as independent workers and professionals.

THE MANAGERS' AFFILIATIONS: RELIGIOUS, POLITICAL, COMMUNITY

With an idea of the managers' family background and marital status, the profiles of the managers are beginning to take shape. For a more comprehensive view, we also need to inquire about their beliefs and affiliations within their communities.

Religious Preferences

The managers' religious preferences are shown in Table 2-3. Of the blacks, the largest percentage who express a preference are Baptists—29 percent. Closely following this is 28 percent of the blacks with no religious preference. Of the whites, the most frequent religious preferences are in the high-status Protestant religions (Presbyterian, Episcopalian, and Methodist) for a total of 32 percent. These preferences are closely followed by 29 percent who are of the Catholic faith, and 17 percent who have no religious preference.

The sizable secular minority and the large Catholic minority among the whites are striking. A study made 20 years ago, and generally believed since, pointed out the large discrepancy between the Catholic population in the United States, 33 percent, and the Catholics at the executive level in business, 9 percent (Newcomer, 1955, pp. 46–48). But the high percentage of Catholic managers in the present study gives clear testimony that, at least

TABLE 2–3   MANAGERS' RELIGIOUS PREFERENCES (in %)

Religion	Black Managers (N = 116)	White Managers (N = 156)
Baptist	29	1
None	28	17
Methodist	11	7
Catholic	9	29
Episcopalian	5	9
Lutheran	4	5
Other Protestant denominations	4	3
Church of Christ	4	0
Presbyterian	2	16
Protestant—no specific denomination	2	8
Jewish	1	1
Other denominations—not Protestant	1	1
Mormon	0	3
Total	100	100

in the West, religious discrimination against Catholics in the business community has substantially decreased. (However, it should be noted that Catholics may still be highly discriminated against in the East and Midwest, where negative associations of Catholics with working class ethnic backgrounds may be stronger in the business community than in the West.)

There is apparently still much discrimination against Jews. The fact that only 1 percent of the managers are Jewish indicates that Jews are still finding it extremely difficult to pursue careers in Protestant-dominated firms. When the managers are asked whether they think being Jewish helps, hinders, or is irrelevant to promotion, almost one in three of the blacks and one in four of the whites say that it is harmful in the business world in general. With regard to their own firms, one in five of the blacks and one in ten of the whites believe that being Jewish is a detriment.

The Protestant denominations are still the favored religions. Although only 49 percent of the white managers are Protestant, compared to an earlier finding of 70 percent for the business world (Bowman, 1964, p. 8), the proportion of the white managers who are Presbyterian, Episcopalian, and Methodist is still very high in relation to the small proportion of these religions in the overall United States population.

It is apparent that most of the whites who succeed to high managerial levels in the participating firms belong to one of these high-status Protestant denominations. For example, of the white upper level managers, almost half

(42 percent) are members of these denominations, as are 29 percent of the middle level managers, and 6 percent of the lower level managers. This is not the case at all for blacks. Thus it seems that the business community not only favors Protestantism in general but favors those individuals, especially whites, who belong specifically to the more prestigious Protestant denominations.

The majority of the managers in this study attend religious services infrequently, if at all. More than half of both black and white managers attend church only a few times a year or not at all, although attendance is higher among Catholic managers than among Protestants.

Low church attendance reflects a general societal trend away from organized religious observance and seems to have an ironic relationship to racial prejudice among the managers. Among the whites who attend church only a few times yearly or never, 86 percent express no negative racial attitude toward blacks (the managers' negative racial attitudes will be dealt with more completely in Chapter six). Among the whites who occasionally attend church, 60 percent express only a few negative racial attitudes. But those white managers who attend more frequently hold more racist views than the preceding groups—35 percent of the managers at least frequently attending church express few negative racial attitudes.

It has been noted that those who attend church frequently have not been affected greatly, if at all, by the Christian doctrine. Angus Campbell comments in his study of 2945 whites and 2814 blacks that the churches' contribution "to racial patterns in this country has been to preserve the status quo. . . . Despite [the churches'] historic dedication to the inculcation of moral values, their influence on the racial attitudes of their constituents appears to have been very limited" (A. Campbell, 1971, p. 68). Among the Christian religions, Catholic as well as the Protestant denominations, there is little difference in racial attitudes, a finding also noted by Campbell (p. 47). But there is a difference when it comes to Jews. Because of the few Jews in the present study, a comparison between their attitudes and those of Christians was impossible, but Campbell was able to compare them: "The pattern of Jewish attitudes presents a striking contrast to that of Catholics and Protestants; Jews are consistently more positive in their orientation toward . . . racial issues (pp. 47–48).

However, more recently Jewish support for civil rights has been decreasing. This is because of the differences between blacks and Jews on government-required goals and timetables for business employment and enrollment in educational institutions. The Jewish response is generally that these goals are discriminatory in the blacks' favor and against Jews, whereas most blacks and other minorities feel such requirements are necessary, at least for the present and near future, to help them gain their equal rights.

Political Orientations

Like religious preferences, the managers' political philosophies and affiliations divide substantially along racial lines. The largest percentage (43
percent) of the black managers consider themselves liberals, and the largest
percentage (41 percent), almost the same, of the white managers consider
themselves moderates. Table 2-4 shows how the managers categorize
themselves.

Significant variations occur when age is used as the control variable.*
Among the white managers, the younger ones see themselves as liberals and
the older ones see themselves as conservatives. It is significant also that with
regard to racist attitudes, the whites who are conservative and "right
winger" have stronger racist views than those seeing themselves as moderate
and liberal. With age as the control variable for blacks, the younger ones
are more likely to consider themselves liberals, and the older ones more
likely to see themselves as moderates.

With sex as the control variable, there is not much difference between the
white men and women, except that none of the women see themselves as a
"right winger." But an interesting contradiction among the black managers
occurs when the results are controlled by sex. More women than men
consider themselves moderates: two-thirds as opposed to one-fourth.
However, throughout this study the black women are much more critical

TABLE 2–4   MANAGERS' POLITICAL PHILOSOPHIES
(in %)

Political Philosophy	Black Managers (N = 116)	White Managers (N = 156)
Radical	8	1
Liberal	43	27
Moderate	33	41
Conservative	6	27
"Right winger"	0	3
Other	10	1
Total	100	100

* Application of a control variable is a method for looking at certain responses by
means of certain characteristics. Thus here we are able to see how responses about
political affiliation differ by age groups.

than the men about the opportunities for blacks in business. In addition, black women have assimilated less into white society than black men (this will be discussed further in Chapter 9). One would expect a moderate or conservative to be less critical on racial issues and more assimilative than a liberal or radical.

Given the managers' political philosophies, the pattern of political affiliation shown in Table 2-5 is no surprise. Analysis of the managers' political philosophies and affiliations clearly shows that the older, more educated, higher level whites are most likely to be moderate or conservative Republicans. The older, middle level black managers are more likely to consider themselves moderate Democrats rather than liberal Democrats or Independents. Thus, age and corporations may exert considerable influence among executives toward a convergence to a moderately conservative political stance.

Community Activities

It has long been known that, in addition to the desirability of certain religious and political affiliations, one of the more helpful factors for success in the business world is participation in community and civic activities and membership in the "right" clubs. In an earlier study of 2000 managers, it was found that the vast majority believed that community and cultural interests ideally should help bring promotions to supervisory positions and above (Bowman, 1964, pp. 18, 22). In the present study, as might be expected, the higher the position, the more likely is the manager to belong to various civic, social, and professional organizations. Thirty-two percent of the black managers and 26 percent of the whites belong to no organizations at all, but most of these managers are on the lower levels of management.

For our purposes, whether the managers' organizations are racially mixed or not becomes important, and Table 2-6 shows the managers' organizations with these breakdowns. Although in general large differences do not occur between the racially mixed and unmixed organizations, important differences do occur when certain variables are controlled. The younger, lower level black managers, especially women, are more likely to belong to all-black organizations than the older, middle level black males. There are several reasons for this difference. Younger black managers have grown up in a time when black pride and black awareness were being increasingly emphasized. These people are therefore more likely to gravitate toward organizations that either have few whites or totally exclude them. In addition, the younger black managers are almost all at the lower rung of the managerial ladder and thus are not required to participate in many social and nonsocial organizations that might have white members.

The white middle and upper level managers are older and more conserva-

TABLE 2–5 MANAGERS' POLITICAL AFFILIATIONS (in %)

Political Affiliations	Black Managers ($N = 114$)[a]	White Managers ($N = 154$)[a]
Democrat	72	33
Republican	4	61
Independent	22	5
Other	2	1
Total	100	100

[a] There were missing data in two black and two white cases.

TABLE 2–6 MANAGERS' ORGANIZATIONAL AFFILIATIONS (in %)

Organizational Affiliations	Black Managers		White Managers	
	Whites Belong ($N = 116$)	Blacks Only ($N = 116$)	Blacks Belong ($N = 156$)	Whites Only ($N = 156$)
Civil Rights	34	0	9	0
Professional	20	3	30	3
Business or civic	19	4	30	9
Fraternal	11	15	3	19
Charitable	9	5	14	1
Church-oriented	7	3	13	13
Social	7	8	4	10
Political	5	2	7	0
Neighborhood	4	7	10	8
Veterans	2	0	2	1
Organizations of the same race (generally social and company organizations)	0	9	0	0
Country club	0	0	1	8
Other	2	1	1	8
Belong to no organizations	32%		26%	
Total[a]	120	57	124	80

[a] The percentages do not equal 100 because many of the managers belonged to more than one organization.

24

tive and, because there are only a few blacks above the lower level, the whites have less interaction with blacks at work. These middle and upper level older whites' positions require them to belong to more organizations, and it is not surprising that more of these organizations are all-white than racially mixed.

INTERRACIAL SOCIAL CONTACTS

The amount of contact with the opposite race outside of the work environment has much to do with overall racial attitudes and prejudices, as will be seen in the following chapters. Although the percentages of black and white managers who belong to racially mixed and unmixed organizations are quite similar, there is a large difference in their degree of contact at social functions, as Table 2-7 shows. The black managers have a great deal more contact with whites at functions not related to work. Furthermore, white friends of the black managers are generally not from their jobs but from outside contacts. Even though 71 percent of the white managers have frequent contact with blacks on the job, only 26 percent have frequent contact with blacks in social situations. The types and frequencies of social contact are summarized in Table 2-8.

The neighborhoods the managers live in, which can provide many of the opportunities for social contacts, fall into similar patterns. Although almost half the white managers have some blacks living in their neighborhoods, almost three-fourths of the whites live in areas where black residents are 5 percent or fewer. Only one white manager lives in a neighborhood where blacks comprise 50 percent or more of the population.

Almost half the black managers live in neighborhoods where blacks comprise the majority of the population. One-fifth of the blacks live in predominantly white areas, where black residents total 10 percent or less, but

TABLE 2–7 TOTAL FREQUENCY OF NONWORK SO-
CIAL CONTACT WITH THE OPPOSITE RACE (in %)

Frequency of Contact	Black Managers ($N = 116$)	White Managers ($N = 156$)
Very frequent	24	6
Fairly frequent	31	17
Not very frequent	32	47
Never	13	30
Total	100	100

TABLE 2–8 TYPE AND FREQUENCY OF NONWORK SOCIAL CONTACT WITH THE OPPOSITE RACE (in %)

Type and Frequency of Contact	Black Managers (N = 116)	White Managers (N = 156)
NOT VERY FREQUENTLY		
Only at civic functions	8	27
Mostly at parties	24	28
A few friends	14	8
Neighbors	3	1
Church activities	0	5
FAIRLY AND VERY FREQUENTLY		
Civic functions	12	11
Social functions such as parties, dinners, picnics, and the like	33	9
Personal friends	41	16
Neighbors	9	1
Educational functions such as attending classes, teaching	0	2
Church activities	2	9
TOTAL[a]	146	117

[a] The total percentages are more than 100 because many managers have contact in more than one area.

this choice of area for the blacks is usually because of proximity to their jobs. Most of the whites, in accordance with much of the country's mobility patterns, have moved many miles away to all-white suburbs, leaving the urban centers heavily populated with minorities. In general, then, both in activities and neighborhoods, there is relatively little social contact between the races outside of work, a finding supported by the Labor Department study of 500 black managers (Freeman and Fields, 1972, p. 61).

The fact that most of the white managers have very little contact with blacks outside of work at social functions indicates that blacks are not fully accepted, equal members of the work group; they are excluded from participating in activities outside work with their white subordinates, peers, and superiors, activities that not only make a work situation more fulfilling but also play an important role in one's promotional opportunities and successes. As the black social scientist St. Clair Drake has observed: "The life styles of the Negro upper class are similar to those of the white upper middle class, but it is only in rare instances that Negroes have been incorporated into the clique and associational life of this group. . . ." He goes on to note that blacks at the higher class levels are not victimized in the same way as lower class blacks, but there is nevertheless a more subtle type of exclusion that also cuts off their avenues of expression:

Their victimization flows primarily from the fact that the social system keeps them half in and half out, preventing the free and easy contact with their occupational peers which they need; and it often keeps them from making the kind of significant intellectual and social contributions to the national welfare that they might make if they were white (Drake, 1965, p. 119).

The black managers attest to such exclusion from social interaction, and they cite this as a major incidental pressure connected with work, one that whites do not have to suffer. They tell of incidents where they are not invited to lunch with co-workers or to social functions outside of work. If they are invited, no one socializes with them. A lower level black manager at Triple A Bank, in relating some of the incidents he has experienced, recalls: "I've been told many times by white co-workers or bosses, I'm not a racist but my wife is, so I can't invite you home for dinner."

In addition, because of the growing simultaneous emphasis on employing and promoting both women and blacks, a rather ironic phenomenon may be occurring that will prove detrimental to the careers of black male managers. White men probably harbor a great deal of concern of a racist, stereotypical nature about the interaction of black men and white women. Therefore, expecially in companies with large numbers of white women, the black mens' career opportunities could be limited by the white male managers.

Would the Managers Marry Across Racial Lines?

The tremendous concern on the part of white male managers about interaction between black men and white women, as well as the whites' own lack of social interaction with blacks, is related to the fact that substantial numbers of the white managers, 72 percent, would not consider a black as a possible marriage partner. An issue of *Jet* reported similar findings: that only 29 percent of the white population approves of interracial marriage, compared to 58 percent of the black population (*Jet,* Dec. 7, 1972, p. 30, Gallup Poll).

The older whites in the present study are much less likely to imagine themselves marrying a black than are the younger whites, although there is little difference by sex among the whites. Men and women feel quite similarly that interracial marriage is far from likely for them, but women less strongly.

The situation is very different among the blacks. Until the late 1960s there was little opposition to interracial marriage throughout the black community. But in recent years many blacks, especially among the women and the young, have become vocal against interracial marriage. They feel strongly that any black who marries a white is brainwashed and psychologically oppressed by white America.

The black managers bear this out: a very high percentage of the women, 74 percent, compared to only 27 percent of the men, could hardly imagine themselves marrying a white. Furthermore, 50 percent more black managers age 30 or younger than those over 30 could hardly see themselves in an interracial marriage. Again we see that the younger black managers are much more involved than the older ones in the black movement toward racial pride and awareness.

There seems to be a relationship between the degree of contact the white managers have with blacks and their views about marrying blacks. For example, of the whites who have a great deal of contact with blacks, 46 percent could hardly imagine marrying a black, compared to 76 percent of those whites with no contact with blacks at all. In addition, the less contact the white managers have with blacks, the stronger are their feelings against interracial marriage.

The trend is similar for black contacts with whites. Black managers with the most frequent white contact are more likely than those with little contact to believe they could marry a white. Since those blacks with the most contact are the middle level males over 30 years of age, more integrationist attitudes are to be expected than from the lower level, younger managers.

REPRESENTATIVE PROFILES

A White Woman

The picture of the managers is now virtually complete. For some overall views of the managers, I now present representative profiles, the first of an upper level white woman. It will be seen that even for white women, those who reach the top (she is one of the two women to have reached the upper level) are similar to most of the successful white men in every respect except for marital status.

She comes from a middle class background, her father a college graduate and owner of a retail appliance business and her mother a housewife with a high school education. This manager is single and has lived all of her 44 years in California in all-white areas. She has a Bachelors degree in business administration from the University of Southern California. A Presbyterian, she goes to church regularly and considers herself a moderate Republican. Outside of her job she has little contact with blacks, and she could not imagine marriage to one.

Her community civic life is an active one and closely tied to her position in the corporate world. Primarily because of her position, she was a vice-president of the Hollywood Bowl Association. A past president of Women Executives, she also belongs to the Urban League and is on the board of directors of the Los Angeles Chamber of Commerce.

A Black Man

This representative black man is a middle level manager. He is 43 years old and spent most of his life in Illinois but now lives in a predominantly black area in San Francisco.

Coming from a broken home, he knows that his father graduated from high school but does not know how his father earned a living. His mother had a college degree and was a topographical draftsman. Apparently highly motivated by his mother, this manager has earned a Master degree from the University of Chicago.

He is married to a woman who completed one year of college. She works for the same company as he but in the Real Estate Division. Although married to a black woman, he can, he says, imagine marriage to a white. A liberal Democrat, he has no religious preferences and attends church once or twice a year.

Partly because of his business position and partly because of his interracial concerns, he is extremely active in many organizations. For instance, he has been an active member of the NAACP since 1946. He belongs to an integrated community neighborhood group and a Poor People's Council, which is an all-black group formed to pressure industry into providing blacks equal opportunities. Although a member of a college fraternity and the black Masons, he devotes little time to these groups, which he sees as irrelevant, and prefers instead to give more time to the American Society for Training and Development and a boys' club of which he is a member of the board of directors. Primarily because of his community involvements, he has frequent contact with whites outside the job.

A Black Woman

This young black woman, a lower level manager, is 28 years of age and comes from a family in which her father completed high school and was a sergeant in the Army. Her mother had only 10 years of schooling and was a housewife.

This manager has been a lifelong resident of California and now lives with her husband in Oakland in an almost all-black neighborhood. Both she and her husband have only high school educations, and he works as an operating engineer in a construction company.

She was raised as a Baptist but never goes to church. She considers herself a liberal Democrat and has no organizational affiliations. Like many other young black woman managers, although she has frequent contacts with whites on the job, her associations with them outside are infrequent, primarily at parties and with a few personal friends not part of the company. And again like many other young black women, she can hardly imagine herself marrying a white.

These sketches and the data yield profiles of the typical managers. The typical white manager is a 42-year-old man, college educated, a moderate Republican and a Protestant, who comes from at least a middle class background and whose father is generally more highly educated than his mother. The manager is married to a person with similar educational achievements, who comes from a middle class background and who does not work. The manager and his spouse live in an all-white neighborhood, and he belongs to segregated social organizations and integrated civic, business, and community organizations, but has little social contact with blacks.

The typical black manager, with characteristics similar to those found in the Labor Department study (Freeman and Fields, 1972, p.9), is a 32-year-old man, college educated, a liberal Democrat and a Baptist, who comes from a working class background and whose mother is probably more highly educated than his father. The manager is married to a person with similar education, who comes from a working class background and who also works. They live in an integrated neighborhood, and he belongs to integrated social, civic, business, and community organizations and has fairly frequent social contacts with whites.

Thus the black managers are younger, from working class families, more highly educated, and live more integrated lives. The white managers are older, from middle and upper class families, less highly educated, and live more segregated lives.

CHAPTER THREE

The Companies' Affirmative Action Programs

In 1970 it became law for most of industry to have concrete, written Affirmative Action Programs, that is, a written plan of steps that would be taken, with definite timetables and goals, to insure the equal and fair employment of blacks and other minorities. The participating firms all fell under the new legal requirement, but there have been great differences in the development and implementation of the Affirmative Action Programs (AAPs). This chapter attempts to find out why.

To see the sweep of the AAPs, rather than trying to delineate each firm's program and the many details involved, we shall instead concentrate on the extremes and describe the best company, Ace Public Utility, and the worst, Triple C Bank. All the other companies fall somewhere in between.

INITIAL AAP ACTIONS

Because all the firms are federal contractors, for more than 30 years they have been generally subject to laws requiring equal employment opportunity (EEO) for all people, regardless of race. But it was only in January of 1970 that the government, in Revised Executive Order 11246, ordered *written* Affirmative Action Programs with specific goals and timetables. This meant that for the first time the companies had to provide detailed and systematic plans for furthering equal employment opportunities, although they all maintained that they had been making voluntary commitments long before the Executive Order and that they had also had written plans. As Table 3-1 shows, the start of the companies' plans covers a six-year period, the latest in 1970 when the law went into effect.

The companies gave various reasons, stemming from both internal and external causes, for having written programs before they were required by law. For example, the AAP coordinator in Triple C Bank said that in 1964 the bank made an agreement with the California Fair Employment Practices Commission (CFEPC). Both Cousins and Aunts Manufacturing Companies indicated that their programs developed because their firms had always been "progressive" in the area of human rights. For Triple A Bank

TABLE 3-1   START OF THE COMPANIES'
WRITTEN AFFIRMATIVE ACTION PROGRAMS

Company	Date
Triple C Bank	1964
Cousins Manufacturing	1967
Aunts Manufacturing	1967
Triple A Bank	1968
Ajax Manufacturing	1969
Century Manufacturing	1969
Deuce Public Utility	1969
Ace Public Utility	1970

the impetus was pressure from civil rights organizations. Three of the companies, Ajax and Century Manufacturing and Deuce Public Utility, stated that their programs resulted from a new awareness by management that equal opportunities for all was a pressing necessity. (However, Deuce Public Utility would not release a copy of its program. I was told by the firm's representative that the senior manager in charge believes the information is privileged and not for outside perusal.) Ace Public Utility was the only company to say it had had no written AAP before the government order, although it did indicate that as early as 1962 it was taking concrete steps to improve minority employment.

TWO CASES

The dates of the companies' written AAPs and the reasons for their implementation actually have little relationship to the quality of the present AAPs. Although last in formulating a written policy, Ace Public Utility has the most detailed and elaborate plan. Lengths and specifications of the AAPs range down to the short 3½ page statement of Triple C Bank, which is not an official Affirmative Action Program. It simply reiterates the firm's longstanding claim of hiring and promoting on the basis of ability and merit rather than race, color, creed, or national origin. A comparison of these two firms will show the wide variety both in written policies and degrees of commitment.

The Best and the Worst: Ace Public Utility and Triple C Bank

Ace Public Utility's plan is extremely comprehensive. It has established the goal of reaching population parity in every district, department, and divi-

sion no later than 1980. (This means achieving an employee group the
ethnic composition of which more or less directly reflects the racial mixture
of the community in which the corporation is located.) In addition, the company has established the goal of employee parity at all levels, from the
lowest level of clerk to the Board of Directors, by 1990. (Employee parity is
a more or less direct relationship between the ethnic and sex compositions
of the work force and of all major job categories and all managerial levels.)
To reach these parities the company has also established goals in all recruiting and training programs. In contrast, in Triple C Bank's affirmative action effort there are no specific goals or timetables for either population or
employee parity or recruiting and training programs.

One of the main differences in the companies' programs, as exemplified
by Triple C Bank and Ace Public Utility, is how the companies view
government and social pressures. The officials in Triple C Bank resent
government and social pressures, feeling that outsiders, as one official says,
"should not tell us how to run our business." Thus compliance with the law
is minimal, shown by a reluctant and unenthusiastic AAP. But in Ace
Public Utility, a number of the influential policy makers have interpreted
the external pressures positively and have used them to help change past discriminatory behavior.

For example, Ace Public Utility has taken its AAP seriously and has
gone about implementing it with sincerity and concreteness, employing
aware and sensitive people in key positions. Responsibility is delegated in a
direct and efficient hierarchy. The vice-president of personnel is directly
responsible for the working of the company AAP. In turn, regional assistant
vice-presidents of personnel report to him. The assistant vice-presidents are
aided by a corporate AAP coordinator and nine area regional AAP coordinators. These coordinators are responsible for preparing AAP documents,
compliance reviews, and progress reviews, and investigating discrimination
complaints. Finally, in each area or company department there are Urban
Affairs representatives who recruit, select, hire, and place minorities and
women. These representatives are also available to counsel minorities and
women and their supervisors. The representatives' job, basically, is to help
the company in any way possible to fulfill its affirmative action obligations.

To coordinate the activities of all these managers, Ace Public Utility has
set up two committees, the Interdepartmental Personnel Committee and the
Interdepartmental Urban Affairs Committee. The first is made up of middle and upper level managers responsible for personnel matters in their
respective departments. The committee is charged with the difficult
responsibility of insuring that the smaller units throughout the company are
complying with the AAP; and in regular meetings the committee reviews
and discusses activities of general personnel and affirmative action.

The second committee, the Interdepartmental Urban Affairs Committee, is composed of personnel managers involved in affirmative action and urban affairs activities. This committee meets at least monthly to coordinate activities in these areas.

The structure of Triple C Bank's affirmative action organization is as far from that of Ace Public Utility as possible. The bank's senior vice-president of personnel is primarily responsible for the affirmative action effort. His main assistant is a lower level human relations officer, who must do alone what the nine regional area AAP coordinators do at Ace Public Utility—prepare and handle compliance and progress reviews and investigate discrimination complaints. There are no other managers in the company effort. This lower level manager is in effect responsible for the total program, has no assistance, and must cover the entire state. When he was asked about assistance in fulfilling his many tasks, he said: "Everyone is my assistant. If I see a problem, I tell the parties to correct it and it is corrected." To say the least, this is a cavalier attitude and one that does little to imbue a sense of responsiblity down the line and promote real action.

The AAP of Ace Public Utility has not been without its problems, however, problems that reflect those of many of the other companies. For instance, many of the utility's managers have used similar rationales for not hiring blacks—lack of qualifications and high salary demands—as other companies. But one senior white manager says that when the managers, as part of their duties, were given definite goals and timetables, for which they would be held accountable, many of those who said they could not find any black managers suddenly were able to find them.

The setting of goals and timetables has also had its attendant problems. At several seminars conducted by me for some of the senior managers at Ace Public Utility, it came out that the country's economic slowdown and the resultant discovery of overstaffing at the middle and upper management levels had created two serious problems. First, the company has had to revise downward its goals and timetables, and as a result some of the black managers who expected promotion have not gotten it. They attribute this not to the slowdown or overstaffing, or both, but to racial discrimination. Second, many white managers have suffered loss of promotion also, and they attribute this to a similar reason as the blacks, only in reverse. The fault is not in economic slowdown or overstaffing, they think, but in the company's strong emphasis on affirmative action.

As many students of job discrimination have observed, only in a brisk labor market can integration progress rapidly and smoothly. A recession heightens conflict between minority and majority groups (Wilensky and Lebeaux, 1965, p. xxxiii). The white and black managers in charge of Ace

Public Utility's AAP substantiate this. They indicate that in their own company the blacks are less discontented because many have recently received promotions, whereas many of the whites have not. Furthermore, the white managers are discontented because they are generally threatened by the emphasis on minorities and women. Many white managers, especially males, see their company's AAP as being preferential toward these groups and discriminatory toward white men.

Although some of the black managers are dissatisfied, in general they are much more positive in their views of the opportunities available in their firm as compared to those in the corporate world in general. This is a direct result of the establishment of goals and timetables in the AAP. The percentage of black managers in Ace Public Utility who believe blacks do not have equal opportunities in the corporate world is the highest of the six large companies, 80 percent. In contrast, the same company has the lowest percentage of black managers who believe blacks do not have equal opportunities in their own firm, 50 percent.

By comparison, in Triple C Bank, 70 percent of the black managers do not believe blacks have equal opportunities in the corporate world and 63 percent believe black managers have unequal opportunities in their own firm. As one might notice, the black managers in Triple C Bank see little difference in the opportunities available to black managers in their firm and the corporate world. The bank's weak affirmative action effort has a lot to do with this view. A strong AAP, such as that in Ace Public Utility, does much to create more positive black views of company employment policies.

Many of the white managers in Triple C Bank, like those in Ace Public Utility, believe that reverse discrimination is taking place and they too are apprehensive. The similarity in white managers' views between these two companies, the one with the weakest AAP and the one with the strongest, is explainable by the fact that the bank's leadership has issued many public relations statements that have created the impression among its white employees that blacks are getting more than equal opportunities. Thus the white resentment. The attitudes of both black and white managers were substantiated by a recent company-wide poll by the personnel department. It seems that very little is being done to bridge the racial differences and remedy the discontents.

Ultimately, a large part of the success or failure of an AAP depends on the individuals in key positions, as a later section will discuss. In many of the firms the managers who have primary responsibility are not specially selected but have simply been rotated into the positions without prior evaluation of their racial attitudes or qualifications. The positions are often looked on as undesirable, deadend jobs for incompetent (primarily white male) managers. It is quite possible to have a highly elaborate and specific AAP structure, but if it is staffed by insensitive and unqualified people the program will fail.

One of the reasons for Ace Public Utility's success is that its vice-president is young, intelligent, and forward-thinking. He has developed an AAP team of dynamic, young, intelligent managers who are enthusiastic but realistic in seeing that their company has a long way to go in providing true equal employment opportunity. One of the AAP coordinators is 37 and a college-educated former journalist who has taken several graduate courses in sexism and race relations. His views exemplify the vigor that is a hall-mark of the company's AAP: "Sure we're making efforts and try-ing—really hard—but there is still a lot of racism around here. Consciously or unconsciously blacks are discriminated against. A lot of our people either find excuses not to hire or promote blacks or seek out only the 'super blacks."

The corresponding managers at Triple C Bank offer a striking contrast. The senior vice-president who oversees the affirmative action operation is old, conservative, and rather racist. He has appointed as the human rela-tions officer, who is actually in charge of the program, an old, lower level manager who belongs to racist organizations such as the Elks and believes that blacks are simply pushing too hard. Both these men believe that their company is fair, and they deny any discrimination against blacks, conscious or unconscious. The human relations officer speaks for both himself and his boss when he says: "Whites at the bank aren't racist. The firm has always been fair. The fact is that if blacks were more qualified, they'd have no problems at all."

It can easily be seen from the contrasting views of the individuals in charge of the AAPs at Ace Public Utility and Triple C Bank how such views can contribute to the effectiveness or lack of effectiveness of a program. Both in plan and personnel, Ace Public Utility is the only com-pany among those participating in this study to have taken the time and ef-fort to develop an elaborate, well-defined, constructive Affirmative Action Program. It is also evident that Triple C Bank has not yet decided to face the fact that to assure blacks equal employment opportunities, the company must take real affirmative steps.

In other companies in the study most of the AAPs are somewhere between these two extremes. For example, Ajax Manufacturing recently set a goal for minority recruits to include three blacks out of every nine managers hired. Triple A Bank recently told its black managers to recruit and hire a certain number of blacks for managerial positions, with the im-portant improvement that the black manager hires the individual before sending him/her to personnel. The usual practice is to leave the hiring to the personnel department. Because of Triple A Bank's new method, it reached its goals for black managers four months ahead of schedule. Before this procedure was instituted, minority hiring goals were seldom reached, primarily because hiring was generally done by white male managers who would attribute their small recruitment of blacks to black lack of qualifications or high salary demands. But more of this later in Chapter five.

Although Ajax, Triple A and Aunts Manufacturing are taking a few steps forward to provide equal opportunities, the rest of the companies are still not convinced that the requirements of the law must be met sooner or later. These firms prefer to ignore rather than attack the problems of employment discrimination. But the problems cannot be ignored. They will not disappear by themselves, and it is rather startling that some of the companies seem to think this way.

It is obvious that the companies' AAPs vary tremendously. There are many reasons for this. To pinpoint them it will next be necessary to examine a number of external and internal factors that affect each firm.

WHY THE COMPANY PROGRAMS DIFFER

Government Influence

It has already been noted that one of the primary motivating forces for the employment of blacks in corporations has been the role of the government. The participating firms have been subjected to more than ten Executive Orders since 1941, when President Roosevelt issued the first one (8802) prohibiting government contractors from racial discrimination in employment.

But it was not until 1964, with the passage of Title VII of the Civil Rights Act, that the first truly comprehensive equal employment law went into effect. This law provided for the establishment of the Equal Employment Opportunities Commission (EEOC) as the main administrative and enforcement agency. Its powers were limited, though, to the right to conciliate; it could not compel employers to conform to the new law. But in the spring of 1972, Congress passed H.R. 1746, which gives the EEOC the direct power to sue firms found not complying with Title VII, without the individual employee having to file a suit.

Although the government has not enforced its own laws strongly or consistently, federal courts have provided a strong impetus for equal employment opportunities. The AAP coordinator of Aunts Manufacturing makes this observation about the nature of this impetus:

Concerning the power of law—in retrospect, the most significant accomplishment toward achieving EEO has occurred through the federal courts by virtue of definition and mandate, or *threat of the same,* rather than by any voluntary action on the part of the government. The examples are too numerous to mention. . . . (Seminar Report prepared by the AAP coordinator of Aunts Manufacturing, p. 7).

This coordinator goes on to describe the effect on Aunts Manufacturing of the government actions and pressures:

It has been five years since the Corporation identified Equal Employment Opportunity as a new and important management responsibility and objective. The concept was acknowledged as early as 1963 when the Company joined "Plans for Progress." However, it is clear that the Title VII lawsuit at _____ in early 1967 (which is still unresolved), charging us with violation of the Civil Rights Act, served as the spur to our declaration of commitment to Equal Employment Opportunity and the establishment of a corporate function responsible for directing the implementation of that commitment (Seminar Report, pp. 7–8).

Aunts Manufacturing is not the only firm to commit itself as a result of government pressure. In 1971–1972, Triple C Bank increased its employment of black women managers by 120 percent (from 17 to 37) and of white women managers by 36 percent (from 1325 to 1801). These increases came about only after a suit alleging sex discrimination was filed against the company.

Put another way, the government is making the cost of discrimination greater than the companies can afford and/or are willing to pay. A most notable example of such costliness is the EEOC case filed against American Telephone and Telegraph, which was finally settled in mid-January of 1973 for $38 million, a sum that does not even include the additional millions spent for legal, administrative, and management services.

It was only in 1967, when the implications of Title VII began to be realized and understood by the business community, that the firms in this study started to make a little more than token efforts to employ black managers, as Chapter Four will show in greater detail. But the firms' programs are quite diverse, which means that other factors are at work and that government pressures are not equally effective. Nevertheless, there is no doubt that government laws and regulations have played a central part in industry's development of programs to provide blacks with the means for equal opportunities.

Riots and Other Social Pressures

The government did not act completely voluntarily; from the very first legislation to the most recent, outside pressure has been the catalyst. The first Executive Order was issued by President Roosevelt only after black leaders agreed to call off a threatened march on the nation's capital. The passage of the Civil Rights Act of 1964 can be directly attributed to social pressures on the government from black civil rights groups and their white allies. As the social scientist John E. Means has said, white America was little interested in understanding or providing blacks the opportunities to better their position: "Only through militant action was better economic opportunity for all minority groups to be gained: by demonstrations, protest meetings, mass marches" (Means, in Ferman et al., 1968, p. 459).

Probably one of the strongest social pressures to coerce many urban corporations into acting to increase their black employment in the middle and late 1960s was the urban riots. This is attested to by the participating managers. A substantial number believe that the 1960s riots had a positive effect on their companies' black employment policies. Table 3-2 shows the managers' opinions. The table reveals that the black managers in general feel more strongly that the riots had a positive effect on their companies' employment policies than do the white managers.

As one would expect the views of managers from different companies vary greatly. For instance, in Ace Public Utility the riots signaled to the management a need to put forth greater efforts in the employment of blacks. In Triple C Bank, no significant positive response was elicited from the management to change its policies. A lower level black manager at the bank says: "The riots had very little effect here. There was no change for the managerial level at all."

More positive effects are seen by other managers at other companies, whose AAPs are better than Triple C Bank's. A white lower level manager at Triple A Bank notices: "The riots affected everyone's attitude. They prompted a realization of the problem. It was an unfortunate way to do it, but it helped. And it's not an unusual way for this country—it's always been

TABLE 3-2 EFFECT OF RIOTS ON THE COMPANIES' EMPLOYMENT POLICIES (in %)

Type of Effect	Black Managers (N = 116)	White Managers (N = 156)
Tremendously–positively	35	5
Positive effect	27	37
Awareness–positively	10	20
No effect–negatively	10	2
Affected only nonmanagerial positions	4	0
No effect–positively	4	16
Indirectly–positively	1	10
Negative effect	1	2
Don't know	8	8
Total	100	100

violent." Another white manager, on the middle level at Ace Public Utility is even more positive in his assessment: "The riots spurred the company on. I'm sort of glad they happened. They brought to attention the fact that blacks weren't going to wait around. They made whites realize the frustration and desperation of the blacks in the ghetto."

Thus riots have been one factor in exerting pressure for change or at least bringing the need for change to awareness in the firms. All the companies have also felt the effects of pressure from various civil rights groups, and all the firms have responded to some degree. Negotiations with civil rights groups have also varied in intensity.

The history of Triple C Bank is an example of extreme friction in dealing with civil rights groups. There is much behind the bank's 1964 "commitment" to improve its employment policies regarding blacks. This "commitment" was generated by pressures from civil rights groups. In January, 1964 CORE, NAACP, and the Ad Hoc Committee to End Discrimination began a protracted confrontation with the bank. At the time blacks made up 2.2 percent of the company's total employment force and almost all the blacks were in the lowest paying, nonmanagerial positions. The first six months of 1964 were spent in negotiations and demonstrations and resulted in no more than an impasse between the bank and the civil rights groups.

However, an agreement was reached with the California Fair Employment Practice Commission but not with the civil rights groups. This agreement resulted in the bank's appointing a black to a managerial position. He was well known, with many years of government experience, and was given the rank of assistance vice-president, a middle level management post. This appointment did nothing to help the blacks in the company. It was mere window dressing. Thus after the pressure from the civil rights groups subsided, the company returned to its previous policy of noncommitment to hire blacks at any level.

Other firms have made commitments with less friction but like Triple C Bank have not followed through. Outside pressure from civil rights groups, although having some effect on the companies' Affirmative Action Programs, has had minimal impact because generally there has not been continuous pressure on the firms over a long period of time. Once the crisis is over and the pressure has been relaxed, most firms revert to their previous discriminatory employment policies toward blacks.

A few firms have not been so recalcitrant. In the summer of 1970 Triple A Bank's employment policies toward minorities and women were investigated by the government after the firm was named in a civil rights suit filed by minority groups and the California Rural Legal Assistance Association. The federal review found Triple A Bank's employment policies commendable, but the bank took further affirmative steps. On November 27,

1970, it reached an agreement with the civil rights groups to formulate a hiring program with timetables that would reflect the population ratio of the state. The goal was to increase the bank's minority work force (blacks, Chicanos, and Asians) to 20 percent by 1972, and this was accomplished.

In addition to external pressures from community civil rights groups, many firms have felt the effects of internal pressures as black employees have begun to organize and demand their rights. This is true not only of the participating firms but of other firms in industry as well. The Labor Department study has noted:

In order to deal more effectively with these problems [unfair employment policies toward blacks] blacks are increasingly finding the need to organize and present a united front to management. . . . One case involved the refusal of blacks to talk with any lower level executives, feeling that only the President had the authority to commit the corporation to corrective action. [The blacks] formed a non-profit corporation to sue the corporation on compliance (Freeman and Fields, 1972, p. 110).

Such action may seem extreme but it is necessary because of corporate apathy.

This type of militancy has been a direct result of the lack of attention that has been given to the issue of equal opportunity by management. Unfortunately, it has resulted in "crisis" attention and [company] programming without benefit of substantive information and thought (Freeman and Fields, 1972, pp. 110–111).

The effects of internal black organization have been mixed in the participating firms. In Ajax Manufacturing, organized protest by black workers resulted in the upgrading of blacks into better blue-collar jobs, the promotion of two blacks to management positions, and a more detailed Affirmative Action Program. Because of pressures from Triple C Bank's black managers, a black recruiter was employed in 1970, although the position was phased out two years later. In 1971 the top management and the black managers of Triple A Bank met and began to develop innovative methods to improve the number of blacks in the firm as well as their level of achievement. In both Ace and Deuce Public Utilities, black employee groups and management have held a series of meetings concerning issues of black employment and the companies' relationships to the black community.

With the exception of Century Manufacturing, all the firms have black employees who are organizing themselves. Because these organizations are new, their impact on the companies' employment policies cannot yet be evaluated. However, the assurance of equal treatment for blacks can be attained only by well-organized, strong, and sustained efforts by blacks, their allies, and the federal government.

White managers are generally biased or pathetically unaware. Seminars at the participating firms about the findings of this study always brought out the surprised remark: "We didn't know our blacks were so dissatisfied with the company. We thought we were making real progress." These companies can no longer avoid the issue by insisting that outside groups are creating their problems when their own employees are organizing to pressure them into providing equal employment opportunities for blacks.

Overall, both external and internal pressures have had a minimal effect on the companies' employment policies. Most of the companies have reacted by satisfying immediate pressures with the smallest positive change and then have either not gone beyond it or have actually reverted to their previous practices. Thus unless social pressures from both the outside and the inside are continuous and determined, little change will take place.

A number of other factors also explain why the companies' Affirmative Action Programs are so varied, and these have more to do with the individual characteristics of the firms and especially individual views of the firms' managers who are in key positions to pursue the programs. An examination of these factors will begin to narrow down the reasons for the extreme differences in company programs.

Special Characteristics of the Firms

It has been argued by social scientists that particular characteristics of various types of firms contribute to different employment policies toward blacks (Northrup and associates, 1968–1970). It would seem reasonable to expect service-oriented firms to be less progressive than others because of fear of white customer reactions to black employees. For instance, in a study of blacks in the public utilities Bernard Anderson explained the attitudes of management with regard to "a strong residential customer orientation":

The burden of public contact rested upon the linemen, meter readers, trouble clerks, and cashiers in the business office. Because the managers of public utility firms were deeply concerned with maintaining a favorable public image, there was widespread reluctance to employ Negroes in nontraditional public contact jobs (B. Anderson, 1970, p. 54).

This concept is certainly not limited to utilities but can apply as well to other industries, especially service-oriented firms such as banks.

On the other hand, one might expect service-oriented firms to be more progressive in order to corner the lucrative black consumer market. A survey of the managers in the participating firms will help verify the truth or falsity of these assumptions.

There are four participating service-oriented firms, the two banks and the two public utilities, and four non-service-oriented firms, the manufacturing concerns. When the managers were asked if they believe any of their customers or distributors from other companies would feel at all uncomfortable if the firm hired or promoted a black into a management position, almost half of the black managers and one-third of the white managers responded affirmatively. Interestingly, a much higher proportion of the black managers in the two banks, two-thirds, said yes to the question than the black managers from the other companies. Possibly the black bankers have more extensive contact with the public than the black managers from the other firms, and this greater exposure and the resulting experiences may make them more aware of the realities. However, the white managers in the two banks did not deviate from the average.

When asked about possible discomfort on the part of managers from other companies in dealing with black managers from their own firms, half the black managers and only one-fourth of the white managers thought outside managers would feel uncomfortable. Again the black bankers answered affirmatively more often than their black counterparts in the other companies. However overall service orientation seems to have little relationship in the participating firms to progressiveness and equal employment opportunities; the firm with the best Affirmative Action Program, Ace Public Utility, and the firm with the worst, Triple C Bank, are both service-oriented.*

Another distinction among industries is whether or not they are regulated monopolies. A regulated monopoly has the advantage of pursuing equal employment opportunities as vigorously as it wishes. This is possible because it is largely free from customer retaliation—it can hire blacks with little concern over losing white clients or, conversely, it can continue discriminatory practices without worry about losing clients who favor black equal employment opportunities. Because of their monopolistic position, these firms are relatively immune to the costs of discrimination. Competitive firms feel the considerable costs more and can readily lose white customers who might resent either the employment of blacks or company discrimination against blacks.

In this study two firms are regulated monopolies, Ace Public Utility and Deuce Public Utility. The other six companies are not. When one looks at the AAPs of the firms, status as a regulated monopoly seems no guarantee of fair practices toward blacks—Ace Public Utility is the best and Deuce one of the worst. That a particular type of industry is more fair than others

---

* As will be seen, the AAP coordinators believe that they have had few, if any, problems with customers or the communities in general because of their employment of black managers.

is not true either—Triple C Bank is extremely backward and Triple A Bank is making some sincere efforts.

Thus regardless of the type of industry there are no specific firm characteristics that make for more or less progressive action in equality and employment opportunities for blacks. We must look for other factors to explain more satisfactorily why the companies differ so widely in their AAPs. Very pertinent here are the attitudes of individual managers on a number of questions.

What Do the Managers Think Is A Successful Affirmative Action Program?

The managers have very different views as to what constitutes a successful Affirmative Action Program. For the official views company spokespersons from each firm were interviewed. These are people closely involved in the programs. White managers from each of the eight firms were asked for their views; five of these are directly responsible for the formulation and implementation of their companies' AAPs, and three of them work in the Affirmative Action Departments. Black managers from six of the firms were questioned, because the two small firms, Ajax and Century Manufacturing, have no blacks in either personnel or the affirmative action departments. Two of the black managers are corporate APP coordinators in Cousins Manufacturing and Deuce Public Utility, and four are the highest-ranking blacks in the affirmative action areas of their companies.

All the managers were asked one question comprised of several parts: Which one of the following would be considered a major, good, minor, or no measure of success by your company in a program of equal employment opportunity? The subdivisions for consideration were as follows:

1. Number of black employees in relation to the number of blacks in the community (population parity),
2. Distribution of blacks through job classification,
3. Income levels of blacks in the company,
4. Visibility of blacks in the company,
5. Job mobility of blacks in the company,
6. Presence of black employees in the management, technical, or supervisory levels of the company,
7. Number of entry level jobs that have been filled by blacks,
8. Other.

For the frequency distribution of the managers' responses see Appendix C, page 259.

The black and white managers generally agree that major or good measures of success should be population parity, distribution of blacks through job classification, job mobility of blacks in the company, and presence of black employees in the management, technical, or supervisory levels of the company. A minor measure of success is agreed to be visibility of blacks in the company. The least agreement between the races is on the number of entry level jobs filled by blacks. Here seven of the white managers and only two of the black managers consider this as a major or good measure of success.

How do individual white managers' ratings relate to their companies' AAPs? The white AAP coordinator for Triple C Bank indicates that the number of entry level jobs filled by blacks should be considered a major measure of success and that visibility of blacks in the company should be considered a good measure. But, in contradiction to most of the other managers, he feels that distribution of blacks through job classification, income levels of blacks, their job mobility, and the presence of black employees in the management, technical, or supervisory levels of the company should all be considered as only minor measures of success. This manager's views are representative of his company's kind of leadership and reflect the very weak Affirmative Action Program. The views of the white manager from Ace Public Utility are almost the complete opposite, and significantly Ace Public Utility has the most elaborate and successful AAP. In another variation the AAP of Deuce Public Utility is quite weak, but the white manager who answered for the company agrees with the views of the personnel of more successful companies. However this manager is young and on the lower level. He admits that his views differ from those of the senior management, which of course is the most influential level in policy making.

From personal contact with some of the senior managers in most of the companies, I believe their views are quite similar to those of senior personnel at Triple C Bank—they feel there are no real problems. It is becoming evident how the attitudes of the white AAP coordinators and senior management as to what constitutes a successful AAP are reflected in the companies' programs. Here one sees how ideology and practice come together.

Problems: Anticipated and Actual

How do the programs reflect the managers' perceptions of anticipated and actual problems? Again the official company spokespersons, the six black and eight white AAP coordinators, were asked for their views on problems they would anticipate resulting from the implementation of an Affirmative Action Program. If the company anticipates many problems from many sources, it will seek to meet these by developing a strong AAP; if no problems are anticipated, there is no necessity seen to develop a strong program.

The AAP coordinators of the companies were asked for their responses to the following questions, designed to compare their degree of anticipation of problems with the problems that actually occurred:

1.   What problems did you anticipate to be major, some, minor, or no problem prior to the adoption of your firm's minority group employment practices?

2.   Looking back since the development of your AAP, which of these problems, if any, did occur? Again please rate them as to magnitude: major, some, minor, or no problem.

There were seven types of problems the managers could select from:

1.   Resistance by white workers,
2.   Lack of qualified blacks to fill available jobs,
3.   Interference with productivity or worker efficiency,
4.   Community opposition,
5.   Poor customer relations involving blacks dealing with whites,
6.   Resistance by supervisors and executives,
7.   Black dissatisfaction with available job opportunities.

(See Appendix C, pages 259–278, for the frequency distributions of managers' responses to the questions.)

The black and white AAP coordinators generally agree that resistance by white workers to their companies' APPs was anticipated as a major or some problem, but there is less agreement on anticipated resistance from supervisors and executives. The black coordinators believe resistance by whites from all levels was anticipated as a major or some problem, but the white coordinators anticipated a large problem only among the workers and hardly any trouble from the managerial ranks. Along the same lines almost all black coordinators believe that resistance to their companies' APPs has actually occurred at all levels, whereas the white coordinators believe there has been more resistance from the workers than from the managers. In other words, the blacks consistently see more problems with resistance to AAP efforts, and more so from the upper levels, than the whites.

Lack of qualified blacks to fill available jobs was generally anticipated by all the coordinators as a major or some problem, and it has actually become an important problem in the opinion of three of the six black managers and six of the eight white managers. For community opposition and poor customer relations involving blacks dealing with whites, all whites and most blacks generally agree that these were anticipated as minor or no problems, and there has been little actual disturbance in these areas. For black dissatisfaction with available job opportunities, anticipation and actuality have also turned out to be close. All six of the black and four of the eight white coordinators foresaw this situation as somewhat of a problem, and three of the black and four of the white coordinators believe it actually has assumed large proportions.

Again it is telling that Ace Public Utility anticipated many problems and thus developed a comprehensive effective Affirmative Action Program; Triple C Bank anticipated hardly any problems and its AAP is little more than lip service. Differences in anticipation of problems definitely do influence the strength of a company's program in moving from a predominantly white male-dominated work force to one integrated in terms of sex and race.

Where Affirmative Action Programs Are Most Resisted

Although there is some agreement between black and white AAP coordinators about resistance by white workers, there is less agreement between them with regard to the anticipated resistance by supervisors and even less agreement about anticipated resistance by executives. All the black AAP coordinators believe that resistance by whites—from all levels—was anticipated as a major or some problem; however, the white AAP coordinators believe that the resistance decreased the higher up the occupational ladder the managers are. And there is considerable disagreement among the black and white AAP coordinators as to where the resistance actually occurred. These differences exist among the *entire* sample of black and white managers in this study.

Table 3-3 shows more specific breakdowns by managerial level in the managers' responses. As can be seen from the table, there are great dif-

TABLE 3–3   AT WHICH MANAGERIAL LEVEL IS THE COMPANY AAP MOST RESISTED? (in %)

Level of Management	Black Managers ($N = 116$)	White Managers ($N = 156$)
Lower management	25	36
Middle management	37	19
Upper management	42	18
No resistance	2	22
All levels	5	3
Resistance is individual	0	3
Don't know	1	5
Total[a]	112	106

[a] The total percentages are above 100 because some managers selected more than one level.

ferences in opinion between the black and white managers. The explanation for this is that over 60 percent of all the white managers participating are on the middle or upper level, and over 70 percent of the black managers are on the lower level. Thus because of the general tendency to shift blame from oneself, one would expect the white managers to select the lower level as the most resistive rather than the middle and upper levels. When managerial level is used as the control variable, this assumption is indeed borne out by the data. One upper level manager from Ace Public Utility speaks for many managers when he says: "We never believe we are the problem; it is always the other guy."

An example of how such an attitude can impede a company's Affirmative Action Program is seen by the fact that none of the upper level managers believe there is any resistance to their firms' AAPs at their own level. They feel there is the greatest resistance at their companies' lower managerial levels. However the AAP coordinators tell a different story. Four of them indicate they have difficulties getting the upper management to do more than pay only lip service to their AAPs. One coordinator says that he must continually struggle to get the senior people to accept any of his programs, and if they are accepted it is in a very watered-down form. This coordinator believes that the upper management still thinks all it has to do is issue statements and everything will automatically be taken care of (an attitude reminiscent of that stated by the Human Relations Officer at Triple C Bank).

With the company as the control variable, the black managers' views directly reflect the strength of their AAPs. The black managers in Triple A Bank and Ace Public Utility, which have two of the best programs, believe that upper management presents the least resistance, whereas the black managers in Triple C Bank, which has the worst AAP, believe that the greatest resistance comes from the upper ranks.

The managers have different reasons for selecting the various levels of management as most resistive. (See Appendix C, pages 259–278, for the frequency distribution of all the reasons why the managers selected various managerial levels as most resistive to affirmative action efforts.) For example 67 percent of the blacks and 59 percent of the whites select the lower level because there are many more blacks competing with whites at the lower level. Thus the whites feel more threatened, fear blacks more, and as a result become more antagonistic toward blacks than the middle and upper level white managers. One black lower level manager in Triple C Bank does not have much hope for blacks at any level: "Most of the blacks are hired at the lower level and there is a lot of resistance because of the competition. But the resistance will increase even more as blacks move up the ladder." A white manager on the middle level at Cousins Manufacturing tends to agree: "The lower level managers have the most day-to-day contact with blacks. They have to make the AAP work—they're directly involved, and they're often up against blacks for jobs. That's why their viewpoint is different from the people at the top."

The black managers also cite the fear of competition, such as that voiced by the white manager just quoted, as the most frequent reason for resistance at the middle level. But most of the white managers believe that the middle ranks are older and more conservative, and thus it is difficult to change their attitudes (a situation also true of the upper level, where most managers are over 40). A white upper level manager from Aunts Manufacturing describes it this way: "At the middle level you find an age level less capable of handling change. These people aren't interested in assuming additional risks or jeopardizing their careers. Most of them are harder to get at or influence." Another white from the same company, a lower level manager, concurs: "There is an innate discrimination by middle management. They've never come to accept black people—they haven't changed their ways."

Of those managers who selected the upper level as giving the most resistance to company AAPs, many blacks believe this is so because upper management does not want to give blacks real power and so does not promote them to the upper level (there are no blacks at this level). A black lower level manager at Triple C Bank says: "The white man doesn't want to see niggers making major policy decisions." Another black manager, from Cousins Manufacturing, gives a similar reason, compounded by the "super black" concept: "Blacks must be twice as good as whites—they must be extremely superior to make it to the top. At the top there are fewer jobs and more competition, and they usually give the break to the white man." Just as disheartened with upper management resistance is a black woman manager from Duece Public Utility: "When I heard about the program I thought it seemed made up just to pacify the minorities and not because the company really was committed to improvement. It's just trying to get people off its back. Management won't really do anything."

White managers' reasons are not significantly different from blacks' to explain the resistance at the upper ranks. A middle level manager from Duece Public Utility comments: "When a minority gets more power to make decisions, upper level managers get uptight. They believe in affirmative action until it begins to affect them." Another manager, at the lower level at Triple C Bank, sees the resistance in terms of social discrimination: "Social intercourse comes into play in all large industries and blacks are not accepted socially—so they just won't be promoted to the upper level of management."

Some of the white managers say they see no resistance at any level, and these are the ones who indicate that their companies are strongly committed to affirmative action. But several feel that although their companies are committed and nonresistive, blacks themselves are creating resistance, and they agree with a white upper level manager at Cousins Manufacturing: "As the black people push, they will create their own resistance. It is entirely possible that there is more subconscious resistance now than there was ten years ago."

Whether such a reason is true or not—and it may be overly simplistic—many of the managers of both races select different levels of management as most resistive to affirmative action efforts but for very similar reasons. Although the black and white managers differ as to which level puts up the most resistance, the most consistent theme throughout all the responses is that as blacks move up the occupational ladder and begin to compete with whites the resistance at the middle and upper levels will increase because of the threat posed by blacks to white positions.

The Main Explanation for AAP Differences: Individual Managers

It has been seen that major differences in the companies' Affirmative Action Programs cannot be attributed to any specific internal or external pressures or characteristics, but rather that the differences are connected in great part to views and attitudes of managers within the companies. A company not only adapts, as William Quay has pointed out, to the social, economic, and political climate but varies individually "according to particular managerial desires, inclinations, and insights" (Quay, 1969, p. 1). From extensive contact with the managers, I believe that differences in their programs can be explained primarily in terms of how the top managers interpret and react to pressures to provide equal employment opportunities.

The two companies with the extremes in AAPs again provide striking contrasts. One of the main reasons for Ace Public Utility's progress in hiring blacks since 1968 is, as noted earlier, because a young, senior level manager responded to pressures to provide blacks with equal employment opportunities in a positive and progressive manner. When he was appointed vice-president of personnel in 1969, he immediately took aggressive steps to develop an elaborate, effective Affirmative Action Program that anticipated many of the more recent government regulations dealing with equal employment opportunities. His ability to get the company president's support and to develop a loyal, forceful staff has been without a doubt a major factor in the company's progress.

In contrast, at Triple C Bank the corporate personnel senior vice-president and top leadership, for the most part, have shown extremely negative and defensive attitudes. When the personnel senior vice-president was asked, at a seminar conducted by me, about the negative views his black managers have about the company's employment policies, as revealed by the present study, he was extremely defensive and tried to discredit their views by questioning the validity of the number of participating black managers and the selection procedures. When a vice-president from the research division pointed out to him that of the company's black managers a large percentage had been interviewed and the managers had been selected through a random procedure, the information produced little change in the personnel senior vice-president's attitude.

Such attitudes on the part of white top management filter through an entire company. I met with a group of Triple C Bank personnel managers in January, 1973 to discuss a survey the bank had conducted of all its employees; the survey found that most of the black employees were very displeased with the company's employment policies and most of the whites, on all levels, thought the blacks were getting, as one manager said, "more than a fair break in employment." Because the white managers believe this, their attitudes toward equal employment opportunities for blacks are hardly positive or constructive. Since the whites see no real problems, it is little wonder that they tend to react very defensively and negatively to any pressures, external or internal, to make black employment opportunities more equitable in the firms. The bank's extremely weak, almost nonexistent affirmative action effort is a direct outcome of such managerial views.*

THE OVERALL PICTURE

Although all the firms have written Affirmative Action Programs, these programs have been prompted by government laws and regulations and vary immensely in comprehensiveness and effectiveness. Only one company, Ace Public Utility, has specific goals and timetables to insure real action in the coming years. The other companies, in varying degrees, have not seriously committed themselves to the admittedly difficult task of formulating and implementing strong Affirmative Action Programs. The basic attitude of most of these firms, that of "minimal compliance" and its results, was well described in 1972 by the chairman of the Equal Employment Opportunities Commission, William Brown, and the situation has not materially changed:

Too much of both private industry and the public have been concerned not with carrying out the spirit of the law but rather with achieving minimum compliance. Some very ingenious minds, when told that discriminatory treatment was unlawful, devised some very subtle ways to continue excluding minorities and women from

---

* It is interesting to note that Aunts and Cousins Manufacturing Companies, which have the same chairman of the board, have very different approaches to AAP. Aunts is more progressive than Cousins primarily because of the stronger commitments to EEO by the top leadership, that is, the president and his senior staff.

better jobs. They created standards which treated everyone equally on the surface but which had the effect of disadvantaging and screening out certain groups (Brown, 1972, p. 161).

As we have seen, government and social pressures from civil rights groups and more militant actions such as riots have all had some effect in making companies begin to take some action. Also effective have been internal organization and pressure by black employees. But what seems to have the most effect, after the initial impetus, are the white managers' attitudes and opinions as to what constitutes an effective AAP, what problems they anticipate in relation to those that actually occur, and how they react to the various pressures placed on them. When top level management responds positively and dynamically, as in Ace Public Utility, the AAP is strong; when top management is reactionary, as in Triple C Bank, the AAP fails.

Resistance to affirmative action, then, is greatest at the top, as the black managers believe, rather than at the lower levels, as the white managers assert. Because of the entrenchment of such resistance, immediate and positive action is necessary to provide blacks with true equality in employment. The late Whitney M. Young, Jr., former executive director of the National Urban League, stated the case eloquently:

Neither the Negro nor the Urban League is asking for three hundred years of preferential treatment such as white citizens have had. We are asking for only a decade of dedicated special effort. . . . At this point, when the scales of justice are so grossly unbalanced, it is impossible to balance them by simply applying equal weight (quoted in Aunts Manufacturing Company's Affirmative Action Program Director's 1972 Annual Report).

Except in one case, and possibly two others, the firms in this study are either not committed to providing equal opportunities for blacks or they do not realize that unless positive efforts are made to offset the effects of past discrimination, formal abolition of present discrimination will have limited benefit at best. It is not sufficient simply to reiterate commitment to the idea of equal employment opportunity. What is necessary is a strong, well-developed plan, carefully formulated and implemented, one that is closely overseen by responsible and sensitive people.

CHAPTER FOUR

Black Managers in the Participating Firms

Certainly most of the firms' Affirmative Action Programs fall far short of the ideal. Nevertheless, there are some blacks in management. This chapter explores the representation of blacks in the business world, both in the participating firms and industry in general, with a view toward ascertaining what the companies have done and how far there is to go. Evidence for the situations described will be found in Chapters 5, 6, and 7; this chapter presents the general picture.

BLACKS IN GOVERNMENT SERVICE

It is first necessary to examine the representation of blacks in government service. This will also serve as a comparison with private industry and will show how much the government is adhering to its own laws. Studies have shown that progress is slow at best. Although blacks comprise 12 percent of all government employees, until the past few years they have been relegated to the lowest positions, both managerial and nonmanagerial. The few blacks who have attained higher status jobs are generally in research or staff positions directly related to interracial concerns, rather then in decision making and supervisory positions (Krislov, 1967, pp. 90–91; Rosenbloom, 1972, p. 38).

Such findings were supported by the former chairman of the Equal Employment Opportunity Commission, Clifford Alexander, who wrote in 1971 that the government has made "loud noises" about doing away with its own employment discrimination but has not followed through with concrete action. The Department of Defense, Alexander pointed out, has been one of the "noisiest" but in action is one of the most silent, employing less than 1.3 percent blacks at the supergrade levels of management (Alexander, 1971, p. 7).

One of the most telling reports may well have been that issued by Ralph Nader in June 1972, a report prepared by the nonprofit Public Interest Group. It asserted that the Civil Service Commission has done very little to improve the lot of the 2.5 million blacks, Chicanos, and women in government service. Most of the commission's successes, the report concluded, have been in public relations and gimmickry rather than in significant social change (in Brewer, 1972).

Although the government record is poor, in the last two decades, it has still been better than the corporate world's in the employment of blacks in managerial and professional occupations. By comparison with the corporate world the government actions look impressive (see Wilensky and Lebeaux, 1965, p. xxxvi). For example, the government has had black managers for many years, but of the eight firms in this study, five hired or promoted their first black into a management position only in the early 1960s, and none of the firms had any black managers before 1955. Compared to the 2.4 percent of middle level black managers in government service, in the participating firms there are only .4 percent, an appallingly low figure.

BLACKS IN PRIVATE INDUSTRY

Because the federal government has not consistently or carefully followed the law of the land in providing equal employment opportunities for all, it is not surprising that industry in general and the firms in this study likewise have been lax. The participating companies are far behind the government in their employment of blacks, although most are quite representative of their particular industries and reflect the dismal state of the corporate world in black employment.

In fact, the data indicate, as summarized in Tables 4-1 and 4-2, that only in the past decade have the companies made any worthwhile efforts to practice what they preach. And only in the last four years have some of the firms undertaken any meaningful action at all. In Table 4-1 it will be seen that the first black workers in low status jobs were hired long before the first black managers.

When a four-year period of the companies' black managerial employment

TABLE 4–1   DATES WHEN FIRST BLACKS WERE EMPLOYED

Companies	Black Managers	Black Workers
Ace Public Utility	1955	1935
Deuce Public Utility	1957	1945
Triple C Bank	1958	1952
Ajax Manufacturing	1961	1952
Cousins Manufacturing	1963	1942
Aunts Manufacturing	1963	1947
Triple A Bank	1963	1956
Century Manufacturing	1964	1963

TABLE 4-2 INCREASE IN TOTAL MANAGEMENT AND BLACK MANAGEMENT: 1967–1971

Companies	Increase in Total Managerial Work Force (1967–1971)	Percentage Increase in Total Managerial Work Force (1967–1971)	Black Managers (1967)		Black Managers (1971)		Percentage Increase of Black Managers (1967–1971)
			(#)	(%)	(#)	(%)	
Ajax Manufacturing	60–85	42	1	1.7	3	3.5	200
Ace Public Utility	19,666–21,434 9%	9	169	0.9	508	2.4	201
Cousins Manufacturing	1,403–1,613 14%	14	8	0.6	35	2.2	338
Century Manufacturing	New function	New function	,1	0.6[a]	2	1.6	100
Aunts Manufacturing	4,444–4,790 8%	8	33	0.7	76	1.5	130
Triple C Bank	6,135–7,230 17%	17	25	0.4	111	1.4	304
Triple A Bank	2,171–3,238 49%	49	14	0.6	47	1.4	236
Deuce Public Utility	3,537–4,273 21%	21	10	0.3	37	0.9	270

[a] Figure is for 1968.

increases is compared with increases in the total managerial work force for the same period, the increases in black managers appear to be phenomenal, as seen in Table 4-2, especially in the last column. The overall growth of the companies' managerial work forces between 1967 and 1971 varied from a low of 8 percent for Aunts Manufacturing to a high of 49 percent for Triple A Bank, yet all of the companies increased their black managerial forces from 100 to over 300 percent for the same period. These percentages seem extremely impressive, but it should be remembered that in 1967 the companies had *very* few black managers, amounting to a total of only .7 percent. Thus in 1971, even after the extreme percentage increases occurred, black representation was still very low, only approximately 1.9 percent of the managerial forces of the eight firms.

Another way to find out when the companies began to make a little more than token efforts to place blacks into management positions is to consider the black managers' lengths of service. Many black managers, especially in Ace Public Utility and Aunts Manufacturing, did not start out as managers but were promoted from nonmanagerial to managerial positions. When lengths of service of the black and white managers are compared, the results are significant (see Table D-3, Appendix D, page 281, for the length of service of all the black managers in the companies and Appendix C, page 259, for the frequency distribution of the participating managers' lengths of service with their firms).

Of the participating managers, 45 percent of the blacks have four or fewer years with their company, compared to 9 percent of the whites. In addition, 83 percent of the black managers have ten years or less of service, compared to only 26 percent of the white managers. When managerial level is used as the control variable, it is found that of the blacks in middle management 71 percent have been with their firms less than eight years, compared to 15 percent of the white managers, and 38 percent have been with their firms less than four years, compared to only 6 percent of the white managers. These figures add further support to the contention that it has been only in the last few years that the firms have made any real efforts at all to hire blacks into the managerial ranks.

Six of the eight companies describe their growth as rapid and their increase in employment as substantial since 1960. If these firms had begun to practice equal employment at that time, in conjunction with their growth their numbers of black managers should be much greater. Until the past few years the labor market has been brisk, and in such a market, as noted in the previous chapter, increase in the black managerial work force creates less opposition by white employees. But in these firms the numbers of black managers have not been increased as much as one would expect—expanding labor markets and greater employment of blacks, especially in managerial positions, do not go hand-in-hand. No matter what the labor market, blacks will not be provided with more opportunities unless the firms are seriously committed to equal employment policies.

The small number of black managers in these firms is even less excusable in terms of their locations and population composition. Except for Aunts Manufacturing in which 50 percent of the plants are located in areas where blacks comprise less than 1 percent of the population, all the other firms are situated primarily in the San Francisco Bay area, which has a black population of 12 percent, and the Los Angeles area, which has a black population of 17 percent. Furthermore, these firms are located in the state that leads all others in the number of college-enrolled black students—72,000. This figure represents approximately 10 percent of the nation's black college students, and they are attending one of the best college and university systems in the country. Thus sizeable numbers of educated blacks are part of the labor market.

The participating firms are quite representative of their industries and the corporate world in general. For instance in 1966 when the Equal Employment Opportunity Commission began to require firms with 100 or more employees to provide statistics on the number of employees by ethnic groups, and sex, the banking industry reported that blacks constituted approximately .4 percent of its managerial forces, a figure very close to the banks in this study (Thieblot, Jr., 1970, p. 27). In its 1967 Annual Report, the EEOC noted that blacks represented approximately .2 percent of the officials and managers and 1.5 percent of the professionals in the gas and electric industry (EEOC's Third Annual Report, 1967, p. 26). Again these percentages concur with those of the gas and electric (utility) firm participating in this study. Finally, for total managerial representation, black managers comprise only 1.1 percent of the black work force compared to white managers, who comprise 6.2 percent of the white work force (Freeman and Fields, 1972, p. 113).

CAREER PATTERNS

Industry has obviously been reluctant to hire blacks at the managerial levels, but it has been pressured into hiring at least some. Many of the blacks who have been hired have demonstrated skills in other work experiences before being hired by the companies—72 percent of the participating black managers held jobs in other firms directly related to their present jobs, compared to 52 percent of the white managers. The black managers, especially those at the middle level, were employed in previous

* Now firms with 25 or more employees must provide these statistics.

jobs much longer than the white managers. Table 4-3 shows the managers'
total number of years of relevant work experience.

Experience in other institutions is one of the primary factors cited by the
black mangers themselves as helping them attain their present positions.
Table 4-4 shows the responses of both races as the main factors they believe
aided them in reaching their present positions. Forty-five percent of the
white managers, compared to 19 percent of the black managers, believe
experience in their present companies was the *only* factor helpful in obtaining their present positions. In addition, almost as many blacks believe their
educational experience was *at least* one of the factors helpful in obtaining
their present positions as believe experience in their present companies was
helpful.

With managerial level as a control variable, the black middle level
managers present a particularly interesting picture. Only 12 percent of
them, compared to 47 percent of the white middle level managers, believe
experience in their own companies was the *only* factor that helped them to
their present position. This suggests that many of the black middle level
managers have been brought in at middle level positions.

It is very possible that the corporate world is beginning to discover and
utilize the many capable, qualified black managers who have thus far been
working almost exclusively in government, social agencies, academic institutions, public organizations, and their own businesses. Many firms have used
these sources for years to seek white managers, but the firms, reluctant to
have black managers, have ignored the black potential in these areas.

TABLE 4–3   TOTAL YEARS OF RELEVANT WORK EXPERIENCE (in %)

| | Black Managers | | White Managers | | |
Years	Lower (N = 82)	Middle (N = 34)	Lower (N = 47)	Middle (N = 79)	Upper (N = 30)
1–4	26	3	15	3	0
5–8	29	18	19	6	0
9–12	21	18	13	14	0
13–16	13	17	13	19	10
17–20	6	15	11	19	10
21–24	4	24	9	14	30
Over 24	1	6	21	25	50
Total[a]	100	101	101	100	100

[a] Some percentages are over 100 because of rounding errors.

TABLE 4–4 FACTORS THAT HELPED MANAGERS ATTAIN THEIR PRES-
ENT POSITIONS (in %)

Factors	Black Managers ($N = 116$)	White Managers ($N = 156$)
Experience within the company	60	97
Experience in another company	16	21
Experience in the government	7	3
Experience in the military	21	17
Experience in social agencies	6	3
Experience in the academic world	55	33
Initiative in organizing the company	0	2
Other	26	10
Being black (Previously listed under "Other")	9	0
Total[a]	200	186

[a] The total percentages are over 100 because the managers could select more than one factor.

Although only 9 percent of the black managers, almost half of them at the middle level, believe being black was a primary factor in their achieving their present level, their comments show the kinds of pressures imposed on the firms from various sources. For instance, a black middle level manager from Triple C Bank says: "I'm a black banker because of the Watts riots. They need blacks to put in branches in black communities." And a black manager from Ajax Manufacturing comments: "I have this position only because I helped lead a protest movement which demanded better treatment of black employees and more black managers. They gave me the job to try to shut me up. Being black helped."

From all the data presented so far, it will be surmised that black and white managers have reached their present positions, especially those at the middle level, by very different paths. To elucidate this difference, the backgrounds and career experiences of two middle level managers, one black and one white and both from the same company, are now presented.

The white manager, Mr. W., is 37 years old and married to a woman who does not work although she has a Bachelor of Science degree in education from Purdue University. Mr. W. comes from an educated middle class family. His father had a college degree and was a sales engineer for a local utilities company in the family's native state of Ohio, and his mother, a housewife, had 14 years of school. Mr. W. is a Presbyterian and attends church once a week. He is a moderate Republican and belongs to many re-

ligious, social, business, civic, and political organizations, most of which
have no black members.

The black middle level manager, Mr. B., is also 37 years old, unmarried,
and from an educated family. Both parents had four-year college degrees,
and his father was a pharmacist in Oklahoma (Mr. B.'s family background
is above that of the average black manager). Mr. B. has no religious
preferences, never attends church, and considers himself a moderate Independent. He belongs to a number of organizations—veterans, civic,
professional, charitable, and civil rights—and all except one have white
members.

The work experience of the two managers differs significantly. Mr. W.,
the white manager, attended Purdue University on an ROTC scholarship,
majoring in engineering. On graduation he spent 3 years in the Navy as an
engineering officer and then applied to his present company for a job. He
was brought in as a commercial lighting representative and stayed in that
position for 2 years, then was transferred to a post as power engineer for $1\frac{1}{2}$
years, then spent another $1\frac{1}{2}$ years as a senior industrial engineer, 2 years as
a sales trainer, and has been in his present position as a marketing supervisor for the past 2 years.

In addition, in the course of his career with the company, Mr. W.
received a Master of Business Administration degree at San Francisco State
College. When asked what he thought contributed most to his reaching his
present position, he says: "No doubt about it—experience inside the company. I've had a lot of training in a lot of areas." Mr. W. reached middle
management by assignment to various experience-building jobs within the
company. Such movement is very typical of white managers, but as we shall
see blacks must rise through other avenues.

Mr. B. earned his degrees long before entering his company—a Bachelor
of Science degree in civil engineering from New York University and a
Master of Science degree in civil engineering from MIT. His first job was
with the federal government as a junior designer, and within the government
he progressed over 3 years to designer, engineer, and civil engineer. At the
end of this time he joined a private corporation as a chief civil engineer but
left after $3\frac{1}{2}$ years because he felt there were no further opportunities there
for him as a black man.

A friend told Mr. B. that there were increased opportunities in middle
management in the federal government, and so he accepted a post with a
government agency as deputy district director. He remained there 5 years
and then worked for the Atomic Energy Commision as an investigator for 1
year. After this he took a job with the General Service Administration as a
resident engineer, where he remained for 4 years. This was followed by a
year in a large corporation as a project manager and another year as

resident engineer for the City of San Francisco. He was recruited 2½ years ago by his present firm as an engineer designer, and in that time he has been promoted to staff engineer.

Mr. B. attributes his present level to his experience in government, the academic world (his education), and work in other companies: "It's been sort of a checkerboard but this is where I've gotten the necessary experience that has led to my job here." In contrast to Mr. W.'s job history, which has been primarily within the company, Mr. B.'s has encompassed a variety of experiences, especially in federal and local government agencies. Apparently the business world has not yet reached the point where it will invest in blacks enough to allow them training and background experience within the company; blacks must still "prove themselves" beforehand.

Black Positions and Levels

Career patterns of whites and blacks are quite different, and it is reasonable to assume that the types of positions held, the levels, and the salaries will also vary. Here too our companies reflect white business in general.

Although most businesses are slowly increasing the number of blacks in lower management positions, there are still very few blacks at the middle levels and none at the upper ranks. There are no black corporate officers in the major *Fortune 500* firms and none who are on boards of directors.* Only 19 black managers in the participating firms are considered middle level managers, and a slightly higher number are considered lower middle level managers. That is, only approximately 0.4 percent of all middle level management positions are filled by blacks. The 34 middle level managers in this study represent approximately 80 percent of all the black middle level managers in these firms. As in the larger corporate world, none of the companies have blacks at the upper levels of management or on the boards of directors.

The blacks' salaries are also much below the whites' salaries. Of the 819 black managers in the eight firms, only three people earn between $22,000 and $23,999 and only two earn over $25,000. As the next chapter demonstrates, black managers with similar relevant work experience and education to whites earn less in comparable jobs.

Such facts lead many blacks to believe that they have little chance of going beyond lower level management positions. Seventy percent of the black managers in this study agree that most corporations have simply shifted the point at which they apply discriminatory practices (an illustration of William Brown's observance of "very subtle ways to continue excluding minorities and women from better jobs," quoted in Chapter 3). The com-

* Since this study was conducted, a few blacks have been named to the Board of Directors of a few firms.

panies now hire blacks but will not allow them to realize their full potentials. And the blacks who are hired are, 78 percent of the managers believe, just being showcased—put into conspicuous positions to show that the company is a "fair" employer (see Appendix C, pages 259–278, for the managers' reasons for their views on companies shifting their point of discriminating against blacks and showcasing).

Recent studies have supported the black managers' views about limited placement. Those blacks who have advanced to a relatively high level, for blacks, are normally placed in positions specifically related to the black "sphere," such as special markets, industrial and community relations, AAP director, urban affairs, and personnel (Jackson, 1969, p. 6). Even those blacks assigned to technical and professional areas are not normally put into jobs that would lead directly to administrative supervisory decision making positions. In the Labor Department study, 64 percent of the black managers were in staff positions, most without supervisory or managerial responsibilities (Freeman and Fields, 1972, p. 18; see also Fogel, 1968, p. 61, and Quay, 1969, p. 36).

The black managers in this study are no different. Of the 19 middle level managers, the two highest ranking blacks are vice-presidents in public relations and urban affairs. They were hired in 1964 and 1971, after long and distinguished careers in the federal government. Thirteen of the remaining 17 middle level managers hold positions where they deal with either urban affairs and personnel or with the black consumer market; for example, they may manage a branch or supervise a district in a black area. The remaining four middle level managers hold professional-technical positions that are nonadministrative in nature.

These new types of discrimination—the limiting of blacks who are in middle and upper management positions and placing them primarily in black jobs—is documented in a study by Freeman and Fields (prior to their large study for the Labor Department) in the case of a young black M.B.A. graduate from a top business school. He entered his firm with educational credentials similar to two white holders of the Master of Business Administration degree who came in at the same time, but they were assigned to duties where they interacted with clients and exercised authority in money allocations and policy decisions. He, however, was assigned to work with the Urban League, NAACP, and other minority-oriented groups.

His white counterparts were gaining broad experience, and when he began to take steps to enlarge his own experience within the firm, he found that the whites thought he had been kept in limited posts "because he lacked real ability." The black approached his white manager with the problem, who rationalized his treatment by saying that it was important that, as the first black hired, he simply be "seen around." But the study reports: "Underlying his statements was the fear that business would be lost if clients had to deal with a black." And the young black, discouraged at the barriers to advancement, started to seek another position. The authors conclude: "Unfortunately, this case is typical. Blacks and whites enter as equals, but whites get the experience needed for promotions, while blacks do not" (Freeman and Fields, 1972a, p. 78).

The experience of a young black manager in Triple C Bank bears out the typicalness of this plight (as do further experiences reported by black managers in succeeding chapters). A new branch was established in a black community as a result of riots. This black became manager of the branch in $3\frac{1}{2}$ years, an extremely rapid advancement. But his position was little more than a showcase: His salary was much lower than his white counterparts, many of his decisions were reversed, white managers could make exceptions and he could not, he did not receive promotion after doing a conscientious job. He wanted to be a "full" banker, he said, and left after $1\frac{1}{2}$ years to become district manager for six branch banks at a salary 40 percent higher than he had received at Triple C Bank.

In discussing his job with the bank, he voiced objections not simply to the lower salary and the difficulties in getting his decisions approved, but more important to the lack of opportunity to be a banker for all customers: "I'd just be a black banker for the black customers, and this is neither fair to my abilities nor to the customers themselves." He recognized the need for black bankers in a black community but suggested that there are a sufficient number of black bankers who could be rotated to branches in the black communities. That way the bankers would not be restricted in their growth or deprived of further opportunities.

BLACK MANAGERIAL POWER?

The experiences of the black M.B.A. reported by Freeman and Fields and the black banker at Triple C Bank both dramatize a very important facet of the subtle discrimination against black managers. They are given very little power—in exercising authority and making decisions about money, subordinates, or policies—no matter what managerial rank they hold.

In the participating firms only 24 percent of the black middle level managers control a budget, compared to 58 percent of the white managers at that level. At the lower level only 10 percent of the blacks control a budget, compared to more than twice that number of whites, 23 percent. As to subordinates, 64 percent of the black managers have five or fewer, compared to 31 percent of the whites. By managerial level 24 percent of the black middle level managers have no subordinates, compared to 14 percent of the white managers. At the lower level twice the percentage of blacks as whites have no subordinates—34 percent as opposed to 17 percent (see Appendix C, page 259, for the frequency distribution of the number of subordinates the black and white managers have).

Although there is little difference on specific decision-making powers between the races at the lower level (31 percent of the black managers and 36 percent of the white believe they have little or no influence in hiring and promoting in their departments and divisions) at the middle level there is a large discrepancy. Only 25 percent of the white managers feel this way, but 59 percent of the black managers do.

Most of the black managers hold positions formerly held by whites; only one in 12 does not. And one in three blacks do not feel they have the same power and authority as the whites who previously held their posts. (See Appendix C, page 259, for the reasons the managers do not believe they have the same powers as the white managers who held their jobs previously.) In fact, it is in personnel, ironically, where more blacks feel this than in any other area 53%.

The black managers see their own power as almost nil for two major reasons. First, whereas the white managers are immediately given authority, the blacks must prove themselves first before being given any authority. Second, because of the suspicion of their abilities, the blacks are always being checked on. The white managers easily gain the complete power, authority, and latitude to which the black managers are equally entitled, but the blacks must overcome obstacles put in their way before they are given the same powers—if ever.

There are many black managers in the participating firms who have the titles of authority but who are not permitted the power that should go with their positions. Two managers, one on the lower level and one on the middle, illustrate the dilemma of most blacks in the business world.

Mr. F., a black, now 35 years old, has been with his company for 5 years as a lower level manager. Before coming to the company, he worked for 4 years in the military as a ground radar technician and before that held jobs in various garages as a mechanic. During his 5 years with the firm he has been promoted twice, and his present position is urban affairs representative for a regional department. However, he has no subordinates and controls no budgets.

Although he is responsible for assuring employees in his department of equal opportunities, he feels he has little influence over his department's hiring and promoting policies, and as a result, too little authority to carry out his duties. A white person held the job before him, and Mr. F. feels acutely that he has much less power than his predecessor and knows why: "The attitude of upper management says you don't have to abide by the rules when blacks are involved. Another white in my position would have the same authority as the guy before me. But they don't want blacks to have the control and power to make decisions." Mr. F. gives an example of how his efforts at fulfilling his responsibilities have been frustrated because of lack of power: "I've tried to help certain blacks who were terminated by bigoted supervisors—with little success. One black employee was terminated while he was on a leave of absence, which is hardly a fair time, and all my efforts to get him back on the payroll failed."

Because of his unique position in urban affairs, Mr. F. sees little hope for blacks reaching their full potential. He points out that there are few if any blacks in policy-making positions and those in relatively high places are simply being showcased to appease the government and the black community: "As of yet, even though the company says it's enforcing certain policies, the reality is very different, because there is no impetus from the people who are in the positions to enforce those policies."

One would hope the views of a middle level black manager would be somewhat more optimistic. However this is not true of Mr. P., a 39-year-old middle level manager. His views reflect the general attitude of the black managers at his level. His only work experience has been 14 years with his present company, where he started out as a laborer and has risen to his present position as field supervisor of 40 men, although he controls no budget. This is a line position, which is a decision-making and administrative post, but Mr. P. feels just as powerless as many other black managers in black-oriented staff positions, such as those related to equal employment opportunities.

Quite often Mr. P. feels that he has too little authority to carry out his responsibilities, primarily because he cannot influence his immediate supervisor about decisions and actions that affect Mr. P. himself. Thus he must frequently do things against his better judgment. As is common, a white person held his job previously, and Mr. P feels that the power of the job did not pass to him: "Whites just don't accept your mental reasoning ability. They feel blacks are mentally inferior." He too is pessimistic about blacks in business. Like Mr. F., he believes they are just being showcased and kept in lower level positions. He says: "Blacks have never been accepted and so they've never been given the opportunities to do a good job."

Unfortunately, the data support such opinions as Mr. P.'s, especially in the case of private industry. Although the federal government has by no means been an exemplary equal opportunity employer, it has far surpassed the business world. The firms in this study reflect their industries in general, and it is only in very recent years, despite their years of claiming real commitment to equal employment opportunities, that the firms have made any attempts to hire and promote black managers. Because of their past practices, they have very few blacks in management positions, and those they do employ are in lower level posts where they relate almost exclusively to black employees and the black consumer market. Those few black managers not in black-oriented positions have equally little, if any, decision-making power or authority to influence company policies.

This situation is not very hopeful. One of the ways to seek a remedy is to explore in greater depth the reasons behind this situation. This is the focus of the next chapter.

CHAPTER FIVE

Why There Aren't More Blacks in Business

As Chapter 4 has shown, there are very few blacks in managerial positions in the firms participating in this study. This chapter explores some of the reasons why this is so. The firms here reflect the corporate world in general in the number of black managers, their managerial levels, and the types of positions they hold: in 1967 blacks represented 0.7 percent of the managerial work force, and by 1971 this figure had increased to only 1.9 percent.

As we have seen, most of the managers are in lower management positions and are generally associated with the black consumer markets and/or black employees. There are no blacks in upper management, and only 2.2 percent of the black managers are in middle management. At this level they are generally associated directly with the black community, in Affirmative Action Programs or public and industrial relations programs, or they hold technical or professional positions, with no administrative or supervisory duties. The participating managers are aware of the small number of black managers, but do they see this as a problem? And if so, how do they explain it?

The managers were asked for their views on fairness in the hiring and promoting of blacks, both in their own companies and in industry generally. As might be expected, the responses of the black and white managers differ significantly. Most whites regard the hiring and promoting policies of their own firms as very fair. They do not see industry in general as nearly as fair as their own firms. To the majority of blacks unfairness is rampant, both in their own companies and the corporate world as a whole.

Again there is a wide discrepancy between the races when the managers are asked why they think there are not more blacks in business. To the whites the most important explanations are black differences in "culture" and lack of the necessary "qualifications"; to the blacks, by far the most important explanation is racial discrimination.

What accounts for these extremely different views? What are the reasons and rationales behind them? This chapter attempts to answer these questions.

EMPLOYMENT: THE MANAGERS' OWN COMPANY POLICIES

To assess the black managers' situation, let us first look at the way in which both black and white managers view their companies' employment policies concerning *any* employee, regardless of race.

"Are you in agreement with the hiring and promoting policies of this company?" To this question the black and white managers give very different answers. Only 37 percent of the black managers think their companies are fair, as compared to the vast majority of the white managers, 82 percent (see Table D-4, Appendix D, page 282, for reasons for the managers' views). Again the races differ when asked why they disagree with their companies' policies. The largest number of blacks, 34 percent, cite as their primary reason "discrimination against blacks," in contrast to only 4 percent (one person) of the whites. Table 5-1 shows the total picture.

"Politics" (that is, the practice of hiring or promoting based not on ability and merit but on personal contacts and proper playing of the corporate "game") is given second importance by the black managers (see Table 5-1). This practice is described by a black lower level manager in Ace Public Utility: "My company doesn't always put the right man in the right

TABLE 5–1   WHY THE MANAGERS DISAGREE WITH THEIR COMPANIES' HIRING POLICIES (in %)

Reasons	Black Managers ($N = 72$)	White Managers ($N = 28$)
Discrimination against blacks	34	4
Politics	28	14
Policies not carried out	13	11
Seniority system should be de-emphasized	13	4
Agrees with hiring policies but not with promoting policies	7	4
Discrimination against women	7	0
Does not like testing system	6	4
Seniority system should be emphasized	6	14
Disagrees with selection and evaluation procedures	3	18
Disagrees with Affirmative Action Program	3	25
Other	3	14
Total[a]	123	112

[a] The total percentages are over 100 because several managers gave more than one reason and also because of rounding errors.

place. . . . You have to have contacts regardless of whether you can do the job or not." Twice the percentage of blacks as whites cite "politics" as a primary influence in company employment decisions. A possible explanation for this large difference is that because of their race, most blacks have been prevented from forming relationships on and off the job with their white subordinates, peers, and superiors that could be helpful to their careers. As will be seen further in Chapter 10, black managers emphasize that they would advise new blacks entering their firms to be especially cautious about and aware of corporate politics. (See Appendix C, page 259, for the frequency distribution of the advice black managers would give to other blacks entering their firms.)

Table 5-1 also shows a large difference in opinion on the seniority system between the black and white managers. Many of the blacks want to de-emphasize the system. The most reasonable explanation for their feeling is that now, after working very hard for the education and training required by the business world, they have finally received limited opportunities to demonstrate their abilities. They do not want to be held back by a seniority system they consider unfair because of the corporate world's past closed-door policy toward blacks.

When age is used as the control variable for all the questions dealing with the managers' views of the seniority system, it becomes clear that among the black managers of all ages there are no large differences. But the white managers are divided—the younger ones want to de-emphasize seniority and the older ones want to hold onto it. The older whites probably feel that their secure, monopolistic positions are being threatened by the new competition from minorities and women. If the seniority system is emphasized, the whites need not fear losing their promotional opportunities since they have served their companies for a longer period of time. In three of the large firms participating in this study, women and minorities make up more than 50 percent of the employment work force. With the old seniority system the white managers would have a substantial advantage. Another reason most of the white managers prefer to emphasize the seniority system is that many of the minority managers and women are better educated than they are, an additional cause for feeling threatened. Many of these white managers probably feel threatened by any educated person, even another white man; however, the threat from minorities and women is newer and of greater potential and is therefore of more concern to the older white managers.

Seniority is not the only practice that hinders blacks. Among the most damaging are the "unwritten" policies affecting individual decisions in both hiring and promotion. Such policies are based on factors having nothing to do with ability, such as physical appearance and social and political attitudes. Because an extremely high percentage of the white managers believe the formal employment policies of their firms are fair, one might expect that they would deny the existence of unwritten policies. But fully half of the white managers do admit to such policies, as shown in Table 5-2. A candid white middle level manager in Cousins Manufacturing remarks: "Some of the unwritten practices are standards of dress and personal appearance. Also political viewpoints—individuals must not be too militant or want to change capitalism. There is not enough room for divergent opinions. . . ." Another white manager, in the lower managerial ranks at Ace Public Utility, gives a very clear picture of how an unwritten dress code can work: "Someone who dresses rather bizarrely indicates a lack of maturity, and it would be an obstacle to his or her promotion to management. This is a conservative company."

As might be expected from their feelings on company fairness, 75 percent of the black managers acknowledge unwritten policies in their firms. High on the list of specifics are "discrimination" and "conformity," each cited by a fourth of the blacks. The interrelationship of these two factors is pinpointed cogently by a white middle level manager from Triple A Bank:

TABLE 5–2   HOW DO UNWRITTEN POLICIES AFFECT HIRING? (in %)

Unwritten Policies	Black Managers ($N = 116$)	White Managers ($N = 156$)
None	25	50
Discrimination	25	2
Conformity	24	8
Politics	21	10
Informal appearance	9	12
Individual biases	7	6
Sex favoritism for males	7	9
Blacks must not be militant	7	0
Affirmative Action Program	3	7
Careful placement of blacks	3	2
Sex favoritism for females	1	3
Other	12	24
Total[a]	144	133

[a] The total percentages are over 100 because the managers could give as many unwritten policies as they believed existed.

"People look for individuals who resemble them; therefore if you are different [black], you are at a disadvantage if your boss is white, which is the
case 99.9 percent of the time."

In addition to the emphasis on conformity for blacks, a recurring theme
is discrimination against women. The same white manager just quoted observes: "The discrimination against women in the past was not apparent,
and to many people it was not an obvious policy because of their conditioning. But realistically they [the companies] do discriminate against women."
Women are very much aware of this, as illustrated by the fact that four of
the five managers under 30 who emphasize the seniority system are women.
Their reason? Even though they have capably served their firms for a
number of years, they know that many less able white men have been
promoted over them. A white woman, one of the two women at the upper
level at Ace Public Utility, says: "If I'd been a man I would have reached
my present position faster and would have gone further." And a black
woman manager from Cousins Manufacturing sums up her own dual plight
and that of many like her: "Race and sex are unwritten employment
policies. Women can't reach high positions and the same is true for
blacks. . . . Blacks can't be too militant or aggressive."

Many of the black managers tell of cases they know in which blacks were
fired or transferred because, in the opinion of white superiors, they held
"militant" attitudes—which usually meant they spoke up about discriminatory company policies. Although white managers are affected by such
unwritten policies, blacks are affected to a much greater extent because so
many of the unwritten policies are applied more frequently and severely to
blacks simply because of their color.

The managers' views of their own companies' policies, then, divide quite
sharply along racial lines. Whereas 82 percent of the white managers believe
their company policies are fair, 63 percent of the black managers believe
their company policies are unfair. Fifty percent of the white managers
admit awareness of unwritten policies, compared to 75 percent of the
blacks. Put another way, although a significant number of whites do see unfairness in hiring policies within their own firms, the number of blacks who
see this is much higher. Such a situation can only prove harmful to those
who do not fit the corporate image, especially blacks, other minorities, and
women. In the long run the corporations will be adversely affected too.
They will lose large pools of exceptional talent.

To state it differently, most whites believe that their firms are color- and
sex-blind and therefore that company policies are fair. But most blacks
believe that the firms' claims of color- and sex-blindness are false and that
hiring and promotions are still white male-oriented. The reason the system
is still white male-oriented, even though the companies are supposedly

color- and sex-blind, is because the white man has received great advantages in terms of experience and seniority owing to past sexual and racial discrimination. In addition, because past discriminatory practices are hard to change and most decisions are still made by white men, the white man will have the advantage. White male managers will promote the individuals who fit their images of the most promotable managers, which, of course, will be white males.

But before we look more deeply into the reasons for support of this kind of inequity, the managers' views of black hiring and promoting in their own firms must be seen in a broader context. This context will reveal a wider overview less biased by managers' personal experiences, good or bad, or by their loyalties to their companies. On the question of fair employment of blacks, how do the managers see the corporate world as a whole compared to their own firms?

EMPLOYMENT: OTHER COMPANIES' POLICIES

The answers to this question were obtained by asking the managers a series of questions specifically related to the fact of race, for instance, "Is being black a helpful, harmful, or irrelevant factor for promotion in business in general?" Then, from the managers' responses, indexes were compiled (Tables 5-3 and 5-4) to see the general patterns and range of responses (see Appendix E, page 287, for the lists of questions that make up the indexes for Tables 5-3 and 5-4).

TABLE 5–3   HOW FAIR IS THE CORPORATE WORLD? (in %)

	Number of Questions Answered Negatively	Black Males ($N = 93$)	Black Females ($N = 23$)	White Males ($N = 133$)	White Females ($N = 23$)
Corporations are completely fair.	0	1	0	16	22
	1	15	0	23	17
	2	18	30	23	22
	3	34	17	29	26
Corporations are extremely unfair.	4	32	53	9	13
Total		100	100	100	100

TABLE 5–4   HOW FAIR ARE THE MANAGERS' OWN COMPANIES? (in %)

	Number of Questions Answered Negatively	Black Males (N = 93)	Black Females (N = 23)	White Males (N = 133)	White Females (N = 23)
Companies are completely fair.	0	8	0	29	39
	1	3	0	29	22
	2	8	4	17	0
	3	13	9	14	9
	4	11	17	5	17
	5	22	17	3	13
	6	18	23	2	0
Companies are extremely unfair.	7	18	30	2	0
Total[a]		101	100	101	100

[a] Some of the total percentages are over 100 because of rounding errors.

Not surprisingly, Table 5-3 shows that a much larger percentage of whites than blacks feel that the corporate world is completely fair in hiring and promoting blacks—a total of 18 percent of all the whites as opposed to 1 percent of the blacks. It is noteworthy that unfairness is felt most by the black women managers—53 percent agree that the corporate world is extremely unfair. Such a high percentage attests to the double stigma carried by this group of managers.

When an index was drawn of questions relating to the role of race in the managers' own firms, the results obtained from the white managers are surprising considering their responses in the previous section. Only about a third of the white managers think their companies are completely fair. Not even a tenth of the black managers think so, as shown in Table 5-4. Again Table 5-4: the black women managers are the most dissatisfied—30 percent feel that their companies are extremely unfair. Although not as strongly the white women managers feel their firms are much less fair to blacks than white men. Discrimination is making an alliance between blacks and white females. The white women, like the blacks, are feeling the effects of discrimination and are therefore much more critical of their companies' policies than the white men. For example, a young white woman manager at

Ace Public Utility states: "I had to start out in a clerical position even though I had a college degree, while the males started out in management. Women and blacks are being hired and promoted only because of civil rights and pressure from the government."

Views of company policy are also affected by how much contact a white manager has with blacks on the job. When frequency of contact with blacks is used as a control variable for the whites' overall views of their company employment policies, the results are significant. Generally those white managers with the most frequent contact with blacks on the job are likely to be more critical of their companies' policies toward blacks, and those white managers with the least frequent job contact with blacks are likely to be less critical of their companies. In addition, the white managers involved in personnel, affirmative action, and industrial relations, more than white managers in any other work area, disapprove more strongly of their companies' employment policies toward blacks. Because of their firsthand observations and experience, the white managers in these areas and the managers with the most job contact with blacks probably are assessing the situation more correctly and realistically than those who work in other areas or those who have no contact with black managers.

Another perspective on the responses among the white managers may be gained by comparing their contact with blacks not only on the job but outside of work. Again those white managers who have generally greater contact with blacks hold more critical views of their companies' employment policies toward blacks.

So far we have seen some differences (in Tables 5-3 and 5-4) in the managers' views about their companies and the corporate world's black employment policies, but the differences have not stood out that clearly. A sharper delineation is evident in Table 5-5, which breaks down the managers' responses by company. In general, the black managers do not see that much difference between the opportunities that exist for blacks in the corporate world and those in their own firms. This is especially true in the companies with weak Affirmative Action Programs. But in the company with the best Affirmative Action Program, Ace Public Utility, the largest number of blacks believe their firm is much fairer than the corporate world generally. This is despite the fact that 50 percent of the black managers interviewed from this firm are women, who are more critical than the men, as we saw above.

In addition, the table shows that the white managers are much more positive about their companies' black employment policies than about the corporate world's. The white managers have several reasons for this preferential view. First, most are not ready to criticize a system in which they have "made it." To do so would be admitting they have succeeded in

TABLE 5–5   A COMPARISON: FAIRNESS OF THE CORPORATE WORLD AND THE MANAGERS' OWN COMPANIES (in %)

Companies	Black Managers ($N = 116$)		White Managers ($N = 156$)	
	Firm	Business	Firm	Business
Ace Public Utility	50	80	20	52
Triple A Bank	55	77	19	54
Aunts Manufacturing	59	70	28	65
Cousins Manufacturing	63	70	36	43
Triple C Bank	63	70	13	37
Deuce Public Utility	72	74	21	49
Ajax Manufacturing	77	85	33	58
Century Manufacturing	88	85	8	35
Overall Mean	61	73	21	49

an illegitimate system. Second, the managers subscribe to the old adage that "it's the other guy who's unfair." And finally, the white managers are much more loyal to their companies than the blacks, and therefore do not want to denigrate their firms' policies. Opinions of their own companies' fairness most directly reflect the bias of the whites' favored positions. This is why the more realistic of their views are those on opportunities for blacks in industry as a whole.

It should also be noted that blacks in small operations of larger companies, such as Ajax and Century Manufacturing, are extremely critical of their companies' employment policies toward hiring and promoting more blacks. This is primarily because these small operations are generally staffed with older less-educated white men who, as Chapter 6 shows, have the most racist attitudes toward blacks. Thus sending blacks to smaller operations might hinder their changes of advancement. It should also be noticed that the black managers' views from the two parent companies, Aunts and Cousins Manufacturing, are not much different; however, Aunts comes out just a bit better because at the time of this study some concrete action was being planned and some halting steps toward EEO were beginning to have their effect on some of the black managers. Under the same chairman of the board, Cousins has not begun to tackle the problem of EEO as vigorously as Aunts—thus the difference.

Some of the managers' attitudes are strikingly and typically illustrated by a young white man in lower management. From a middle class family, he has 2 years of college and hardly sees blacks either on the job or off. When he looks at the general employment picture in the business world, he acknowledges that to be white and male are helpful for promotion, and to be black and female are not. But concerning his own firm, he sees no racial or sexual barriers to promotion: "Our company has a very aware group of managers. They are open-minded and have developed a progressive employment policy." But this man's company probably has one of the least aware and progressive managerial staffs of all the participating firms.

This same manager sees racial prejudice as the reason blacks are not rising, but to him it is the prejudice of other companies: "Most whites in this society are prejudiced and you can't overcome centuries of prejudiced thinking about blacks in a few years." Apparently the whites in his own firm, to judge by his first comment, are exceptions.

A number of older blacks, especially those without college degrees, hold views closer than most younger blacks to such white managers' views. Older blacks can remember when they were victimized by many worse injustices than those of the present. Many of these managers have learned to live with the system, even though they do not like it. But most younger blacks have their eyes open wider and are much more vocal (this is true also of some younger white managers). A primary ingredient for their awareness is better education than the older blacks. The younger ones now have the same credentials as whites and better credentials in many cases, but they are still being held back. A young black woman manager, who comes from a welfare family and graduated with honors from San Francisco State College, is strong in her opinion. She feels that her company is no better than the corporate world in general, that white men have the advantage, and that black hiring and promoting are mere tokenism: "Government has told our company to have blacks so they have a few blacks. Whites say blacks aren't making it because they aren't educated. I don't believe this—blacks simply aren't given the chance."

Ramifications of this situation have been predicted by more than one social critic. As H. L. Wilensky has written:

If educational opportunity whets the appetite for a better life but does not lead to job opportunity and income, it serves less as a compensatory reward than as a source of resentment. Thus, as their educational opportunities exceed their economic rewards and living standards, American Negroes will become more militant (Wilensky, 1966).

This is what is happening in some measure in the world of business. One of the older black middle managers at Triple A Bank gives this advice to new blacks entering his firm: "I tell them—be overly competent in your job, don't be afraid to speak up, watch your back at all times, and don't assume smiling white faces are friends." These are strong words, but they may be the only kind that will be effective in breaking through the racial barrier.

We have seen that many more blacks than whites believe they are discriminated against in numerous ways within their own firms and in industry in general, by both formal company policies and unwritten policies. In contrast although some white managers are willing to admit unfair practices, a much greater proportion of them overall see no unfairness at all in the treatment of blacks, especially in their own companies as compared to the corporate world. The black dilemma in the predominantly white business world is described in no uncertain terms by a white middle level manager at Ace Public Utility: "Everyone wants a clean-cut, white, all-American boy who won't be a problem."

Because they do not fit this description, blacks are being excluded. It would seem that the business world is not ready to confront the problem of racism. In fact to explain the exclusion of blacks, white managers make use of several seemingly rational explanations. In the next section the most important of these are examined and reveal the extent to which the stereotypical image has hampered the advancement of blacks in business.

THE REASONS FOR FEW BLACKS IN BUSINESS

"What are the explanations for the presence of blacks in business?" When the managers were asked this question with regard to their own firms, the black and white responses again differ markedly. As Table 5-6 shows, most black managers ascribe black employment not to fair or progressive policies but to external pressures, those of civil rights, society, and the government. A black middle level manager from Aunts Manufacturing gives an opinion heard before: "The only reason there are any black managers in this company is because the government has to be satisfied." But most white managers believe blacks are in their firms because of the company's "fairness."

There is one point of general agreement between the managers though. This is seen in Table 5-7. When asked their opinions about the small number of blacks in the corporate world at large, *both* races give as the primary cause "racial discrimination"! However aside from this point there are the usual extreme differences between the views of the blacks and the whites.

The reasons listed in the tables that managers give for the low representation of blacks in industry and their firms fall into three broader groupings. Admittedly, these are all interrelated and in practice are often inseparable; but for a clearer understanding of the factors involved, the groupings are dealt with individually. Two of them are used almost exclusively by white

TABLE 5–6   WHY THERE ARE BLACKS IN THE MANAGERS' FIRMS (in %)

Explanations	Black Managers (N = 116)	White Managers (N = 156)
Civil rights and social pressures	36	12
Governmental pressure	33	12
Racial discrimination	30	2
Company's fair employment policy	19	50
Blacks are qualified	14	21
AAP just beginning	10	15
Blacks are becoming more interested	4	1
Blacks are a new excellent resource	4	5
Lack of qualifications (education)	3	12
Blacks are not interested	1	4
Blacks are lazy, and so on	0	1
Other	3	4
Total[a]	157	139

[a] The total percentages are over 100 because many managers gave more than one explanation.

TABLE 5–7   WHY THERE AREN'T MORE BLACKS IN BUSINESS (in %)

Explanations	Black Managers (N = 116)	White Managers (N = 156)
Racial discrimination	84	62
Firms just beginning to practice EEO	9	13
Lack of education	8	30
Lack of awareness of business opportunities because of past discriminatory practices	6	6
Lack of qualifications	5	31
Showcasing (token hiring of blacks)	4	0
Different life styles	3	10
Lack of ambition and initiative, undependable	0	12
Blacks lack entrepreneurial attitude	0	10
Other	8	3
Total[a]	127	177

[a] The total percentages are over 100 because many managers gave more than one explanation.

managers as principal rationales for not hiring blacks. They are:

1. *The Cultural Argument.* Blacks lack the necessary entrepreneurial attitude or ethic, as well as the ambition, initiative, and dependability for success in the business world. Furthermore, the argument goes, blacks' lifestyles make them unable to fit well into corporate life.

2. *The Qualification Argument.* Blacks lack the educational achievement and other necessary qualifications, such as experience and technical know-how, to rise in business.

The third grouping is much broader than these two and encompasses them both. In a sense this third area is the subject of the entire book.

3. *Racial Discrimination.* As must be evident by now, this term can describe many different elements, a number of which are listed in Tables 5-6 and 5-7. The term itself is cited by a very large percentage of all the managers as the main reason for the small number of blacks in industry. Therefore racial discrimination in its widest sense must be considered as an extremely prominent factor. It is dealt with in this chapter by means of certain mathematical applications, regression analyses which use significant characteristics of the managers to determine salaries. The results of the analyses show dramatically the concrete effects of racial discrimination on the individual black manager.

THE CULTURAL ARGUMENT

Lack of the Entrepreneurial Ethic

A number of white managers believe that blacks have been brought up in an environment antithetical to a strong interest in or aptitude for business careers. This remark from a white middle level manager at Cousins Manufacturing is representative: "Many of the white college graduates are raised in a cultural world that has a bearing on their business ability. The environment in which blacks are raised does little to contribute to their understanding of the business world."

Is this contention true? Most black parents who attended college in the past normally pursued degrees in professional fields such as social services and teaching rather than business administration or the sciences. This is evident in the present study; Chapter 2 showed that the vast majority of the black parents with college degrees were clergymen, teachers, lawyers, doctors, or business owners in black communities. However, blacks selected social services, teaching, and helping professions not out of personal choice but out of necessity. They realized that a college degree in business administration or business-related subjects would prove of little use because of the white business world's exclusion of blacks. One of the black managers aptly summarizes this aspect of the cultural argument: "There is an opinion or myth that only sons of businessmen can make it. Whites are associated with the business world and people think blacks can't make it because their fathers never made it in the business world." But because a black comes from a non-business-oriented background does not necessarily mean he or she lacks the aptitude for business.

It is true that most of the white managers in this study come from families with entrepreneurial backgrounds. Their fathers were professionals, owners of small businesses, and managers themselves. It would seem very natural for children of these men to choose business. Many fathers of the black managers, though, were skilled or unskilled laborers. But *their* children have also chosen business. Why is this happening?

The most likely explanation is that blacks have been aware of and have possessed the entrepreneurial attitudes all along. After all, our entire American culture was founded on the Protestant ethic and is based on a capitalistic, business-oriented system. Blacks have been subject to the same private and public influences in this culture as whites and from the same early age. Blacks have had the same desires to become a contributing part of our system and receive its rewards. And blacks, especially the younger ones, are finally gaining the opportunity to break away from the cycle of the low paying and low status jobs to which their parents were condemned. This is primarily because various external pressures have forced black hiring on managerial levels. The fact that blacks are succeeding in business in the hostile atmosphere that exists toward them in this country is ample proof that they have the aptitude for the entrepreneurial ethic and have developed it. They need only a reasonable chance to demonstrate it.

Personality Characteristics

Another important aspect of the cultural argument says that blacks cannot succeed because they lack the necessary characteristics of personality, such as ambition, initiative, and dependability. Here are the typical comments of two middle level white managers, the first at Century Manufacturing and the second at Triple C Bank:

Caucasians are the most ambitious—blacks aren't interested in becoming a part of the business world.

There are a lot of things we take for granted that we better not when we bring black people to work here. Most of these people are not initially ready to take on the discipline of a job. We expect certain work habits from the white employees that can't be taken for granted from the black employees.

An experienced black middle level manager from Triple A Bank has seen much evidence of this type of attitude. He feels very strongly that both his firm and industry do not give blacks any decision-making power because "they don't trust blacks' abilities to make decisions."

Much sociological literature has dealt with the so-called "superior" values inculcated in children from middle and upper class families. These values increase motivation for higher educational and occupational achievement. It is expected then that middle and upper class children are more likely to attain higher positions as adults than children from lower, working class families (see Collins, 1968). When applied to blacks, who often come from less privileged backgrounds, the "personality characteristics" factor cuts two ways: Not only do blacks lack the necessary characteristics because of their race, but they lack them also because of their class.

The argument based solely on race is quickly seen as highly racist, but the argument based on class is less easily dismissed, especially because a number of past studies have produced data to support this argument (such as Warner and Abegglen, 1955). Recent re-evaluative work has yielded new evidence, which is contrary to previous findings. For instance, as noted in Chapter 2, a 1972 report entitled *Do The Poor Want To Work?* found very strong desires among welfare mothers and other poor people *and their children* to pursue good educations and good careers (Goodwin, 1972).

Most of the black managers interviewed in this study as well as most black people in general do not come from "superior" family backgrounds. But studies such as the one mentioned above and my experience and observations, bear out the fact that the black family, which has survived despite extreme racial oppression, has always attempted to instill in its children the desire for self-betterment and achievement.

More recently, the effects of the civil rights movement and the emphasis on "black pride" throughout our society have helped create and sustain "superior" values in blacks. Most telling of all is the fact that so many blacks today have already bettered their economic status in the face of overwhelming oppression. What better evidence is needed to show the forceful presence of the very personality traits—dependability, ambition, initiative—whites say that blacks lack?

The black managers in this study realize the importance of such traits. When asked what adivce they would give to a young black for achieving a high managerial position and for living a prosperous life in this society, many of the managers answer: Become well educated, develop your skills, set and pursue high goals and appropriate priorities, work hard, do the best you know how, and stand up for your rights. (These views are discussed in more detail in Chapters 9 and 10.)

It is not hard to imagine a white manager giving similar advice to young white men or women. In fact, the goals and ambitions of the two races are not very different. If anything, blacks are more ambitious and have higher goals, as will be seen further in Chapter 8. When the white managers are asked about positive and negative factors of the black managers they know, about one-fifth admit they see no real differences between the blacks and whites. In addition, a number praise the black managers in their companies for their self-confidence, high motivation, dedication, and ambition. Such praise adds further evidence that blacks do indeed possess the necessary characteristics for success. Unfortunately, this white view is in the minority.

It should be noted that many of the managers, both black and white, are aware of an ironical inconsistency in the attitudes of a large number of the white managers. At times they complain that blacks are lazy and have little or no ambition, initiative, and aggressiveness. And then these same white managers are heard to accuse the blacks of being *too* ambitious, independent, and aggressive. A young black woman lower level manager at Ace Public Utility observes: "They always find a problem with the blacks, such as their personality, aggressiveness, appearance, etc., etc." And a white middle manager from Triple A Bank corroborates this view: "Blacks are stereotyped as being lazy. When people are looking for a reason to find fault, they will use anything."

In other words, some whites will never be satisfied. This is yet another reason to question very seriously the validity of the "personality characteristics" component of the cultural argument.

Subculture Characteristics

The third variation of the cultural argument used to justify the small percentage of blacks in the business world, especially in the middle and upper ranks, is that of subcultural differences. At the extreme blacks are seen as a completely different, almost alien, species of human being. One white manager, at the middle level in Triple A Bank, minces no words: "I don't like the majority of black people. They are loud, noisy, and boisterous. I'm not so sure about the morals of the black race. Where blacks live in large numbers there are always a lot of problems."

At a less extreme level, even though blacks may have the requisite education and work experience, it is believed by many white managers that blacks cannot interact effectively with whites in higher business circles, particularly in social activities where much business is informally transacted. Why? Because their styles of dress and speech, personal mannerisms, and social mores produce what has been called a "culture gap" (Ferman, et al., 1968). For instance, a white lower level manager from Ace Public Utility comments: "The values and culture of whites have been an obstacle to blacks. It's more than just skin pigment. . . . Most blacks don't have the necessary cultural background to assimilate into the white business world." Another white manager from Triple C Bank supports this view by describing the only black male manager in his area: "He will do well. . . . He is from the upper middle class and has married a white woman, so it is easy for him to understand the white corporation."

Two black managers tell of experiences that do more than hint that perceived cultural differences are a definite factor in black hiring and promotion. The first manager, on the lower level at Triple A Bank, recalls: "I was thoroughly reviewed through normal channels, but I feel that they were also digging deeper, like checking with my schools and into my personal activities." The second, a middle level manager from Deuce Public Utility, relates a friend's experience: "I know a black who is up for promotion—he's the president of a black employee organization—and not only are his work activities being evaluated but so are his social activities."

White managers can find support for their contention that a culturally homogeneous group of managers is necessary for smooth organizational functioning. This very claim was the basis of a book by Chester I. Barnard called *Functions of the Executive,* which has been widely read since its publication (Barnard, 1948; for a critique of Barnard, see Packard, 1962). Barnard's observations have been borne out by at least one study of 76 large corporations, in which 90 percent of the terminated managers were dropped not because of professional or technical incompetence, but because of what were considered undesirable personality traits (Sayles and Strauss, 1960). Whatever the intention of Barnard's book, it has been interpreted by white managers as a recommendation and a defense to maintain the status quo—to hire the white male Anglo-Saxon Protestant, the "clean-cut, white, all-American boy. . . ."

But what happens when blacks completely assimilate into this culture as some have, and in accord with Barnard's "smooth functioning" theory tailor their behavior to the white majority? (For a discussion of this phenomenon, see Frazier, 1957.) One might then expect the blacks to have no trouble in being hired and promoted, but this is not the case.

The subcultural differences cited by white managers as reasons for excluding blacks are, to me, no more than an excuse for what is actually racial bias. The situation is well summarized by a middle level black manager, the assistant equal employment opportunity coordinator of Triple A Bank: "Until Blacks are accepted socially they will never move above middle management, because senior management necessitates socialization. Although whites and blacks work together, whites are reluctant to 'play' with blacks because of their racist attitudes."

Blacks have a double burden in our society. As Afro-Americans they must be bicultural. Social scientist Charles A. Valentine has said, "They must be able to behave with a certain effectiveness in terms of the standards prescribed by both worlds" (Valentine, 1972). This bicultural competency develops and must develop for survival from a very early age. It is developed both consciously and unconsciously, through all of our society's organizations—the community, educational and political institutions, news media, and the arts, to name a few. The necessity for blacks of dual cultural competence in our society is clearly explained by Valentine:

Most Black people are prevented from activating or actualizing their lifelong socialization into white patterns, the same patterns which so many Euro-Americans easily use to achieve affluence and ease. Most Blacks are reduced to peripheral manipulations around the edges of a system which might have crushed them entirely long ago if they had not acquired and developed such multiple competences as they could (Valentine, 1972, p. 33).

These observations have been illustrated by our emerging picture of black managers in the business world.

The entire cultural argument is unjustifiable, first because it is used in a racial manner, and second, because it is used in a class manner. Although many blacks do come from lower class backgrounds, this does not exclude the possibility of many variations of lifestyle and attitude within a given class, much less an entire race. It is more than likely that a poor, uneducated, lower class, black ghetto inhabitant would have trouble functioning in the corporate world because of his or her background—but the same could be said of a poor, uneducated, lower class white. A white middle level manager from Cousins Manufacturing admits, "The white community considers blacks to be different without really knowing them. Their lack of social and business contact with blacks has tended to segregate them in their own minds. Therefore, they categorize blacks into one group."

The truth is not that blacks, especially those aspiring to become managers, possess cultural differences that would hinder their becoming a part of the business world. Rather, they have been stopped because of racial barriers and have been given little chance to disprove the white attribution of undesirable characteristics. The truth is not that blacks are unable to interact with whites—they are forced to do so every day—but that many whites will not or cannot admit that blacks can interact successfully if given the slightest opportunity. It is the many whites who have isolated themselves, as the manager quoted above observed, who are unable or unwilling or both to interact successfully with the blacks.

THE QUALIFICATION ARGUMENT

The argument that blacks lack the education, technical and professional knowledge, and experience to do the job properly has been the main explanation of white writers who have studied the low proportion of blacks in the business world. (See, for example, Gourlay, 1965; Quay, 1969; Thieblot, Jr., 1970.) It may not be readily evident from Tables 5-6 and 5-7, but this argument is also the one the white managers in this study use most often. Their rationale is that emphasis on qualifications shows their companies' fairness; the implication is that blacks were rejected in the past not from racial or cultural bias but because they lacked the qualifications. Here is a typical comment by a white middle level manager in Triple C Bank: "Our company has a fair employment policy. The blacks whom we employ as managers are qualified. If they weren't, we wouldn't have hired or promoted them."

The majority of white managers believe the opportunities exist but that blacks do not have the necessary qualifications. This is expressed by a white upper level manager from Ace Public Utility:

My department [engineering] is unable to find any colored fellows to hire—they are not qualified. We're under pressure to find colored people and minorities and we'd like to get some. There just aren't many colored people in engineering. I'm going to have a terrible time trying to fill my affirmative action quota. We have one colored summer student I'd like to keep, but these people are in great demand by other companies too.

And a white upper level manager from Cousins Manufacturing has this to say:

At present we have a few blacks in inside sales, but we won't put them into outside sales until we're sure they can handle the job. We'd put a white in there first because he could handle the job better.

On the other hand, most blacks believe that blacks *do* have the necessary qualifications and that it is only the opportunity that is lacking. The philosophy of the white manager just quoted affected a black lower level manager in his company in exactly this way. He recalls: "I was placed in a temporary position for four months before I was made a senior salesman. My white peers have spent at most six weeks in the training program—but I was the first black." Another black manager, from Triple C Bank, relates a parallel story: "Before I was promoted I was a supervisor and I was kept there for five years, which is an abnormally long time. I was told this was because there was no one to replace me. Probably being black was the cause." The black and white views are completely contradictory. To get to the root of them it is necessary to look further into the qualification argument.

Importance of Education

Education is a cornerstone of the qualification argument, and so the relevance of educational requirements to managerial positions should be examined. Studies have found that the average American worker holds 12 major jobs during his or her normal work life (45 years), and that only one-fifth of the workers hold the same occupation throughout their careers. Thus to the average worker specialized educational training is not likely to be of indispensable value (see Wilensky, 1967). Many researchers concerned with the relationship of educational achievement to success have questioned the business world's emphasis on college degrees. The researchers have reached several conclusions. First, educational requirements are overemphasized. Second, the primary function of education for business is a socializing one, and most of the necessary training is learned not in school but on the job. Third, and possibly most important, during their careers most managers hold positions *not directly related* to their major field of college study (see Dalton, 1951; Gordon and Howell, 1959; Wilensky, 1967.)

The white male managers in the present study bear out this last finding. Many of the white men who were trained in engineering and other physical sciences are employed in financial and personnel sectors. Others trained in the social sciences have been placed in production and technical areas. And many others with no college degrees hold technical, financial, and production jobs. Also it is common practice to transfer the more competent managers every two or three years to a new area, as part of the grooming process for upper management positions.

But most of the black managers, especially those in the middle ranks, are almost exclusively placed in fields in which they received college training. Almost all (96 percent) of the black middle level managers with college degrees are employed in the areas of their college specialization, compared to a little over half (57 percent) of the white middle managers. The 24 percent of the black managers who have technical or scientific degrees are all working in these areas, which is not the case with the white managers. Of the women managers, all the blacks and five of the six whites work in the areas of their college training. These statistics indicate great restrictiveness—because of bias— on the part of the firms towards both women and blacks. A black manager from Deuce Public Utility tells of his experience with educational requirements: "I had an A.A. degree and I was replaced by a guy I had to train because he had no knowledge of the job he was supposed to do. . . . In order to get my present job I had to get a B.S. Whites don't have to have college degrees."

It is not that educational achievement is unnecessary or umimportant. What is questioned here is the extent to which specific educational training is made a prerequisite for blacks and not for whites. Because of this prerequisite blacks are kept locked into certain jobs, with fewer opportunities for diverse experience and training, while whites are promoted over them.

Many whites especially males who have no specialized education in their occupational fields have become very successful managers, and some, as observed above by the black manager, have had no college training at all. It is
axiomatic that most of the knowledge for a given job is learned in the doing
and not in the classroom. But so far this seems to be a white axiom. The
time has come to extend it to blacks too, rather than continue to emphasize
overly high educational achievement as a primary qualification for black
employment.

Difficulty of Evaluation

It is often very difficult to evaluate and even to define what qualifications
are necessary for a particular job. Although most people might agree that a
social worker would not be qualified to deal with a complex problem in
chemical engineering, it is much harder to determine the best qualified of a
number of chemical engineers or a number of nontechnical managers. As
hard as technical and professional skills are to evaluate, more difficult are
the intangible skills especially needed for managerial positions: leaderslip,
organizational and planning abilities, and reasoning and communicative
skills. Added to this is the fact that evaluation ultimately depends, as Theodore Caplow has put it, "on the judgment, and hence on the good will, of
one's superiors . . . [where] even objective achievement usually requires the
active cooperation of occupational superiors" (Caplow, 1954).

Evaluation is difficult enough for white managers within their own race;
there are greater problems when whites try to evaluate blacks. Until
recently many white managers saw nothing objectionable in blacks being
confined to certain levels and certain jobs, regardless of their qualifications.
So now when blacks are demanding the same opportunities as whites, it is
even harder for the whites to reverse their longstanding racially biased
views. (For discussion of this situation, see Gourlay, 1965).

Black Overqualification

The white managers' biased views are resulting in a new method of discriminating against blacks: If blacks must be hired and promoted into all
areas and levels of business, then higher qualifications will be required of
them. This attitude is revealed by the managers' responses to two statements:

1.   Blacks must be a little better than others to get ahead in this company.
2.   My firm is more careful in promoting black employees than white
employees because it wants to be certain that blacks will succeed before
promoting them.

From the managers' responses to previous questions in this chapter, it would seem reasonable to expect the vast majority of the white managers to disagree strongly with the first statement and disagree with the second, and the vast majority of the black managers to strongly agree with the first and agree with the second. As to the first statement, more than one-third of the white managers agree. The lower level white managers, who have the most on-the-job contact with blacks, believe more frequently (49 percent) that blacks in their companies must be a little better to get ahead. Only 34 percent of the middle level whites and 23 percent of the upper level whites believe this. A lower level white manager in Ace Public Utility puts it this way: "A black individual has to be really talented to make it . . . ."

The responses of the white lower level managers are probably more accurate and knowledgeable reflections of the real situation than the middle and upper level managers' responses. The higher in rank managers are, the further away they are from actual supervision and evaluation of black managers. This is because there are very few blacks in the middle level and none in the upper level of management. Therefore the higher managers may very well be indulging in wishful self-congratulation. Since they have little actual contact with blacks, they may be reacting not to the situation as it really is but as they think it should be.

Of the black managers the overwhelming majority, 88 percent, agree that blacks indeed have to be better to get ahead. A black woman manager from Ace Public Utility comments: "Blacks must be twice as good as whites." Another black, a middle level manager from Aunts Manufacturing, knows the situation well: "I have to be better—I can't afford to make the mistakes my white counterparts can. If I do, I'm never allowed to forget it." Statements such as these support the black managers' view that blacks must be "superblacks"—highly overqualified and achieving—before they are hired or promoted. The white managers' contention that blacks are not or were not hired or promoted because they lack the necessary qualifications seems highly suspicious in light of the managers' responses thus far. (See the discussion on educational qualification in Chapter 2).

The managers' opinions on the second statement, whether they believe their companies take greater care in promoting black employees, show that many more blacks than whites think this is the case. Two-thirds of the black managers agree with the statement as compared to more than one-fourth of the white managers. Interestingly enough, more upper level managers agree—one in three whereas less than one in four of the lower and middle managers agree. For the two statements a total of more than 50 percent of the white managers believe blacks must be better and/or their promotions are considered more carefully by the firms. (The reasons for the managers' beliefs are given in Appendix C, pages 259–278.)

Comments from the managers reveal more of the story. A middle level white manager from Cousins Manufacturing says: "Blacks are more competent than their white counterparts. I am careful with my black managers."

Further insight into the white position is provided by an upper level white manager from the same company: "I think it [the company] only wants to be right when it puts a black in a position. It's too important to get blacks into positions and not be careless in promoting them. They can't turn out to be failures." And finally, a white middle level manager from Ace Public Utility aptly sums up the present situation in the corporate world regarding qualifications: "Most black executives are super-blacks—mediocrity is the privilege of the white male."

To recapitulate, eight out of 10 of the white mangers believe their companies' employment policies are fair; nine out of 10 believe their firms are not simply paying lip service to equal opportunities for blacks; and more than one out of two believe blacks in their firms must be better than whites to get ahead and/or that the firms are most careful in promoting blacks to be certain of their future success.

There are some obvious contradictions in the white managers' views. If black managers must be above average and if blacks are more carefully evaluated because their firms want to be certain they will succeed before promoting them, these companies are discriminating against blacks. Such practices are extremely futile and extremely unfair to blacks, primarily because no one can be certain that any manager, regardless of color, will succeed before promoting him or her. In addition, requiring blacks to be overqualified could lead firms to institutionalize dual selection and evaluation systems that would set unrealistic standards for blacks.

In other words, if firms require blacks to be overqualified, blacks would be expected to have superior records. Anything below superior would be considered unacceptable. Again this would be a far cry from offering equal employment opportunities. Furthermore, requiring black overqualification can have harmful effects on the attitudes of the black managers toward themselves and their work. If blacks believe they must be better than whites in qualifications and job performances, the resulting pressure can damage their work attitudes to the point where qualified, capable blacks become ineffective, and/or frustrated managers ready to leave their firms. Evidence of this situation will be seen in Chapter 8.

True equal employment opportunities will exist when an average black can secure a job and promotion with the same efforts as an average white. Blacks must have the chance to fail or succeed by the same rules and criteria that govern whites. Until this happens, no firm can truly be considered an equal opportunity employer.

Reverse Discrimination

Even though the majority of white managers believe blacks must be "super blacks," a persistent undercurrent among the whites is that if you are black "you have it made." As a white middle level manager from Triple C Bank comments: "Now it's the other way around. Blacks are given promotions faster than they deserve them." Managers of both races have several general explanations for such a belief by whites: (1) many companies use extensive public relations strategies in the area of equal opportunities that present an image of the companies' doing everything in their power to give blacks equal employment opportunities; (2) any movement toward more equitable employment policies is seen by many white managers as giving blacks an advantage; and (3) there is a general belief in white society that blacks are getting all the advantages and that whites are being pushed into the background. A white middle level manager exemplifies some of these views: "I had some trouble adjusting to the recent policies of promoting blacks. I felt that at times the blacks were not the most able people for the jobs and that the company was trying to overcome its guilt and make up for it in six months."

Both the cultural and the qualifications arguments as explanations for the black mangers' position in the white corporate world are highly questionable, but many white managers believe these arguments. To show how these attitudes can coexist, with all their contradictions, as part of an individual's overall outlook, a profile is presented of a white male manager on the middle level.

This manager is 35 years old, with an masters degree in Mechanical Engineering from Claremont College. He comes from a middle class family, his father having been a middle level manager for Southern Pacific Railroad. Our manager has frequent contacts with blacks at work but little, if any, contacts with them outside work.

On the one hand, he believes that being black is a helpful factor for promotion in his firm and that being white is irrelevant. He also feels that this firm is not simply paying lip service to equal employment opportunity efforts but that the difficulty lies in finding qualified blacks: "The company's policy is fair. We have few blacks because most are not qualified. The firm is making every effort to recruit and hire qualified blacks." But on the other hand, according to this manager, blacks do have to be better than whites to get ahead in his firm. And the firm, he admits, is more careful in promoting blacks than whites, to insure that the blacks will succeed: "Blacks have to be more competent in more areas than their white counterparts. With the black managers under me, I'm more careful."

Finally, in another set of contradictory views this manger believes that blacks can rise only as far as middle management because they lack the qualifications to go higher. But he also says that even the blacks who are qualified for upper management could probably not attain this level "because of the social implications."

RACIAL DISCRIMINATION

Another term for the kind of "social implications" the manager quoted above is talking about is racial discrimination. The cultural and qualifications arguments cannot be taken as valid explanations for the blacks situation in the corporate world. A more plausible reason, which is at the root of these arguments, is discrimination: To be black is, simply, unacceptable.

That this statement has far-ranging effects in today's business world can be shown quite forcefully by approaching the manager's situation from a mathematically based standpoint, in which many of the factors associated with the cultural and qualification arguments can be measured. The method used is the multiple regression analysis, a statistical means by which to determine the effects of a number of independent variables on a dependent variable. In this case, the independent variables are:

> Job Duration (JD)
> Education (ED)
> Outside Job Experience (Duration) (OJD)

The dependent variable is:

> Salary

One would expect these variables to have an essentially additive effect on salary. Therefore the regression equation is determined by using B_1 as a constant term and other B terms as partial regression coefficients, which measure the effect of a unit change in each independent variable on the dependent variable. The equation is then

$$\text{Salary} = B_1 + B_1 JD + B_2 ED + B_3 OJD$$

Each individual variable was assigned coded values: job duration 0 to 21, education 0 to 9, and outside job experience (duration) 0 to 21. In order to determine the different or similiar effects job duration, education and outside work experience have on the salary of black and white managers separate regression equations were run for them. With the appropriate statistical tests, the following equations were found to have significant explanatory power: 37 percent for the black managers and 34 percent for the white managers (see the more detailed explanations and table in Appendix F, pages 288–289):

For blacks only:

$$Salary = -1.2 + .36(JD) + .48(ED) + .09(OJD)$$

For whites only:

$$Salary = -4.9 + .52(JD) + 1.0(ED) + .31(OJD)$$

From the partial regression coefficients it can be seen that a unit change in any of the individual variables means a greater increase in salary for whites than for blacks. How does this work in actuality?

Applying the characteristics of our sample manager with two years on the job, a college degree, and no outside work experience, if he or she is black the formula reads:

$$Salary = -1.2 + .36(0) + .48(8) + .09(0)$$

When converted to dollars, the black manager's salary would be $9200. With the same characteristics, if he or she is white, the formula reads:

$$Salary = -4.9 + .52(0) + 1.0(8) + .31(0)$$

After conversion it is found that the white manager's salary would be $10,200.

It is clear that in such a case a college degree alone would mean about $1000 more for a white than for a black. The white gains more proportionately with the other variables also. Further calculations show that a one-unit change in job duration means an increase per year of $360 for a black but $520 for a white. And for each additional year of outside work experience the white would earn $220 more per year than the black. As noted, detailed discussion of the regression analyses may be found in Appendix F, pages 288–289. The important point here is that these equations vividly and concretely add further proof that education and work experience have much more influence on the salaries of white than black managers. In short blacks are not making it in the corporate world not because they don't have the necessary qualification, but because they are black.

A CONCLUSION

The picture presented here is a disturbing one. There are great differences in the beliefs and explanations of the black and white managers for the low presence of black managers both in their own firms and in the corporate world generally. It is quite obvious from the material presented in this chapter that real equal employment opportunities for blacks still do not exist. One of the most pervasive of American myths holds that, regardless of race, creed, color, or national origin, in this land one can get ahead solely on his or her own abilities. A great many whites are living proof of this myth, but so far for blacks in this country, there is very little evidence that the myth has become a reality.

CHAPTER SIX

Racial Atmosphere and Company Employment Policies

Chapter 5 concluded that the vast majority of the black managers and a significant minority of the white managers in this study do not believe that real equality of opportunity for blacks exists in their firms. The discrimination noted by the managers takes a number of forms: overt discrimination, emphasis on the "right" type or the overqualified black, and greater care in promoting black employees than white. This chapter discusses in depth the attitudes that bring about discriminatory actions against blacks.

Because of the crucial role whites play in providing equal employment opportunities for blacks, several aspects of their attitudes will be dealt with here. Among them are: (1) the racial atmosphere in the firms, that is, the attitudes, feelings, and remarks of the white employees that managers of both races hear and believe to exist; (2) the racial attitudes of the participating white managers toward black people, both generally and specifically with regard to the black managers in their firms; and (3) the attitudes of the managers of both races on deviation from formal company employment policies, and how the managers would deviate or have already deviated.

Such considerations are a necessary part of an analysis of the position of blacks in the business world and of the improvement of this position. Because corporate policies, however progressive, can be changed and distorted through complex networks of social relationships as the policies are applied at the lower occupational levels, any effective Affirmative Action Program will depend heavily on the attitudes of the white managers who control the corporation. As we glimpsed in Chapter 3, if the white managers at any level are opposed to the AAP of their company, they can usually make the program quite ineffective in practice, even though it may be strong and elaborate on paper. There must be strong enforcement procedures to create an atmosphere in which these racist attitudes will not lead to discriminatory behavior.

The white managers' attitudes will largely determine to what extent the black managers are allowed to participate in and receive the benefits of the psychology of group life. If the whites generally have negative attitudes toward blacks, they most likely will exclude blacks from playing a part in the network of social relationships. This could limit the cooperation and information needed to carry out specific assignments, and thus the blacks' job performance would suffer and their progress would be hindered. Such negative attitudes could also limit the blacks' opportunities to make those personal impressions on subordinates, peers, and superiors that are essential for any individual's progress. Unfair situations such as these make it essential to discover the extent to which negative racial attitudes exist in the participating firms.

RACIAL ATMOSPHERE IN COMPANIES

The negative racial attitudes the managers hear expressed in their companies fall into several categories. The most frequent attitude the managers are aware of is the stereotypical belief that blacks are lazy, dumb, or slow. As one black lower level manager at Triple C Bank describes it: "Many whites who claim they are not prejudiced frequently say that blacks are slow and dumb, but they never say that about other whites." An upper level manager at Triple A Bank has seen the effects of a hostile racial atmosphere: "Some of my white subordinates treat blacks badly. They are very curt with them and don't give them the courtesy of an explanation because they assume the blacks are too dumb to learn."

The second most frequent attitude of which the managers are aware is the white belief in and resentment of what is perceived as reverse discrimination. A black lower level manager from Triple A Bank reports: "I keep hearing the old clichés like, 'We don't see why you niggers want so much' and 'You blacks are getting all the breaks.'"

Another frequently encountered attitude is undisguised opposition on the part of whites against blacks—they refuse to hire, work with, or promote blacks. A black lower level manager at Cousins Manufacturing tells of the openly admitted prejudice in his firm: "One white manager at the lower level sent a written memo to personnel saying he didn't want any more blacks in his department because they were lazy and didn't want to work. Many departments say they have their quotas and don't want any more." And a white lower level manager in Ace Public Utility says: "I have associates who are definitely prejudiced. They would not promote a black person." Two black managers at the same firm relate their experience with uncooperative white co-workers: "One employee wouldn't talk to me even though it was his job." And: "When I first got here, even though I was assistant manager, my authority was questioned by my subordinates."

Superiors as well as subordinates demonstrate hostility that excludes blacks from the psychology of group life. A black lower level manager from Aunts Manufacturing recalls: "When I became an accountant supervisor, my boss didn't introduce me to anyone in the department or assist me in any way."

To determine the extent and awareness of such types of hostility, the managers were asked a number of questions. These questions did not ask for the managers' own opinions but were aimed at pinpointing their awareness of the views of white people in their companies. The four questions were as follows:

1. Are you aware of any carryover into the work situation of negative white attitudes toward blacks?
2. Would any of your peers and subordinates feel in any way uncomfortable if you hired or promoted someone who was black into a management position?
3. Would your immediate superior feel in any way uncomfortable if you hired or promoted someone who was black into a management position?
4. Would any of the managers above your immediate superior feel in any way uncomfortable if you hired or promoted someone who was black into a management position?

An index measuring perceived racial hostility was compiled from the managers' responses to these four questions, with a score of 1 given for each affirmative response. When a manager scores 0, this indicates that he or she answered none of the questions affirmatively and thus believes the racial atmosphere in his or her company to be free of any racial hostility. A score of 4 indicates affirmative answers to all the questions and the manager's belief that his or her company is quite hostile to blacks. The frequency distribution of the managers' responses is shown in Table 6-1. The table indicates

TABLE 6–1   THE MANAGERS' OVERALL VIEWS OF THEIR COMPANIES' RACIAL ATMOSPHERES

	Number of Questions Answered Affirmatively	Black Men $(N = 93)$	Black Women $(N = 23)$	White Men $(N = 133)$	White Women $(N = 23)$
No racial hostility	0	10	9	27	31
	1	25	17	28	39
	2	25	35	33	13
	3	24	26	12	13
Extreme racial hostility	4	16	13	0	4
Total		100	100	100	100

that a substantial majority of both black and white managers are aware of negative racial attitudes and/or employees' uncomfortable feelings toward blacks. Only approximately 10 percent of the black managers and 27 percent of the white managers believe they are working in a situation where whites do not seem to have any negative racial attitudes.

Differences Among the White Managers

The white managers were asked another question that was not included in the index: Do your hear derogatory remarks about blacks in your company? The white managers' responses are very interesting. If their answers to this question were included in the index, the results would show that only 17 percent believe their firms are free of negative racial attitudes, a decrease of about 10 percent from the original index. When the question is narrowed as to who the managers hear making derogatory remarks, it is found that all managerial levels indulge in this. Of the upper level managers, 47 percent indicate that they hear such remarks from their peers and 30 percent indicate hearing such remarks from their superiors.

The managers were also asked what they do when they hear derogatory remarks. Only 50 percent of the whites who hear them from their peers and subordinates express dislike for such hostile remarks, and only 20 percent who hear them from superiors express dislike. One manager who not only sees prejudice among his subordinates but does something about it is this upper level manager at Aunts Manufacturing: "The people who work for me have prejudiced attitudes and I talk to them about it. Just because there's as much prejudice in the company as on the streets is no reason to stand by and just watch."

Those managers who do not object to negative remarks geneally mask their own prejudice by saying that individuals are entitled to their opinions.

Finally, it should be noted that the upper level white managers are more aware of a hostile atmosphere than the middle and lower level white managers. None of the questions were answered affirmatively, indicating no racial hostility, by only 17 percent of the upper level managers, compared to 32 percent of the middle level managers and 26 percent of the lower level managers.

There are several explanations for the differences in awareness of hostile racial atmosphere among the various managerial levels. Many senior level managers have not only heard fellow colleagues express negative attitudes because they have been under pressure from various internal and external sources to implement AAP's, but they have also heard many negative comments directly and indirectly from white employees about affirmative action efforts.

On the other hand, the lack of awareness of a negative company racial atmosphere on the part of many middle level managers is probably explained by the isolation of this group. There are few blacks at this level compared to the lower level. Middle managers also do not receive the brunt of government and civil rights pressures. These managers are much less exposed than those at the other levels to situations that bring out into the open hostile remarks and attitudes. At the middle level there is little direct supervision of blacks, competition from blacks as is the case with lower level managers, or pressures from internal and external groups to improve the employment opportunities of blacks as is the case with upper level managers.

Differences Among the Black Managers

The lower level black managers are more aware of a negative racial atmosphere than those at the middle level. This is owing primarily to the age differences of the managers and to the fact that the young er managers are usually on the lower levels. Of those managers who answered none or only one of the questions affirmatively, indicating that a negative racial atmosphere does not exist, the smallest percentage is in the black managers under 30–22 percent. Next is the group between the ages of 31 and 40–36 percent. And finally there is the group over 40, who see the least evidence of hostility—56 percent.

The younger black managers are probably more sensitive to negative white attitudes and more vocal in their criticism than the older blacks because they have been brought up in the more recent atmosphere of intense black pride and racial awareness. Although the older blacks have had more difficult times in the corporate world and white society generally, they have most likely become immune to negative white attitudes. Too, they may believe that things have improved to such a degree that the present negative white attitudes are nothing compared to the past. Thus the older blacks do not believe these attitudes are obvious enough to say they are aware of them.

It is also quite possible that the older blacks' conditioning has been such that they do not expect to be treated very well (that is, equally) by whites and may therefore have a conception of the meaning of negative racial atmosphere different from the younger blacks. They younger blacks have much greater expectations about their treatment by whites, and so there is bound to be a much wider gap between their expectations and the realities.

Differences Among the Companies

Attitudinal differences, like many other differences previously examined, are directly tied to the effectiveness of the companies' Affirmative Action Programs. Tables 6-2 and 6-3 show the managers' responses, averaged and by company, to the questions cited earlier about negative attitudes and un-

TABLE 6–2 THE MANAGERS' VIEWS OF NEGATIVE RACIAL ATTITUDES AMONG THEIR PEERS AND SUBORDINATES (in %)

Companies	Black Managers	White Managers	White Managers (Includes Derogatory Remark Responses)
Triple C Bank	60	45	43
Cousins Manufacturing	62	50	57
Aunts Manufacturing	71	57	56
Ace Public Utility	73	57	56
Deuce Public Utility	73	53	57
Triple A Bank	74	71	67
Ajax Manufacturing	83	64	69
Century Manufacturing	100	54	58
Overall Mean	69	55	56

TABLE 6–3 THE MANAGERS' VIEWS OF NEGATIVE RACIAL ATTITUDES AMONG THEIR PEERS, SUBORDINATES, SUPERIORS, AND SUPERIORS' BOSSES (in %)

Companies	Black Managers	White Managers	White Managers (Includes Derogatory Remark Responses)
Triple C Bank	47	26	29
Cousins Manufacturing	48	30	37
Ace Public Utility	51	31	36
Triple A Bank	54	46	47
Aunts Manufacturing	57	34	38
Deuce Public Utility	60	32	37
Ajax Manufacturing	66	37	45
Century Manufacturing	75	30	37
Overall Mean	53	32	38

comfortable feelings, first (Table 6-2) among the managers' peers and sub-ordinates, and second (Table 6-3) among their peers, subordinates, superiors, and superiors' bosses. The third column in each table includes the white managers' responses to the appropriate questions as well as the question about the managers' hearing derogatory remarks about blacks.

The managers' responses indicate the bearing of the AAPs on views of the racial atmosphere in the companies. For example, in Ace Public Utility a large percentage of the black managers believe that whites in their company hold racist attitudes (Table 6-2, 73 percent). This is despite the finding earlier (Chapters 3 and 5) that only 50 percent of the black managers in this company felt they were treated unfairly. This could mean that although whites harbor negative attitudes, they are not able to translate their feelings into actions because the company's emphasis on equal employment opportunities has made it more difficult for them to discriminate against blacks. Such a view of white negative attitudes is not held by many black managers in the other companies, although it is held by most white managers. That is, most whites in all the firms believe whites may indeed have racist attitudes but they are not translated into discriminatory behavior.

This belief would be more credible if *all* the firms had strong, well-developed AAPs, with appropriate implementation, compliance, and disciplinary procedures, in addition to a well-developed managerial training program (to be discussed in Chapter 10). Such programs would then insure that the white managers who hold racist attitudes would not act on them by discriminating against blacks. But this is not the case, and thus the consequence of such attitudes can only mean that the firms' AAPs will be distorted, made weaker, or not be carried out at all.

The tables indicate further that good affirmative action may well have the immediate effect of sharpening conflicts and increasing racial hostilities, especially in the lower ranks where most blacks are employed. An illustration of this is the percentages in Table 6-2 of black views on white negative racial attitudes in Ace Public Utility and Triple A Bank, the companies that have the best AAPs. The percentages are quite high—73 percent and 74 percent, respectively—indicating a large degree of hostility between the races (the 100 percent in Century Manufacturing represents only one person). In this connection frequent derogatory remakrs heard by the managers are related to reverse discrimination in blacks' favor; such remarks often go with a strong and effective AAP.

Although Table 6-3 shows the general trend of decreasing racial hostility in all the companies, when the upper levels are included it is noteworthy that Ace Public Utility and Triple A Bank record the greatest percentage decreases in the black managers' feelings about negative racial atmospheres in their firms. When their responses about peers and subordinates (Table 6-2) are compared with their responses including superiors (Table 6-3), the percentage of black managers in Ace Public Utility who feel negative attitudes on the part of whites drops from 73 percent to 51 percent, and the percentage of black managers who feel this way in Triple A Bank drops from 74 percent to 54 percent, decreases of 22 and 20 percentage points.

These drops are testimony to the greater confidence the black managers in these two companies have in their upper level managers. The smallest decreases are in Triple C Bank and Deuce Public Utility, the first from 60 percent to 47 percent, and the second from 73 percent to 60 percent, both showing a drop of 13 percentage points. These are the firms whose AAPs leave a great deal to be desired, where one out of three of the black managers believe their immediate superiors would feel uncomfortable about blacks in management positions, and where the black managers feel much resistance to equal employment opportunities from upper management. A black lower level manager at Deuce Public Utility attests to such attitudes: "In my department you hear whites always saying that blacks don't do their jobs correctly or don't have the ability. The whites say blacks are taking over. You also hear whites say they dislike militant blacks or that blacks come on too strong."

This comment illustrates the prevalence among whites of an attitude of reverse discrimination. In my continuing research on black and women managers, I have found an ever-increasing feeling among white men that blacks are indeed becoming favored over whites. This belief—which is unfounded—is nevertheless building up a great deal of resentment and fear among white men, despite the fact (as Chapter 5 showed) that undeniably whites, especially men, are still given tremendous advantages over blacks. The white men's fears will be discussed in Chapter 10, but here an indication of the strength of this feeling is given by two white managers at Cousins Manufacturing, who tell about some of the remarks they have heard:

I hear comments about reverse discrimination, caustic comments about the term "Black is Beautiful," and comments about the toughness of whites' getting jobs in the labor market because of blacks.

There are hostility and resentment among the whites. I hear them complaining about being forced into situations where they have to hire blacks who they say cannot do the job.

In light of such attitudes it is no wonder that blacks are experiencing the effects of discrimination. But do all the white managers hold such attitudes in the same degree? And if not, how different are their attitudes.

HOW THE WHITE MANAGERS FEEL ABOUT BLACKS

Stereotypical Attitudes

Kenneth Clark has made some significant observations as to how white negative racial attitudes are perpetuated:

In a society, it can become fashionable to dislike some group of people for various reasons: "Everyone else dislikes Jews and Negroes. I can't be different. I must dislike them, too. . . . " In time, these ideas and attitudes become ingrained in the individual, accepted as a normal, natural way of life . . . and become an aspect of lifestyle, enmeshed in status, privileges and personal aspirations.

Clark further explains how disagreement with the in-group can profoundly threaten the individual:

When an individual does appear to have succeeded in freeing himself from these attitudinal and behavioral determinations, it is quite likely that he will lose his status or have his prestige or power modified in the white group. In order to regain it, he must make concessions, however subtle, in the direction of the crystallized pattern of racial attitudes. Few personalities are able to withstand these permeating pressures (Clark, 1972, p. 34).

Considering that ours is a racist society, the white managers in the present study provide ample illustration of Clark's points. In fact, far from trying to hide their prejudices, a number of the managers are sometimes quite vociferous about them. It might be expected that white managers would admit more easily to the negative racial attitudes of other employees than to their own, yet it will be seen that only a very small proportion of the white managers make no negative comments about blacks or disagree with negative statements.

The white managers' racial views were solicited in a number of ways. The first was to ask for their own degree of agreement with several stereotypical statements about blacks. Using almost the same stereotypical statements, a previous study about Jews indicated that if a person were not in absolute agreement with any of the statements, he or she would inevitably strongly disagree with them. That is, the stronger the disagreement, the freer is the manager from negative racial attitudes (Quinn et al., 1968, p. 8). Table 6-4 shows the five statements to which the managers were asked to respond and the frequency distribution of their responses.

The intensity of the managers' disagreement is far less than what one would expect of whites completely free of negative racial attitudes. Although the overall percentage of white managers who agree with each statement is quite small, nevertheless almost one in three agree with at least one of the statements. What is interesting about these responses is that 46 of

TABLE 6–4 AGREEMENT WITH NEGATIVE STEREOTYPICAL STATEMENTS ABOUT BLACKS (in %)

Stereotypical Statement About Blacks	White Managers				
	Strongly Disagree	Disagree	Agree	Strongly Agree	Other
There may be a few exceptions, but in general blacks are pretty much alike.	39	54	5	1	1
Even though there are some exceptions, most blacks have annoying and offensive faults.	29	67	3	1	0
Most blacks who aspire to become managers in the business world do not have the personal characteristics needed to become successful management persons in this company.	24	64	10	2	0
In general blacks have low IQs and less technical and analytical competence.	26	57	15	2	0
In general, blacks are pushy, loud, argumentative, arrogant, obnoxious, and aggressive.	33	63	4	0	0

those managers who agree with at least one of the statements are men; only one woman agrees with one of the statements.

If one considers as having a racist attitude, a manager who agrees that he or she could hardly imagine marriage to a black, and if this statement is included with the previous five in a new index, three out of four of the white managers agree with at least one of these statements. Table 6-5 shows the frequency distribution of agreement with the statements.

When certain variables are controlled for, it is found that the manager most likely to hold these negative stereotypical attitudes about blacks is a white, middle to upper level man, with less than a Bachelor degree, over 40, having contact with blacks only at work and/or through civic and business organizations. These characteristics describe many of the managers who hold responsible, influential, and powerful positions in these firms.*

Are Blacks Pressing Too Hard?

The negative racial attitudes of so many whites, both in terms of stereotypical beliefs and reverse discrimination, lead to another belief on the part of whites—that blacks are pressing their case too hard. When the white managers are asked whether they think this is so, fairly large percentages of both men and women agree—44 percent of the men and 30 percent of the women. As with so many other beliefs, patterns are found related to age and education; more older, less educated white managers agree that blacks are pressing too hard than younger, more educated managers.

TABLE 6-5   AGREEMENT WITH NEGATIVE STATEMENTS ABOUT BLACKS

	Number of Questions Agreed With	Percentage of White Managers[a] Who Agree
No negative views of blacks	0	24
	1	51
	2	17
	3	6
Extreme negative views of blacks	4	2
		—
		100

[a] No managers agree with five or six of the questions.

---

* Family origins do not seem to have any relationship to the managers' racial attitudes (see A. Campbell, 1971, p. 53).

The white managers give several reasons for their belief. Twenty-one percent see blacks as too impatient and wanting everything right now. A lower level manager from Ajax Manufacturing feels this way, especially with regard to education: "They're pressing too hard in the educational area, and money is being wasted on black studies. We're being forced to educate them all at once." Other white managers, 17 percent of our sample, cite the violent tactics used by blacks. A white lower level manager from Triple C Bank says: "They are going overboard. They had the riots and got the attention they wanted. Now blacks are demanding respect and that's one thing you can't demand."

And 14 percent of the white managers believe that blacks want things just because they are black. This view is stated by a lower level manager at Triple C Bank: "The extreme groups are pressing too hard—they feel that just because they are a minority race they should be given everything whether they are qualified or not." Another manager, from Ajax Manufacturing, sees the problem of black intrusiveness in terms of the public media and politics: "Blacks have more publicity on TV and in the papers than whites. White political leaders are taking advantage of the black vote. The government should not force industry to hire blacks."

Obviously, with such views these white managers are going to have problems dealing with black employees. However 30 percent of the whites who agree that blacks are pressing too hard do qualify their statements. For instance, they say that the militants are pressing too hard but the moderates are not. Here, though, the point of contention is in defining who is a militant and who a moderate. A manager may believe that a person who is peacefully picketing a company is a moderate, but if it is the manager's own company that is being picketed, he may well view the picketer as a militant. Many whites may see as nonmilitant a black who always agrees with the whites—an "oreo."

An illustration of this kind of confusion, as well the whites' ignorance of the black movement and the whites' consequent tendency toward distortion, is the comment of a white middle level manager from Triple A Bank:

The militants are pressing too hard and the nonmilitants aren't. Some organizations which are trying to improve the black man's image are definitely pushing way too much. Take the Black Muslims. All I know is what I read in the papers and hear on TV. Even though I don't know that much about them, I have a negative image—I see how they've installed themselves in large houses with big gun arsenals.

The fact of the matter, one which does not get publicized or commented on in the media, is that the Black Muslims have clearly adopted many aspects of the Protestant ethic. To continue their business endeavors in 1972 they received $20 million in loans from several white banks.

Of the white managers who do not think blacks are pressing too hard, some have reasons very similar to those of the managers who think there is too much black pressure. Thirty-seven percent of the managers feel that blacks in general are not pressing too hard but that the militant blacks are. Another 10 percent believe blacks are pushing too much when they use violence. An upper level white manager from Aunts Manufacturing reflects: "There is ample evidence that equality is not achieved through evolution. Human nature must be pushed. But I don't agree with all the tactics." However, 17 percent of the white managers say outright that if blacks do not pressure white society, there will simply be no change. This view is expressed well by a white upper level manager at Ajax Manufacturing:

I think about the Indians who are being peaceful in general and they're not really getting anywhere. Where would blacks be if they weren't pressing?

Black Managers' Characteristics: Good and Bad

The white managers, then, have definite and varied opinions about blacks in general, in terms of stereotypical characteristics and the black movement in general. To find out their views in more specific terms, the whites were also given the opportunity to talk about the black individuals they know personally and work with. They were asked to respond to the open-end question: What are some of the good and bad characteristics you have observed about black managers? Their responses are summarized in Tables 6-6 and 6-7; Table 6-6 shows the white responses regarding good characteristics; Table 6-7 shows their responses regarding bad characteristics.

It will be noticed from Table 6-6 that one out of five of the white managers could not answer the question because they have had little or no contact with black managers. Another one out of five said they see no difference between the races as far as good and bad characteristics are concerned. The most frequently mentioned good characteristics, as Table 6-6 also shows, are that black managers try harder to get along with and understand people, and that they are hard workers, dedicated, confident, and ambitious. As a middle level white manager from Ace Public Utility puts it: "They are trying exceptionally hard to be exceptionally good managers. They know they have a tougher road, and this is more of an incentive. I know of no bad characteristics." An upper level manager from Triple C Bank observes: "They have a genuine interest to want to succeed, to show the world they have what it takes. They understand each other better than whites understand each other. . . . "

The most frequently expressed bad characteristics in the white opinions, as Table 6-7 shows, tend to be the old, often contradictory stereotypical attitudes: Blacks are arrogant and aggressive, yet lazy and undependable; they lack confidence and are culturally different. A middle level white manager

TABLE 6–6   GOOD CHARACTERISTICS OF BLACK MANAGERS

Good Characteristics	Percentage of White Managers Observing these Characteristics ($N = 156$)
Blacks are nicer to people than are whites; they have a greater understanding of people; they try harder to get along with people.	28
Blacks are dedicated, confident, ambitious; they try extremely hard; they have a high motivation; they have a genuine interest to really want to succeed and show the world they have what it takes.	27
Can't answer; doesn't work with black managers or has very little contact with black managers.	22
No difference; there are no outstanding good or bad characteristics that the respondent hasn't observed in white managers.	21
No general good characteristics observed about black managers, but they do have some bad characteristics.	5
Most blacks are slightly better qualified.	3
Blacks have firm characters and are good decision makers; they have good judgment.	3
Blacks are fairer with people.	3
Other	4
Total[a]	116

[a] The total percentage is over 100 because the managers could give as many good characteristics as they wished.

from Triple A Bank concedes technical know-how but is still critical of the blacks he works with: "They do have the technical ability to do their jobs and some of the best blacks have a practical approach to the problems of business. But they have an above-it-all attitude."

Another manager from the same company also admits to some good characteristics but his view is basically negative: "They can relate to the

TABLE 6–7   BAD CHARACTERISTICS OF BLACK MANAGERS

Bad Characteristics	Percentage of White Managers Observing these Characteristics (N = 156)
No general bad characteristics observed about black managers, but they do have some good characteristics.	17
Blacks are too independent, arrogant, and aggressive; they have a chip-on-the-shoulder attitude; too impatient.	8
Blacks tend to back away from confrontations with both black and white employees; blacks lack assurance and confidence.	7
Blacks take advantage of their blackness in the work situation, i.e., they blame everything on race.	6
Blacks have a lazy attitude; they are not dependable or reliable; they are late and never return calls.	5
Blacks have a different culture, i.e., language, life-style, values, attitudes, personality, and so on.	5
Blacks are less likely to express legitimate complaints because they fear whites will think they are too sensitive.	1
Blacks tend to test whites when they really don't have to.	1
Blacks are slow learners.	1
Other	11
Total[a]	62

[a] The total percentage does not equal 100 because not all of the white managers believe black managers have bad characteristics, and some believe they have more than one.

black community like no one else can. But the young blacks won't talk to me. And some of the black managers feel they don't have to produce because, since they are black, the company will promote them anyway." And a middle level white manger from Aunts Manufacturing sums up some of the conflicting negative characteristics, as he sees them: "In some cases they have an overawareness of being black and therefore they are less confident in making decisions. On the other hand, they are overarrogant because they are black."

Overall White Racial Attitudes

With such responses as these by the white mangagers, as well as their responses to previously discussed closed-end questions, a picture of their racial attitudes is taking shape. To check these further, an overall racial index was compiled. The index, made up of previously asked questions, included 14 questions that either directly or indirectly allowed the managers to express racial attitudes about blacks in all areas, such as the incidence of black employees in industry and their particular companies, black opportunities for promotion, personal and professional characteristics of blacks in general, and the managers' own feelings about blacks and the possibility of marriage with a black. Of the 14 questions, nine specifically solicited negative racial attitudes and five did not. (See Appendix G, page 290, for a list of the questions.) Table 6-8 shows the range of the managers' responses.

None of the managers responded negatively to more than 10 of the questions, and only two managers responded negatively to seven or more of the questions. But one should not conclude from this that in general the white managers have favorable views toward blacks. Only 9 percent of the managers showed no agreement with hostile statements and made no hostile statements themselves about blacks. If the question about the possibility of marrying a black is removed from the index, then 19 percent of the white managers voice no negative attitudes about blacks. Table 6-8 also clearly shows that white women have fewer negative attitudes than white men.

The race of the interviewer seems to have no bearing on the managers' responses. For example, of the managers interviewed separately by me, the white woman interviewer, and the white man interviewer, almost one-third of the managers scored 0 to 1, indicating very little antiblack response. In addition, all the interviewers elicited scores of from 4 to 10 from about 20 percent of the interviewees.

Tables 6-4 and 6-5, measuring the white managers' degree of agreement with negative stereotypical statements about blacks, revealed, when certain variables were controlled, that the most negative attitudes are held by the white middle to upper level manager who is over 40, less educated (without a Bachelor degree), and with infrequent contact with blacks. Does this

TABLE 6–8   WHITE MANAGERS' OVERALL RACIAL ATTITUDES (in %)

	Number of Antiblack Responses	White Men (N = 133)	White Women (N = 23)	Total (N = 156)
No antiblack responses	0	8	13	9
	1	20	17	20
	2	25	44	27
	3	23	17	22
	4	8	9	8
	5	8	0	7
	6	6	0	5
	7	1	0	1
Extreme antiblack responses	10	1	0	1
Total		100	100	100

profile of typicality hold when the other eight questions in the present index are added?

Although there is a wide variation in each age group, the younger managers do tend to express the least negative racial attitudes. Forty-four percent of the managers age 30 or younger scored 0 to 1, compared to 35 percent of the managers between 31 and 40 and 26 percent between 41 and 50. Only 16 percent over 50 scored 1 and none over 50 scored 0.

As for education, the tendency of the less educated managers to agree with more stereotypical questions, which was seen in the earlier index, is not evident in the present larger one. Rather, it appears that even though the more educated managers are less likely to agree with direct hostile statements about blacks, these managers are more likely in open-end questions to make negative stereotypical statements about blacks.

When managerial level is compared, even though the managers at the top level represent less than 20 percent of our sample, they make up 40 percent of the 10 whites with the most extreme negative attitudes (scores of 6 to 10). Furthermore, only 3 percent of the top managers did not express some type of antiblack attitude, compared to 9 percent of the middle level managers and 13 percent of the lower level managers. This is owing, in part, to the large number of women at the lower level, who, as noted earlier, have fewer negative attitudes toward blacks than the men.

Because an unequal number of upper level managers were interviewed from each company, it should be remembered that the upper managerial views are generally those from Ace Public Utility, Triple A and C Banks, and Aunts Manufacturing. When compared by company, the managers do not differ significantly, although the upper managers from Ace Public Utility score slightly lower on the racial index. Since all these managers belong to companies whose Affirmative Action Programs vary considerably in effectiveness and strength, it may seem surprising that the managers' attitudes hardly differ. However, as noted earlier, the lack of variation may be an indication that although some managers may harbor negative racial attitudes, continuous forceful external and internal pressures on them to practice equal employment may counteract the tendency toward unfair treatment of blacks as a result of the managers' negative racial views.

Although political affiliation did not specifically enter into the earlier profile, it is interesting here to see that those managers who consider themselves liberals are generally less negative in their attitudes toward blacks than those who consider themselves moderates. The moderates are less negative, in turn, than the conservatives. Since Democrats generally consider themselves more liberal or moderate than Republicans, it is not surprising that they are less negative in their views of blacks than Republicans. The eight white managers who consider themselves Independents are even less negative toward blacks than the Democrats.

When the index on the white managers' frequency of contact with blacks is correlated with the index on negative racial attitudes, it is found that the white managers with a great deal of contact with blacks are more likely than those whites with no contact to have positive racial attitudes. Also those white managers with no contact are more likely to have positive racial attitudes than the whites with only a little, usually work-related, contact with blacks. This finding should not be misconstrued: It is also true that many of the white managers who have a great deal of contact with blacks *do* hold negative attitudes about them. Even though these views may be generally less strongly held and more subtle than the extreme negative views of those whites with little contact with blacks, they are still operative and held to despite apparent inconsistency.

This phenomenon was also found by A. Campbell, who offers an explanation:

[M]any white people have attitudes toward racial integration which have no relation to their own interracial contacts. It is particularly impressive that a substantial number of those people who claim to have had Negro friends respond negatively to our proposals of various forms of contact with Negroes. Assuming these friendships to be real, they seem to be regarded by these people as purely idiosyncratic, having no relevance to the larger issue of interracial contact (A. Campbell, 1971, p. 10).

Thus business executives and government officials should not believe that all they have to do is expose their white employees to blacks and the whites will automatically develop positive attitudes. Particular circumstances play a large part in producing better or worse attitudes in white contact with blacks.

Although we have found that the most negative attitudes toward blacks are concentrated among the white, middle to upper level male managers over 40, who are religious and less educated, with few contacts with blacks, a careful review of the 10 white managers expressing the most negative attitudes and the 15 who express none at all reveals no personal characteristics that could distinguish either group. The only differentiating factor appears to be that the white managers with less negative attitudes are generally more confident about their chances of achieving their desired career goals than the more prejudiced managers.

With these observations in mind let us now look at several individual white managers in greater depth. These four managers illustrate the range of racial attitudes held by whites. They come from disparate backgrounds and have varying personal goals, which further indicates that certain personal characteristics are no guarantee of particular attitudes when it comes to degree of racism. There are certainly trends among certain groups, as pointed out earlier, but special characteristics or backgrounds by no means define, predict, or limit such attitudes.

The first manager is a 39-year-old, good-looking, male banker. He has already achieved an upper management position and feels rather confident about reaching his career goals. Most of his life was spent in Kentucky, where his father was a lawyer and his mother a housewife who had earned a Bachelor degree. This manager is well educated, having received a Bachelor of Arts in economics from Washington and Lee and then a law degree from Stanford University, where he happened to meet his wife, who was pursuing a degree in English.

He considers himself a moderate Democrat and attends the Methodist church at least once or twice a month. His interests range from a church-connected group to business, civic, and professional organizations, to conservation. He lives in San Francisco but in an area where fewer than 5 percent of his neighbors are black. His contacts with blacks are very limited, both on the job and outside of work at social functions; he has only one black friend who is from his law school days.

This highly educated manager manifests extremely negative racial attitudes. Although he agrees with only one closed-end negative statement—that he could hardly imagine marriage to a black—he makes several comments in the open-end questions that clearly illustrate how educated whites rationalize their racist views. A great drawback of blacks, he says, is that they do not embrace the Protestant ethic, and this hinders them from "fitting in" and advancing in the corporate world. He also feels that some blacks "put on a show" in terms of their dress and lifestyles. Important aspects of his consideration of a black for employment or promotion are, not surprisingly, "appropriate dress" and "personality": "I don't like people who are too militant or aggressive. I don't mean they should be timid, but they should have a certain sense of propriety."

His views of black underutilization in the corporate world in the past are related to these opinions. He blames their different cultural lifestyle and "language problem" and attributes their present slow progress to too much aggressiveness and militancy and "flamboyant appearance." He also says that blacks are pressing their case too hard because they want representation in higher management and that they "cry wolf" too often, claiming racial discrimination when there is no foundation for such a claim.

He readily admits that blacks must be better than whites in his firm and that they are more carefully evaluated because failure will help strengthen racist attitudes on the part of whites watching the black managers. At the same time, though, he maintains that his company is definitely not paying lip service to equal employment opportunities and that the firm is totally fair to black employees.

What is especially astonishing here is that most of the remarks of this manager were unprompted and completely voluntary as part of the open-end questions. Despite his friendship with a black (and in illustration of Campbell's observation), he holds stereotypical racist views that without a doubt will constitute great obstacles to his treating the blacks he comes in contact with in an equitable manner.

The second white manager comes from quite a different background, but his attitudes toward blacks closely parallel those of the first manager. He is a lower level manager and is 48 years old. He has only a high school diploma and for this reason feels his chances of advancement are poor. Before coming to California he spent a good part of his life in Iowa and now lives in an all-white neighborhood in the San Francisco Bay area. His father was a paper hanger and his mother a factory worker. This manager is separated from his wife.

He is of the Lutheran faith and attends church once or twice a year. He calls himself a liberal Republican and does not belong to many organizations but is active in the Society of Automotive Engineers. His contacts with blacks are very frequent both on the job and socially outside of work, where he meets them primarily at parties.

This manager's responses to the closed-end questions contrast sharply with the responses of the previous highly educated manager. The present manager agrees with many of the closed-end questions, illustrating the tendency of uneducated whites to do this much more than educated whites. For instance, he believes that blacks have lower I.Q.s and less technical and analytic competence than whites and that most blacks are generally all alike and have annoying and offensive faults. He could not imagine himself marrying a black. However, he does see a few good characteristics in blacks: "They really want to do a good job and are very willing to learn. As far as they go, they are competent." Blacks are pushing too hard, he believes, mainly because they want to get jobs without the necessary experience, but he sees nothing holding them back either in his own company or in the corporate world at large.

Although this manager holds racist views like the first one, he answered the questions in a different manner. On only one open-end question did he say anything negative about blacks (why they are pressing too hard), but he responded to four of the closed-end questions in a way indicating strong racial bias, a pattern followed by only 6 percent of the white managers in this study.

His "liberal" characteristics do not seem to affect his racial attitudes. Although he is not very religious, is a "liberal" Republican, and has frequent contact with blacks on and off the job, he is still as much a racist as the previous manager.

Our third manager is also quite prejudiced against blacks, and his background and personal characteristics fall somewhere between the two just described. He is 55 years old, on the middle level, and does not consider advancement important for himself. Having lived in California all his life, he now resides with his wife in a segregated area of Orange County, California. His father, a large rancher, had 12 years of schooling, and his mother had 10. This manager holds a Bachelor of Science in mechanical engineering from the University of Washington, and a Bachelor of Arts and Master of Arts in religion from a theological college. He has also taken many theology courses at the University of Southern California. He has a second simultaneous career, unusual for a manager, that of a practicing minister. He belongs to a number of church groups and considers himself a conservative Republican. His contacts with blacks are very frequent at work but very limited outside, consisting of only company banquets.

He concedes only one good characteristic (somewhat dubious in its "goodness") to blacks: "On occasion you find one who is willing to grab like everyone else." Blacks are opportunistic, he feels, with their color and cry discrimination without deserved accusation. He also says they have lower intelligence and less technical and analytical abilities than whites. He could hardly ever imagine himself marrying a black.

With regard to blacks in the corporate world, he feels they are being pushed on companies and that the blacks themselves are not ready for the discipline demanded in business. Like a number of other managers, he believes blacks would be more disciplined and inclined to work if there were no welfare system. He sees no unfairness in the treatment of blacks either in his own firm or the corporate world. Progress, he feels, is up to the blacks themselves: "They just have to become qualified and want to work. Then they'll have no problem."

All three of these white managers have different backgrounds but strong racist views. An interesting comparison is offered in another white male manager whose personal characteristics are very like the previous managers but whose racial views are quite different.

This manager is 41 years old and on the upper level in his firm. He has lived most of his life in Minnesota and California, and like two of the other managers lives in the San Francisco Bay area in a town with only a few blacks. He received a Bachelor of Arts degree from Harvard University in electrical engineering and physics. His wife completed two years of college and does not work.

He is a Presbyterian and attends church a few times a year. Although he considers himself a conservative Republican, like the minister just described, he is the only one of a few white managers to belong to civil rights groups and the National Welfare Rights Organization. He also belongs to many business and civic associations. His contact with blacks at work is very frequent and outside is fairly frequent, and he has a few black friends made through civic and charity groups.

He sees no real differences between black and white managers; if anything, blacks have more positive characteristics, especially in being more sensitive to people's needs, he feels. He also could even imagine marrying a black. This manager did not agree with even one stereotypical remark about blacks in the closed-end questions and made no negative comments in the open-end questions. He was one of the few managers of whom this was the case. Instead of agreeing that blacks are pressing too hard, he says: "When injustice is involved, there is no such thing as pressing too hard. . . . People fought for independence in this country for much less serious reasons than those that have caused the blacks so much suffering."

These four white managers illustrate extremely varied backgrounds and personal characteristics, in which no special characteristics can be linked to the extent of their racial attitudes. Racism can occur at any level, any age, and in any social stratum. Only one out of 10 of the participating white managers possess no negative racial attitudes at all about blacks, a very low proportion indeed.

However, it is also important to point out that most whites are neither extremely antiblack nor problack but somewhere in the middle. As A. Campbell has noted:

It is apparent that the white population varies greatly in its feelings about race and that no "typical" person can be identified who might be said to represent the total. The safest conclusion we can draw . . . is that white Americans in the cities are not predominantly located at either extreme of our scales of racial attitudes. . . . In between are those numerous people whose perceptions and attitudes are ambiguous and conflicted, who are variously fairminded, apprehensive, resentful, defensive, ill-informed, and indifferent (A. Campbell, 1971, p. 19).

DEVIATIONS FROM EMPLOYMENT POLICIES

Equality in Hiring and Promoting

From the evidence of the previous pages and the fact that the firms generally have weak AAPs, it cannot be denied that white racial attitudes do have a direct bearing on employment policies. This next section attempts to determine the manner in which both black and white managers choose not to follow the formal employment policies of their companies.

Although the vast majority of both black and white managers believe blacks should be hired and promoted on the same basis as everyone else, there is a subtle difference in their interpretations of what this means. The black managers are saying essentially that all they want are equal opportunities, and they will prove they can do as well as whites. The white managers are saying that blacks should not be given any advantage—in other words, they oppose reverse discrimination. As has been noted before, since whites are so accustomed to having the advantage, they might believe that any movement toward equal opportunities is reverse discrimination. Although one out of eight of the white managers say they believe in the same basis of promotion for blacks and whites, they also indicate that if a white were available, they would not promote an equally qualified black, and they would not promote a black in any case into an important management position.

The fact that the vast majority of the managers give at least lip service to the belief of equality in hiring and promoting is not surprising. In an effort to ascertain the particular reasons the managers use for not hiring or promoting a management candidate, they were asked the following question: What are the kinds of things about a management candidate that might make you hesitate to hire him or her, other than his or her lack of experience and job knowledge? The managers' answers are shown in Table 6-9.

TABLE 6–9 WHY THE MANAGERS MIGHT HESITATE TO HIRE OR PROMOTE A CANDIDATE (in %)

Things Managers Consider Detrimental to Hiring and Promoting Opportunities (Other than Lack of Experience and Job Knowledge)	Black Managers ($N = 116$)	White Managers ($N = 156$)
Lack of ability to relate and get along with people	56	55
Lack of hard work, resourcefulness, initiative, ambition, aggressiveness, and so on	26	30
Lack of leadership ability and/or good judgment	17	23
Lack of personal hygiene and neatness	9	7
Lack of self-confidence	6	3
Lack of maturity, stability, responsibility	6	1
Lack of loyalty, commitment, or identification with the company	5	15
Lack of respect for minorities, i.e., bigotry, racism, prejudice	5	2
Lack of ability to express oneself verbally and in writing	4	6
Overaggressiveness, too arrogant, cocky, too militant, chip on shoulder attitude, and so on	4	9
Lack of conformity to a conservative appearance, i.e., long hair, beards, loud dress, and the like	3	5
Lack of honesty, integrity, ethics, sincerity, morality, and so on	3	5
Other	3	3
None	11	5
Total[a]	158	169

[a] The total percentages are over 100 because many managers gave more than one response.

Deviation in Hiring and Promoting

With the many factors the managers would take into account other than actual job experience, it would follow that, despite a company's written employment policies, many of the managers feel they can freely deviate from the company policies, even though only about a third do so in practice. The black and white managers deviate in different ways. (See Table D-5, Appendix D, page 283, for the enumeration of these ways.) The primary manner in which the blacks deviate is that they overlook work experience—seniority—if the individual has the requisite educational background potential, initiative and drive. Since the seniority system is the most frequent aspect of company policy the blacks would change (see Chapters 5 and 10), this evidence of flexibility is not surprising. The white managers deviate from company policy principally by overlooking education if the individual has seniority, drive, and initiative. This is explainable because some whites want to put more emphasis on the seniority system. However there are also almost as many white managers who would, like the blacks, overlook seniority if the individual had the educational background.

It is especially interesting that none of the white managers indicate that they deviate because of an individual's race, even though nine out of 10 hold various types of antiblack attitudes and one out of eight say they would not hire or promote a black equally qualified with an available white and/or would not promote a black into an important management post. The white managers apparently will not openly admit that they would discriminate against blacks because in the current social and legal climate it is not the proper or prudent thing to do.

An additional way of finding out how the managers deviate from company employment policy was to ask them to what extent they would take into consideration the feelings of those people with whom they come in contact who might feel uncomfortable if the managers hired or promoted a black into a management position. These people include customers and distributors, management personnel from other companies, peers and subordinates, immediate superiors, and managers above immediate superiors. Other studies have noted such considerations, called the "third party argument." For instance, Quinn et al., report: "The decision to hire or promote . . . is not based solely on the behavior of the worker and the judgments of his superior; the second-guessed opinions and reactions of others whom the worker may encounter are also honored" (Quinn et al., 1968, pp. 34–35).

In answer to our questions on this subject, it was surprising to find that blacks would take third party feelings into consideration almost as much as whites in some areas and even more in others. For example, 23 percent of the white managers who said their customers and distributors would feel uncomfortable about dealing with a black said they would take this into consideration, at least to some extent, in hiring or promoting a black. A larger percentage of the black managers, 33 percent, said they would do the same.

The typical reason the black managers give for their response is that blacks must face the reality that their firms are not truly committed to their Affirmative Action Programs. Therefore whether they like it or not, the blacks must consider third party feelings, especially in order to place new black managers in positions where they will be most effective and have the best opportunities to demonstrate their abilities and achieve their objectives. Once the firms really do become committed to equal employment opportunities for blacks and act on this commitment, it is hoped that such compromise will no longer be necessary. In fact, once blacks themselves reach middle and upper management in representative numbers and become more influential and powerful, more of the third parties will be black and the problem should be greatly diminished.

The lower level managers, both black and white, are particularly likely to take into consideration the feelings of the managers in the level above them, an indication of the influence of senior management in directing change in employment policies. Therefore if top management makes it known unequivocally that it wants all employees to receive equal treatment, the managers at the lower ranks will be more likely to comply with such orders. This has been acknowledged in at least one of the companies, Ace Public Utility, by one of its black women managers: "Some whites have appeared to change their attitudes because someone above them told them to." Significantly, as will be remembered, this is the company with the most effective Affirmative Action Program.

Although the managers' responses do not tell us what final action they would take regarding hiring or promoting a black, there are several indications nevertheless. In most of the firms the prevailing racial attitudes and atmospheres are negative, Affirmative Action Programs are weak, and top management apparently lacks any real commitment to equal employment opportunities. Therefore it is probably safe to assume that most managers would not favor blacks at all in their hiring and promoting practices.

Ten Years Ago and Today

To see whether there has actually been any change in attitudes in the past decade, and incidentally to get a sense of how the managers presently feel, they were also asked if they would have responded any differently 10 years ago to questions about various third party feelings in hiring and promoting considerations of blacks. Four out of five of the black managers and three out of four of the whites said that, yes, they would have answered differently a decade ago. Their reasons and the distribution of opinions are shown in Table 6-10.

All of the managers' responses clearly show that their impressions of how other people feel about blacks in management positions have affected their past employment decisions in hiring and promoting blacks. One manager,

TABLE 6–10 HOW THE MANAGERS WOULD HAVE RESPONDED TO ATTITUDES
ABOUT BLACKS 10 YEARS AGO (in %)

Reasons	Black Managers ($N = 100$)	White Managers ($N = 114$)
Would not have been able to answer the questions 10 years ago because would not have had this position then because of the firm's discriminatory practices.	32	0
Was not conscious of himself/herself as a black man/woman 10 years ago, i.e., was apathetic; might have attempted to overlook whites' negative attitudes toward blacks.	26	0
White attitudes have changed, i.e., corporations and white society in general have more positive attitudes toward blacks.	27	52
The company now has an Affirmative Action Program but in the past discriminated against blacks.	12	21
Would have been more influenced by negative white attitudes of workers and customers 10 years ago; therefore, would have been careful in hiring and promoting blacks.	5	13
Was not aware of the racial situation and/or did not have as much knowledge about racial issues 10 years ago.	0	22
Would not have been able to answer the questions 10 years ago because few, if any, blacks were employed in management positions in the company.	0	7
Other	0	6
Total[a]	102	121

[a] The total percentages are over 100 because some managers gave more than one reason.

on the upper level at Aunts Manufacturing, recalls his company's policy 10 years ago: "The company would have been more concerned then about customer feelings. Ten years ago the company didn't recognize the problem and didn't have any real thoughts about bringing blacks into management." An upper level manager at Century Manufacturing is more picturesque in his description of how it was: "Ten years ago people just hated the color of Negroes and if you promoted one your peers and subordinates looked on you as a nut."

It is also clear that employment policies are still very much affected by other people's feelings, as the earlier discussion pointed out, but there has been at least a little change in the attitudes of both the whites and the corporate world as a whole. Two white middle level managers from Triple C Bank sum it up:

There is no way 10 years ago a black would be a supervisor in the bank.

People have changed their attitudes. It is no longer socially acceptable to express derogatory opinions, and it would have been all right in the past. People are better informed now.

The most interesting evidence of change is the response of 26 percent of the black managers who indicate that now they are more aware of themselves as black people and more willing to stand up for their rights. They would have taken third party feelings into consideration much more 10 years ago. As a black woman banker at Triple C Bank comments: "I would have been much harsher in hiring and promoting blacks—because that was the social atmosphere." Now the blacks also believe that standing up for their rights will not be useless i.e. they feel firm stands will have some positive effect. A black male banker at the same bank recalls: "I wasn't a militant 10 years ago. But I've been placed in a situation where I see the obvious problems of racism, and I'm willing now to take the necessary steps to insure equality for blacks in employment."

It is true that there has been some change for the better; but there is substantial evidence, as much of the data in this chapter has shown, that the racial atmosphere in which the black managers must work is still hostile. As we have seen, only 10 percent of the black managers and 17 percent of the whites indicate that they are not aware of any negative white attitudes toward blacks, do not hear derogatory remarks about blacks, and do not believe any of their subordinate, peers, superiors feel uncomfortable about the hiring and promoting of blacks. Furthermore, only 9 percent of all the white managers express no negative racial attitudes at all. Typically the white manager most likely to hold the strongest racist views has been found to be male, over 40, on the middle or upper level, religious, a conservative Republican, without a Bachelor's degree, and having very little contact with blacks. But as the profiles of several white managers show, other personal characteristics do not necessarily lessen hostility toward blacks—many whites at every age and educational and social level hold racist attitudes.

Obviously, negative racial attitudes and the frequent contradictions evident in white responses do not help the implementation of equal opportunity. One black manager, who happens to have light skin, straight hair, and blue eyes, illustrates the type of negative racial comments made by whites among themselves:

Because most people believe I am white, they express all types of negative attitudes about blacks to me. When I disagree with them and tell them I'm black, they don't know how to act or what to say. They usually get all red and say something like they really didn't mean what they said, that they have colored friends and went to school with them. . . .

With such attitudes of whites, the blacks have little hope of equal treatment on the job in large part because they are not completely accepted into informal work groups and social activities that are so important to success. Thus the evidence is abundant that the primary factor affecting the careers of black managers is racial discrimination.

CHAPTER SEVEN

Images of the Most Promotable Manager

The racial atmosphere in a company has a strong impact on the managers' conceptions about the types of individuals they would hire and promote. Although previous chapters have dealt with this subject generally, this chapter deals with the specific image of the most promotable manager in the minds of the participating managers. This permits us to explore further the fairness of the companies' employment policies as they relate to both black and other minority groups, such as Asians, Chicanos, and women. Such an exploration will also enable us to see what, if any, changes have occurred in managers' attitudes during the past decade.

This chapter, then, will ask several questions. First, what are the managers' attitudes about the ideal characteristics of the promotable manager? Second, what are the managers' views of those people who actually do get ahead in their own firms and business in general? Third, what are the people like who do not get ahead, in the managers' opinions? And fourth, how do the managers' views differ by age, educational background, managerial level, and company?

Most of these questions have been explored before by Garda W. Bowman in two important studies. The first dealt with 315 subjects in the New York area and the second with 2000 subjects throughout the United States (Bowman, 1962, 1964). Although Bowman's participants came from various industries and all managerial levels, only a small number of them were blacks and women. There was no opportunity to compare differences in attitudes between the races and sexes. Nevertheless Bowman's main hypotheses are valid.

Bowman argued that conscious or unconscious assumptions as to criteria for who gets promoted are often based on unwritten policies that influence promotional practices more strongly than written company policies. Furthermore once an image of certain personal characteristics is thought to represent the success model, regardless of how few people may have such characteristics, this image of the promotable person tends to be self-perpetuating.

This chapter tests these hypotheses with the participating managers by adapting some of Bowman's methods. She asked the managers for their opinions on which of a list of 72 characteristics ideally should be harmful, helpful, or irrelevant for an individual's promotion to supervisor and beyond. She also asked her respondents how they believed characteristics actually did affect promotional opportunities in their own firms and in the corporate world in general.

Bowman included items under a number of value clusters in her study, as well as some items not readily classifiable, for her total of 72 items. However, this chapter deals with only 25 of these items, chosen for their relevance to the prevailing concerns of the study. Because of my interest in equality, all 17 items in Bowman's "equality of opportunity" value cluster are included. These are items such as age, national origin, race, religion, sex, and social status (indicated, for example, by attendence at an Ivy League school or membership in a local country club). In addition, there are three items directly related to ability—college education, graduate training in business administration, and technical knowledge of a specific job to be done. Another item used, which is sometimes considered an ability criterion, is seniority, although this criterion is not very reliable because an individual may have many years of service with a firm and still be an incompetent manager.

Finally other factors are used that have been found to affect greatly the career patterns of managers, as previous chapters have already indicated, and these are criteria that have nothing to do with ability. They include a spouse who is helpful to career, pull with top management, community interests and activities, and artistic and cultural interests.

THE MANAGERS' IDEAL IMAGES

Ideally Irrelevant Factors

The participating managers were asked for their views on what factors they consider, in an ideal situation, irrelevant, helpful, or harmful for promotion. Some, but not all, of their views, especially those on ideally irrelevant factors, support other opinions they gave on their hiring and promotion practices, such as those discussed in the previous chapter. In Chapter 6 it was reported that none of the managers selected such nonability factors as age, race, sex, or religion when asked what factors other than lack of experience and job knowledge that might make them hesitate to hire or promote a managerial candidate. Most of the managers said their hestitation would be based on ability-related criteria, such as a candidate's questionable ability to relate to and get along with people, or deficiencies in initiative, resourcefulness, leadership, and good judgment. It was also noted in Chapter 6 that when the managers were asked how, if at all, they deviated from their companies' employment policies, none who said they deviated cited selection of managers based on a certain age, sex, or religion. (A few blacks said they would promote an equally qualified black before a white, but no whites selected race.) Rather, they cited such factors as educational requirements, seniority, and salary as their reasons for deviation.

But there was also some variance among the managers noted in Chapter 6. A substantial minority, primarily whites in listing factors that would make them hesitate to hire or promote a potential candidate, chose such things as loyalty to company and conformity to company standards in terms of dress, attitudes, and physical appearance. Such terms may be disguises for managerial judgment based on a potential candidate's class, race, sex, or religion. There was also some indication that some managers of both races would be influenced in hiring or promoting blacks to management posts by the uncomfortableeelings of prospective third parties blacks might have to deal with when hired.

Responding to the question of what factors they believe should ideally be irrelevant for promotion, the managers overwhelmingly cite age, race, religion, and national origin as the most irrelevant factors. Table 7-1 compares the managers' responses with those of the participants in Bowman's study. In comparing the responses, it can clearly be seen that both the black and white managers in the present study and in Bowman's study believe that the factor most irrelevant to promotion should be religious affiliation. In addition in the present study more of the white managers than the blacks feel that race and national origin should be irrelevant. But more of the black managers feel sex, especially male, should be irrelevant.

When the white managers in the three studies are compared, it is seen that the white managers in the present study, who are all California based, tend to believe more that the factors of religious affiliation, race, national origin, and sex should be irrelevant than those managers in New York (Bowman, 1962), and those in New York see these factors as more ideally irrelevant than the managers sampled throughout the United States (Bowman, 1964).

The most significant differences among the white managers in the three studies, as Table 7-1 shows, lie in the areas of church attendance, race, sex, United States citizenship, and club membership. These differences can be attributed to two things, of which the first is the sample makeup. Because of the regional characteristics of Bowman's 1962 study in New York, her 1964 study which was nationwide, and the present one in California, one would expect more liberal views from New Yorkers and Californians than from a sample that includes Southerners and Mid-Westerners, and this is what the table shows. In addition the present study includes 15 percent white women, who are more likely to consider race and sex characteristics as irrelevant than the white men.

The second explanation for the differences among the white participants is the time element. Since Bowman's studies were completed, a decrease in the importance of religion has taken place among many people, as noted in

TABLE 7-1 FACTORS THE MANAGERS BELIEVE SHOULD IDEALLY BE IRRELE-
VANT FOR PROMOTION[a] (in %)

Factors	Bowman 1962 (pp. 99–99B) (N = 315)	Bowman 1964 (pp. 16–22) (N = 2000)	White Managers (N = 156)	Black Managers (N = 116)
Catholic	96	92	97	95
Jewish	95	83	96	93
Protestant	92	86	94	93
Church attendance	62	65	84	91
White	64	53	92	90
Asian	86	67	92	88
Foreigner	91	77	87	85
Ivy league school	84	81	88	84
Country club membership in prominent social clubs[b]	90	63	94	84
Chicano, Puerto Rican[b]	76	62	87	83
Male	50	35	65	82
Black	83	62	89	81
Female	67	50	76	80
US citizen	63	46	80	73

[a] Only those factors which 80 percent or more of either the Black or white managers or both believe should be irrelevant are included.
[b] Bowman used "Membership in Prominent Social Clubs" rather than "Country Club" in her second study and "Puerto Rican" in both of her studies rather than "Chicano."

Chapter 2, and thus church attendance as a factor in promotion has become increasingly irrelevant. Also, in the past decade the civil rights movement and the women's movement have made their influences felt, so that the white managers in the present study tend to consider race and sex less relevant to promotion than Bowman's participants.

Ideally Helpful Factors

Table 7-2 shows those factors that 50 percent or more of either the black or white managers or both believe should be ideally helpful to a manager's promotional opportunities.

Although the differences are small, Table 7-2 indicates that the black managers in this study believe more than do the white managers that the three factors relating to ability—college education, technical knowledge,

TABLE 7–2 FACTORS THE MANAGERS BELIEVE SHOULD IDEALLY BE HELPFUL
FOR PROMOTION (in %)

Factors	Bowman (N = 315)	Bowman (N = 2000)	White Managers (N = 156)	Black Managers (N = 116)
College education	94	94	88	95
Technical knowledge	86	90	86	90
Community interest	71	71	72	67
Graduate work in business administration	78	80	61	62
Cultural interests	75	71	66	53
Helpful spouse[a]	60	—	53	50

[a] This information was not available in Bowman's second study.

and graduate work—should be ideally more helpful. When the black managers' responses on these items are compared with Bowman's white managers, the responses are quite similar except for graduate work in business administration, where more of Bowman's respondents believe this is important.

The three factors not relating to ability—community interests, cultural interests, and a helpful spouse—are all seen as helpful by more white than black managers in all the studies. One explanation for this may be that the black managers place more emphasis on ability criteria because these managers are generally more educated and qualified than their white counterparts. Another possible explanation is that many of the white managers, especially in the present study, are on middle and upper levels. At these levels, as had been noted before, community and cultural interests and a helpful spouse become not only more important but necessary factors in promotability.

Ideally Harmful Factors

With an idea of what the managers consider ideally irrelevant and helpful for promotion, let us now look at what they believe should be harmful in an ideal situation. Table 7-3 shows the managers' responses; the factors that 10 percent or more of both races believe should be harmful are listed.

It should be noted that although in this category Bowman's data could not be exactly compared with ours, her data can nevertheless be used as a basis of comparison. She lists the percentages of managers who believe certain factors should and do hinder promotion. In addition to the items in

TABLE 7–3   FACTORS THE MANAGERS BELIEVE SHOULD IDEALLY BE HARMFUL
FOR PROMOTION (in %)

Factors	Bowman 1962[a] (p. 71) (N = 315)	White Managers (N = 156)	Black Managers (N = 116)
Over 45	15	31	25
Female	19	18	13
Foreign	6	12	12
Seniority	—	4	11
Pull with top management	—	16	4

[a] No data were available in Bowman, 1964.

Table 7-3 Bowman found that 15 percent of the white managers believe that
being Puerto Rican hinders promotion, and 9 percent believe being black,
Oriental, and under age 30 are hindrances.

The sexual factor is especially interesting when the three categories are
compared. Although it was seen from Table 7-1 that approximately 80
percent of the managers in the present study believe that being female
should be irrelevant, Table 7-3 shows that a significant minority of
managers still believe this factor should be harmful to an individual's promotional opportunities. Table 7-2 records only the responses of 50 percent
or more of the managers with regard to helpful factors. But being male was
rated as an ideally helpful factor by 35 percent of the white managers, a
fairly large minority, and 18 percent of the black managers.

These figures contrast with the much higher figures of Bowman on this
factor, 50 percent in 1962 and 65 percent in 1964. The differences between
Bowman's studies and this study clearly suggest that either federal laws and
social pressures against sex discrimination are having a real effect on the
beliefs of white male managers, or less hopefully that many of the managers
are feeling bound as a result of laws and pressures to say the "right" things.

The black and white managers differ on several important points, especially when the tables in this chapter are compared with findings in previous
chapters. In discussions of the seniority system in Chapters 5 and 6, it was
noted that generally the black managers would deemphasize the system,
whereas the white managers would emphasize the system. Supporting these
findings, the present table shows that 4 percent of the whites believe seniority should be harmful to promotion, as opposed to 11 percent of the
blacks; in addition 21 percent of the whites believe it should be a helpful factor, compared to only 9 percent of the blacks.

There is also a large difference in opinions between the black and white managers as to the role of "politics"—pull with top management—in promotional opportunities. Thirty percent of the black managers and only 14 percent of the white believe it should be helpful, and the percentages of managers who believe politics should ideally be a harmful factor support this trend: 16 percent of the white managers and 4 percent of the black feel the political factor should be harmful.

It is surprising that 30 percent of the black managers believe politics should ideally be helpful to an individual's promotional opportunities, because in Chapter 5 it was pointed out that one of the black managers' major complaints about their companies' employment policies is that politics play too great a part. This inconsistency may be the result of differences in interpretation of "pull with top management." One manager may consider as pull the sponsorship of a senior manager, another may look on pull as personal contacts, and a third may interpret pull as his/her own efforts and abilities.

The inconsistency may be explained in another way, as a black middle level manager at Triple C Bank illustrates: "I indicated that pull with top management should be helpful, ideally, in my opinion because the fact of the matter is that people tend to favor those people they know. That's how it works. If a manager knows you, you have pull, if he doesn't you don't." The black managers' opinions probably reflect what they believe is actually taking place, whereas the white managers are being more idealistic and responding as if the situation were better than it is, a pattern we have seen before.

In summary, then, this section has pointed out that overall the managers in the present study, both black and white, believe that more of the non-ability-related factors should be ideally irrelevant for promotion than the predominantly white managers in Bowman's studies. Furthermore, although the managers in our study, as noted in Chapter 6, did not mention consideration of such factors as age, sex, (race with the minor exception noted) and national origin in evaluating a manager with the requisite experience and job knowledge, it is quite clear from their responses in this section that various minorities of the managers *would* take into consideration such non-ability-related factors. This is a further indication of the prejudicial attitudes underlying much of the business world's employment practices.

WHO ACTUALLY GETS AHEAD

In general the black and white managers agree on the factors that ideally should be irrelevant, helpful, or harmful for promotion. As to who actually gets ahead, there is a fair amount of agreement among the managers about who gets ahead in business in general but substantial disagreement with regard to their own firms. If one looks at those factors that 50 percent or more of either the black or white managers or both believe are helpful for promotion in their firms, one finds 11 factors that the black managers consider helpful and only six that the white mangers consider so. These are shown in the middle three columns of Table 7-4.

The black managers believe that the manager who gets ahead in their companies is a white man under 45 years of age, a United States citizen who is college educated and technically oriented. He has a Masters in Business Administration, seniority, a helpful spouse, pull with top management, and is interested in community activities. The white managers' views are somewhat different. The successful manager in their companies, they believe, is a man under 45 who is college educated, technically oriented, with a Masters in Business Administration and interested in community activities. Ten years ago the white managers in Bowman's studies saw basically the same type of manager getting ahead in their firm as the white managers in this study see succeeding now.

With regard to the business world in general (the last three columns in Table 7-4), the majority of the black managers believe a successful manager would have essentially the same characteristics as the successful manager in their own firms. However the successful manager in the business world would also have artistic and cultural interests and belong to a country club. As the table shows, the white managers in both this study and Bowman's generally agree that this is the type of manager who would get ahead in the business world.

The comparative data in Table 7-4 indicate that once again the white managers in this study are generally under the impression that their own companies are much better than those in business in general. As Bowman noted, the managers' responses about their companies may well be influenced by firm loyalty. Their responses regarding the business world in general are more realistic in terms of what the situation actually is, both in the corporate world and their own firms. In addition, as we have noted before and Bowman also pointed out, the white managers' views of the business world may be a projection of how the managers believe it should be rather than how it really is.

Overall, Table 7-4 shows that little change has occurred during the past 10 years with regard to the image of the most promotable manager in business in general. In the minds of a substantial majority of both black and white managers, the most promotable manager is still the native born, college educated white man under 45.

TABLE 7-4 FACTORS HELPFUL FOR PROMOTION (in %)

Factors	Ideally in the Managers' Opinion			Actually in their Firm			Actually in Business		
	Black Managers (N = 116)	White Managers (N = 156)	Bowman, 1964 (pp. 16–22) (N = 2000)	Black Managers (N = 116)	White Managers (N = 156)	Bowman, 1964 (pp. 16–22) (N = 2000)	Black Managers (N = 116)	White Managers (N = 156)	Bowman, 1964 (pp. 16–22) (N = 2000)
College education	95	88	94	85	92	83	94	97	93
Graduate work in business administration	62	61	80	58	68	50	75	81	75
Technical knowledge	90	86	90	74	80	85	81	86	86
Seniority	—	—	—	61	43	—	70	59	—
Under 30	—	—	—	—	—	—	49	50	—
Under 45	—	—	70	60	59	69	60	63	76
White	—	—	—	67	31	—	78	53	74[a]
Male	—	—	65	76	62	79	90	72	87
Cultural interests	53	66	71	—	—	51	60	47	64
Community interests	67	72	71	66	72	51	67	67	64
Country club	—	—	—	—	—	—	66	61	—
US citizen	—	—	54	62	42	80	62	33	76[a]
Pull	—	—	—	79	46	—	82	62	—
Helpful spouse	50	53	—	52	49	—	60	70	—

[a] Data from Bowman, 1962.

WHO DOES NOT GET AHEAD

The managers of both races tend to agree generally on the characteristics that make for the most promotable manager in the ideal situation. When they rate the characteristics that make for the least promotable managers, their perceptions are similar, as they were for promotable characteristics in the business world at large. But the managers differ on the least promotable manager, as they did when asked about the most promotable characteristics within their own firms.

With regard to their own firms, the managers listed six factors, as shown in Table 7-5 (only those that 30 percent or more of the black or white managers believe are harmful are included). As the table shows, of the six factors three are racial, and much higher proportions of black managers than white believe these factors harmful to promotion in their firms. The most harmful factor for the majority of blacks, though, is being a woman, and this is given as the second most harmful factor by a substantial percentage of the white managers.

Notice also that both black and white managers believe that being Chicano is more harmful than being black in their firms. Such a view could possibly result from the fact that pressure on corporations from Chicanos was four years behind pressure from blacks and therefore there has not been as great a shift in attitudes. The managers' views could also show that the recent pressure on firms from Chicanos is having an initial negative effect. Whites are reacting adversely to the Chicano pressures, and black managers are becoming more aware of such negative comments as the following from whites: "Why don't Chicanos use legal means like the blacks, instead of disruptive demonstrations and pressure tactics?"

TABLE 7–5 FACTORS THE MANAGERS BELIEVE
ARE HARMFUL FOR PROMOTION IN THEIR
FIRMS (in %)

Factors	Black Managers ($N = 116$)	White Managers ($N = 156$)
Female	61	44
Chicano	56	21
Black	54	11
Over 45	47	52
Oriental	41	10
Foreigner	39	15

TABLE 7–6   FACTORS THE MANAGERS BELIEVE ARE HARMFUL FOR PROMOTION
IN BUSINESS IN GENERAL (in %)

Factors	Bowman 1962 (p. 61) (N = 315)	Black Managers (N = 116)	White Managers (N = 156)	Bowman 1964 (pp. 16–22) (N = 2000)
Female	58	72	68	77
Black	77	68	58	87
Chicano[a]	71	68	55	77
Over 45	54	67	49	—
Oriental	68	52	38	75
Foreigner	—	40	38	—
Jewish	—	30	23	—

[a] In Bowman's studies she used Puerto Rican.

As one might expect, the six harmful factors to promotion believed to be
in their firms reappear when the managers are asked what they believe is
harmful for promotion in the business world in general. The percentages are
shown in Table 7-6, and there is an additional factor, that of being Jewish.
(Again this table lists only the factors 30 percent or more of both the black
and white managers believe deter one from promotion.)

In comparing Tables 7-5 and 7-6, it is significant that only two factors
were selected by over 30 percent of the white managers as being harmful in
their companies—being female or over 45 (Table 7-5). But for the business
world in general, over 30 percent of the whites selected six of the seven factors also selected by the black managers as being harmful for promotion
(Table 7-6) with being female still very high on the list of detriments. Notice
that here, for the corporate world in general, black and white managers do
not believe that being Chicano is more harmful than being black. This is because the incidence of Chicano pressures is high in California and other
western states and relatively slight in other areas throughout the country.
The fact that in our randomly selected sample only 1 percent of the
managers are Jewish indicates that being Jewish is more harmful to an individual's promotional opportunities both in the business world and in these
firms than the participating black and white managers generally believe.

A comparison of the data in Table 7-6, which shows Bowman's results
and those of the present study, reveals that what managers consider the
most harmful factor for promotion in the business world has changed
slightly in the past 10 years. The predominantly white managers in
Bowman's studies believed that being black is the most harmful factor. But
in the minds of both black and white managers in the present study, being

black has been replaced by being female. This is certainly no sign of progress; it is hard to know whether the racial or the sexual factor is the more discriminatory.

IMAGE VARIATIONS BY COMPANIES

The responses of the managers to selected important factors, when viewed from the perspectives of their particular firms, bear a direct relationship to the Affirmative Action Programs of the firms. Table 7-7 shows the responses of both races broken down by firm.

Ace Public Utility and Triple A Bank, the companies with the strongest AAPs, have created among their black managers the most positive overall views of the promotional opportunities that exist in their companies not only for blacks but also for Asians, Chicanos, and women. In these companies the white managers also have more positive views of the promotional opportunities for these groups than the white managers in most of the other companies.

In terms of consistency of views on the helpfulness or harmfulness of belonging to a certain race, only in Ace Public Utility are the black managers consistent; in none of the companies are the white managers consistent. For instance, 50 percent of the black managers in Ace Public Utility believe that being black is harmful for promotion and 46 percent believe that being white is helpful for promotion, a consistent set of responses. However, in Triple C Bank 48 percent of the managers believe that being black is harmful but the percentage who believe being white is helpful is 72 percent! The greatest inconsistency in the white managers' views occurs in Aunts Manufacturing where only 9 percent say being black is harmful, but 41 percent say being white is helpful.

The white managers' views reveal another important discrepancy. In Cousins, Aunts, and Ajax Manufacturing Companies the white managers almost unanimously agree that being male is a helpful factor for promotion in their firms. Many of these managers say that the type of work their companies do is not suitable for women. But Ajax Manufacturing recently hired 10 women for jobs that were supposedly suitable only for men. It seems, then, that women may indeed be suited for many of the jobs available in these firms but are simply not given the opportunities to demonstrate their abilities.

Several of the companies' groups of managers show consistency on the male-female factor. In Ajax and Century Manufacturing Companies and Deuce Public Utility the managers believe that being male is helpful for promotion and being female harmful. But in the other companies there is much inconsistency on these factors. The most glaring are in the opinions of

TABLE 7-7 RESPONSES TO SELECTED FACTORS BY COMPANIES (in %)

Items		Ace Public Utility	Triple C Bank	Cousins Mfg.	Aunts Mfg.	Triple A Bank	Ajax Mfg.	Century Mfg.	Deuce Public Utility	Total
Negro (−)[a]	Black	50	48	62	68	36	67	100	60	54
	White	8	0	27	9	6	33	0	20	11
White (+)	Black	46	72	85	74	50	100	100	80	67
	White	23	20	47	41	31	53	13	27	30
Chicano (−)	Black	50	52	62	68	43	67	100	60	56
	White	15	7	33	27	19	40	20	20	21
Asian (−)	Black	37	44	39	53	37	33	100	33	41
	White	0	3	13	14	6	40	0	13	9
U.S. (+)	Black	58	56	54	74	57	100	100	67	62
	White	35	33	53	55	50	33	40	40	42
Male (+)	Black	50	80	92	93	57	100	100	87	77
	White	46	47	93	100	63	87	60	40	62
Female (−)	Black	50	60	69	67	43	100	100	67	61
	White	15	7	67	74	38	87	60	40	44
Under 30 (+)	Black	62	28	39	47	29	0	100	33	41
	White	73	40	20	55	31	60	67	0	46

TABLE 7-7 (Continued)

Items		Ace Public Utility	Triple C Bank	Cousins Mfg.	Aunts Mfg.	Triple A Bank	Ajax Mfg.	Century Mfg.	Deuce Public Utility	Total
Under 45 (+)	Black	69	52	54	68	64	33	0	60	60
	White	54	63	67	77	36	53	53	47	58
Over 45 (−)	Black	77	32	46	53	36	33	100	27	47
	White	73	20	33	77	44	87	80	7	52
Jewish (−)	Black	30	20	8	11	21	33	0	27	20
	White	12	3	20	5	6	7	7	7	7
Ivy League (+)	Black	31	36	8	42	64	100	0	20	33
	White	27	17	47	9	31	33	7	20	23
Country club (+)	Black	46	36	39	39	71	33	100	60	47
	White	8	17	13	42	19	33	7	27	14
Pull with top (+)	Black	77	84	69	40	93	100	100	80	79
	White	58	40	40	68	38	60	40	53	46
Negro (+)	Black	23	12	0	21	29	0	0	27	18
	White	42	20	40	23	25	20	20	27	27

[a] The (+) or (−) after the name of the item indicates whether the managers believe the item is helpful or harmful for promotion in their firms.

the white managers in Ace Public Utility and Triple C Bank. Forty-six percent of the white managers in Ace Public Utility believe being male is helpful and 15 percent believe being female is harmful. In Triple C Bank 47 percent of the white managers believe being male is helpful but only 7 percent believe being female is harmful. The higher percentages probably represent the true situations in these firms, and the lower most likely indicate only what the managers believe to be the "proper" response.

In general, however, Table 7-7 does indicate that the stronger a company's Affirmative Action Program the more the program tends to modify the managers' image of the most promotable type of manager. In companies such as Ace Public Utility and Triple A Bank the stereotypical image of the white man is becoming replaced by an image more heterogeneous in nature, and more equitable.

IMAGE VARIATIONS BY SELECTED GROUPS

When the managers' responses to the same selected factors as those in Table 7-7 are compared in terms of managerial level, age, and educational achievement, additional light is thrown on managerial beliefs about non-ability-related characteristics that enter into promotional opportunities in their firms. Table 7-8 indicates several patterns among the managers.

From the data in the table certain patterns become apparent that have been indicated in other ways in previous chapters. The younger, lower level black managers feel more than the older, middle level black managers that being black or Chicano is harmful for promotion in their firms and being white is helpful (see the "Age" columns in Table 7-8). Also more than any other managerial group the older, middle level black managers with college educations believe that being Jewish is a hindrance to promotion. This strong belief may stem from the older blacks' carrying over memories of times when many blacks and Jews were suffering under even more extreme discrimination than at present.

There also seems to be a pattern among the white managers. Those who are younger, more educated, and on the lower and middle levels believe that being black or Chicano is a harmful factor in their firms, whereas the older, less educated upper level white managers believe this to a lesser extent. (All the managers seem to agree that being Asian is not as harmful as being black or Chicano.) Even though more of the white lower level managers than those at the middle and upper levels believe that being white aids promotion, there is still a sizeable percentage of top level managers who believe this, 24 percent, and these are the people responsible for formulating employment policies that determine who is hired and promoted and who is not.

The upper level managers' responses on sex show a telling discrepancy. Sixty-two percent believe that being male is helpful, but only 35 percent

TABLE 7-8 RESPONSES TO SELECTED FACTORS BY MANAGERIAL LEVEL, AGE GROUP, AND EDUCATIONAL LEVEL (in %)

		Personal Characteristics									
		Managerial Level			Age				Education		
		Lower	Middle	Upper	Under 30	30–40	40–50	Over 50	High School	Some College	BA +
Negro (−)	Black	57	47	0	73	45	35	0	30	62	54
	White	11	13	7	17	12	12	7	8	6	15
White (+)	Black	70	62	0	76	62	65	0	30	73	71
	White	40	28	24	56	26	28	29	23	27	36
Chicano (−)	Black	56	56	0	73	49	35	0	30	62	57
	White	22	22	17	33	19	22	16	13	18	26
Asian (−)	Black	42	38	0	51	38	24	0	10	46	43
	White	7	11	7	11	12	8	7	3	9	12

U.S. (+)	Black	59	71	0	67	57	71	0	40	70	62
	White	44	40	45	61	43	45	37	35	39	46
Male (+)	Black	77	77	0	80	76	76	0	30	76	85
	White	76	54	62	83	61	63	55	50	61	69
Female (−)	Black	60	65	0	67	58	59	0	40	60	66
	White	48	44	35	61	44	48	26	28	30	57
Under 30 (+)	Black	39	44	0	42	38	41	0	50	38	40
	White	33	48	59	33	37	50	55	55	49	40
Under 45 (+)	Black	59	60	0	64	55	65	0	20	70	60
	White	54	65	45	61	61	57	52	60	42	63
Over 45 (−)	Black	46	47	0	47	47	53	0	60	51	43
	White	57	48	55	61	58	45	55	55	49	52
Jewish (−)	Black	17	30	0	18	19	29	0	0	24	21
	White	7	8	7	11	7	5	10	5	0	11

believe being female is harmful. Such a difference can be attributed to the bind top management is in when questioned: Upper managers cannot help but admit that being male is helpful to an individual's promotional opportunities—one has only to look at the upper ranks to see there are no women, or very few. Nevertheless, because of the laws forbidding sexual discrimination, many upper level managers will still not admit that being female is a detriment to promotion.

IMPLICATIONS OF THE IMAGE OF THE MOST PROMOTABLE MANAGER

The data in this chapter show that although there have been some changes in the image of the promotable manager in corporations over the last decade, these changes have not been great. Most of the managers, both black and white, believe that the three ability factors—college education, technical knowledge, and a Masters in Business Administration are essential in both principle and practice for promotions. However many of the managers believe that non-ability-related factors such as age, sex, race, and national origin also play crucial roles in the promotional opportunities of managers. In essence the managers are saying that a college education, graduate training, and technical knowledge are important—provided the manager being considered for promotion is a white man under 45 who was born in the United States.

The consequences of this image for business are both predictable and narrow: So long as substantial majorities of the managers believe that the most promotable person is a young, white, college educated, Protestant man, such a person will be the one to receive the special training and promotional considerations. He will preserve the in-group status quo. Minority individuals and women will continue to be excluded for reasons that may appear to be justified but are in fact subtly and strongly sexist and racist. The only practical solution at present is strong Affirmative Action Programs within each company, coupled with better management techniques (which will be discussed in Chapter 10). Such programs as these will do the most to assure minorities and women their equality of opportunity.

CHAPTER EIGHT

Aspirations, Goals, Work Environment, and Job Satisfaction

Information on managers' feelings of progress, their career goals and aspirations, and satisfaction with their environment and job are extremely important for firms that want to improve their Affirmative Action Programs. No less important is the variation in feelings on these subjects between the white and black managers. No company will have a successful AAP if its black managers believe that they are limited in the firm, that they are being rejected, that they will not be able to satisfy their needs, goals, and aspirations, and that their work environment and overall work experience are unsatisfactory. It has been noted before that the nature of a job has a strong effect on motivation, which in turn affects job performance and consequently promotability (Bray et al., 1974, p. 78). Those black managers who are dissatisfied will not readily identify with their company and will not perform to the fullest extent of their capabilities, which will affect their chances of promotion. Thus, black managers' own feelings about their jobs become very important, if not crucial, to the achievement of equal employment.

In this chapter the feelings of both black and white managers will be compared in three principal areas: (1) the managers' views of their own progress within their companies, and their goals and aspirations; (2) their work environment, especially bothersome factors such as vagueness about the scope and responsibility of their jobs, conflicting demands of various people over them, which are impossible to meet, and the carrying out of orders against their better judgment; and (3) job satisfaction in terms of work group, type of work, salary, and company in general.

It has long been recognized that work plays an essential role for the human being. A recent study conducted for the Department of Health, Education, and Welfare documented the crucial nature of work and noted that it is at the center of most adults' lives. It gives them a sense of identity, self-esteem, and order. If an individual's job is unsatisfying and frustrating, this can have serious negative effects on all aspects of his or her life (*Work in America*, 1973, p. 1).

A number of other studies on the importance of work have relevance to the present subject matter. They deal with the needs that are fulfilled for the individual in the work situation. These needs are both egoistic and social. The most important egoistic need is fulfillment in terms of accomplishment, that is, the individual's sense of the importance of his or her own work, rate of progress, completion of the work, and general productiveness. People like to measure their progress, to know whether they are progressing at a satisfactory rate, and to see their assignments completed. Then they can feel they are productive and turning out work that is useful.

Certain social needs are often filled by the subordinate-superior relationship in a work situation. The most satisfactory work environment for a subordinate is when he or she is treated fairly, praised when appropriate, given consideration and understanding when mistakes are made, and told where he or she stands (Sayles and Strauss, 1960, p. 10). Other social needs are also fulfilled on the job with colleagues and subordinates, such as friendships, a feeling of identification with formal and informal work groups, and helping others and being helped by them (Sayles and Strauss, 1960, p. 10).

When jobs do not give these kinds of satisfactions, the result is a state of job alienation. Robert Blauner has theorized that job alienation results from certain missing essential elements. Jobs that do not allow the employees to control their immediate work environment result in a sense of powerlessness. Jobs that do not allow for the development of relationships between the actions of an individual in his or her job and the broader objectives fail to create situations where the individual role is seen as fitting into the overall goals of the organization. In such a situation, the worker develops a feeling of meaninglessness.

Jobs that are boring and monotonous and prevent opportunities for self-growth provoke feelings of self-estrangement. Such jobs are seen as means rather than fulfilling ends. Jobs in which employees are excluded from numerous informal work groups produce a feeling of social isolation. All these negative aspects can, and too often do, lead to alienation and at times even to aggressive antisocial behavior (Blauner, 1964, pp. 15–34).

It has also been noted that a sense of active participation is extremely important in the employee's life. John R. P. French, Jr., and Robert D. Caplan found that lack of participation in decision-making processes can lead to strain among employees and can adversely affect productivity. Their study of 44 organizations revealed that high participation was associated with

... high satisfaction with the job and the organization, high self-esteem, low alienation, high commitment to work and to the organization, more innovation for better ways of doing the job, doing more extra work, reading more books and magazines related to work, a higher performance evaluation by one's manager, and lower absenteeism (Caplan and French, 1972, pp. 49–50).

With such important observations in mind, the feelings of our participating managers about their own career goals and job satisfaction can now be explored.

THE MANAGERS' PAST PROGRESS IN THEIR COMPANIES

The managers were asked whether they have progressed to their satisfaction thus far within their companies in terms of job level. Considering the attitudes of the majority of the black managers, who are pessimistic about the career opportunities that exist in their firms and in the corporate world in general, one might expect the vast majority of the blacks to be dissatisfied with their past progress. But this is not the case, as Table 8-1 shows. The black figure is similar to that found in the Labor Department study (Freeman and Fields, 1972), where 35 percent of the black respondents indicated dissatisfaction with their career progress. This was a small percentage considering that 69 percent were very critical of their companies' employment policies toward blacks.

Not surprisingly, most of the whites—almost four-fifths—are satisfied with their progress and a large proportion of the blacks are also satisfied—almost two-thirds. However both black and white female managers are more dissatisfied with their progress than the men, no doubt a further indication of sex discrimination.

The managers were also asked for the reasons they are satisfied or dissatisfied with their progress to date. Their reasons are shown in Tables 8-2 and 8-3. It was seen in Table 8-1 that approximately 33 percent of the black managers are dissatisfied with the progress they have made in their firms, and that approximately 64 percent are satisfied. This could lead one

TABLE 8–1 HAVE THE MANAGERS PROGRESSED AS RAPIDLY AS THEY THINK THEY SHOULD HAVE? (in %)

Response	Black Men ($N = 93$)	Black Women ($N = 23$)	White Men ($N = 133$)	White Women ($N = 23$)
Yes	69	52	82	74
No	29	48	18	26
Other	2	0	0	0
Total	100	100	100	100

TABLE 8–2 REASONS THE MANAGERS ARE SATISFIED WITH THEIR PROGRESS (in %)

Reasons	Black Managers ($N = 76$)	White Managers ($N = 126$)
Short period of time with the firm and has achieved the position faster than most people	28	8
Goals and aspirations are being achieved either on schedule or faster than was anticipated	20	25
Company has fair promotional opportunities; therefore, has progressed as rapidly as most people	15	22
Can't really say because of the short period of time with the firm, but seems to be progressing all right thus far	11	0
Has progressed faster than most people	6	13
Limited amount of education but has progressed	5	11
Limited amount of experience but has progressed; has progressed according to capabilities; abilities are being fulfilled	5	16
At first did not, but now is progressing	1	4
Other	9	1
Total	100	100

to believe that racial discrimination against blacks is rapidly decreasing, but the managers' responses in Table 8-2 give a clue to the more likely cause for the higher proportion of managers who are satisfied. Their feelings are heavily influenced by the short period of time most of them have been with their firms.

With length of service as the control, although there were no observable differences among the white managers, it was discovered that the black managers with more than four years of service are more likely than those with four or fewer years of service to be dissatisfied. Only 45 percent of those with more than eight years of service express satisfaction with their progress, as do 60 percent of those with more than four years, compared to 72 percent with four or fewer years of service.

Most of the black managers who are satisfied with their progress have been with their firms under four years. One middle level manager at

Cousins Manufacturing has been there three years and in that time has received four promotions and related salary increases. Another manager, who entered Ace Public Utility under the high risk–high reward program 2½ years before the start of the study, was evaluated after one year and found able to assume a middle management district level position within five years. But he actually was promoted after a year and a half. Another middle level manager has been with his firm only nine months and is satisfied: "In terms of entry-level position I'm happy—the future is unknown." And a lower level manager from Aunts Manufacturing who has been there for three years is satisfied but with some qualification: "I think I am more than capable of handling a larger job, but I've progressed as rapidly as I should have. I set goals and I'm on the way to reaching them."

The managers who are dissatisfied with their progress give a variety of reasons, as Table 8-3 shows, but for the blacks the most frequent one by far

TABLE 8–3   REASONS THE MANAGERS ARE NOT SATISFIED WITH THEIR PROGRESS (in %)

Reasons	Black Managers (N = 38)	White Managers (N = 30)
Progress hindered due to race	57	3
Has experience and qualifications, but others with less experience and qualifications have been promoted over respondent	18	10
Not given a chance to prove ability or fulfill potential	15	17
At first did not, but now is progressing	5	7
Lacks political influence	5	7
Not willing to move from the area	3	7
Lack of education	3	10
Progress hindered due to sex, i.e., being a woman	0	13
Superiors have held respondent back	0	10
Came in under the old promotional system, i.e., began at the lowest level rather than where respondent belonged	0	7
Other	5	20
Total[a]	111	111

[a] The total percentages are over 100 because some managers gave more than one reason for their dissatisfaction with their progress.

is racial discrimination (57 percent). A middle level manager at Aunts Manufacturing, who has an engineering degree, a Masters in Business Administration, and five years of previous work experience, earns only $14,500. He says: "For my experience and background I'm not being promoted fast enough. They tell me it's because I'm too young, but the real reason is because I'm black and the company is afraid of employee and customer reactions." A law degree has not helped a black middle level manager at Ace Public Utility: "My first boss indicated I'd be where I am now one year ago. When I changed bosses I got a racist who held me back." A female manager on the lower level at Triple C Bank, who has been there for 14 years, comments: "I knew I had the ability but when I came to the company they weren't promoting blacks." Even one of the black managers who indicated satisfaction with his progress rated his chances of rising from his present middle level management position to the upper level as poor because in his firm, Cousins Manufacturing, there is a prevalence of "ultraconservative" racial attitudes.

The few white managers who are dissatisfied give reasons primarily connected to company politics. This is not true of the women, who cite sex discrimination most often. A white female lower level manager at Triple C Bank relates: I came in with a high school diploma, but in my 20 years at the bank I've taken six years' worth of banking courses. I even took a managers' training program. But I've been held back because I'm a woman."

The dissatisfied white men see their slow progress in other terms. One tells of a staff turnover that put him in "bad graces with the vice-president of industrial relations," and this hindered the manager from two "deserved" promotions. Another, who has been with Deuce Public Utility 24 years and is now on the middle level, acknowledges the need for skills other than ability in his company: "The top job in my department is open now and hasn't been filled. I have the ability and seniority for it, but I probably won't get it—maybe I'm not political enough." Finally, a middle level manager at Ace Public Utility tells how the wrong move can hinder advancement: "I've been at the same level for the past 17 years. And the reason is that I wouldn't take a certain job way back when, and it's been held against me ever since."

These comments by managers of both races, as well as the tables, show that although the vast majority of blacks and whites are satisfied with their progress, the dissatisfied whites attribute their lack of progress to reasons directly or indirectly related to politics. The blacks who are dissatisfied tend to have been with their firms longer and are primarily critical because of the effects of racial discrimination on their careers, a portent for the black managers who are relatively new—they may well become more dissatisfied as their lengths of service increase.

THE MANAGERS' FUTURE PROGRESS AND THEIR GOALS

Satisfaction with past progress has an important relation to anticipated future progress, especially in terms of an individual's goals and aspirations. Thus it is also instructive to examine how the managers feel about their future progress and how compatible it is with their goals for themselves. The managers' feelings in these areas, as well as their views on past progress, have to do with certain factors one looks for in a job.

Most Important Job Factors

The most important job factors were enumerated in the HEW study from the responses of 1533 American workers at all occupational levels. In order of importance, they are:

1. Interesting work
2. Enough help and equipment to get the job done
3. Enough information to get the job done
4. Enough authority to get the job done
5. Good pay
6. Opportunity to develop special abilities
7. Job security
8. Seeing the results of one's work (*Work in America,* 1973, p. 13)

The managers in the present study were asked to imagine they were about to choose a new job. They were given a list of similar job factors and asked for their opinions on the relative importance of these factors. Table 8-4 gives the managers' views.

The managers' responses support the findings reviewed at the beginning of this chapter that the most important aspects of a job to many employees are feelings that the work is important, gives a sense of accomplishment, and is interesting. These categories are selected by the majority of managers of both races, 50 percent of the blacks and 73 percent of the whites.

The higher percentage of whites and the 23 percent difference between the races can probably be attributed to the fact that most of the whites in this study hold secure, well-paying, middle and upper level management positions, but most of the blacks hold low-paying, lower level positions. Higher psychological needs therefore assume greater importance for the whites, and practical needs such as salary and advancement opportunities are of more concern to the blacks. It is also possible that the whites feel that salary increases and advances will automatically be a part of any job they may have, but the blacks cannot jump to this conclusion. Differences between the races decrease greatly in the managers' responses to factors they would consider second in importance and least important (see Appendix C, page 259, for the frequency distribution of the managers' responses).

TABLE 8–4   IMPORTANT FACTORS IN A NEW JOB (in %)

Factors	Black Managers ($N = 116$)	White Managers ($N = 156$)
The work is important and gives a sense of accomplishment.	42	60
Chances for advancement	22	8
High income	20	12
The work is interesting	8	13
No danger of being fired; security	3	2
The work gives lots of chances to meet people.	1	2
Lots of free time	1	1
Other	3	2
Total	100	100

$p \leq .05$

Some interesting findings come to light when age is used as a control variable. Of the white managers age 30 or younger, 94 percent select importance and interest of work as primary, compared to only 41 percent of the black managers in this age group. Income is paramount to only one white manager in this age group, as opposed to 24 percent of the black managers. None of these white managers select advancement as particularly important, but 16 percent of the young black managers do. Variations are also apparent in the 30 to 40 age group and in the group over 40, but as the managers get older the differences between the races become less and less severe. These statistics indicate that younger white managers have satisfied basic or practical job needs and can relate to higher level needs whereas many young blacks have not yet satisfied the basic needs.

Goals and Aspirations

Not only do many black managers consider advancement and salary more important than the white managers, but they also want to advance faster and reach the same, if not higher, levels of management as those to which the white managers aspire. Table 8-5 shows that there are hardly any differences in the advancement desires of the managers.

There is also a realistic attitude on the part of the less educated black managers concerning their goals and aspirations in white corporations.

They realize that for blacks to reach upper management today they must be super-qualified and that the firms are also placing greater emphasis on college degrees. These realizations explain why 24 of the 29 black managers who do not have the Bachelor degrees want only to achieve middle management positions, and it also explains why 52 percent of the black female managers, none of whom have college degrees, select the middle level of management as their goal rather than the upper level.

Although there is agreement among the black and white managers on the levels they desire, there are important differences in the lengths of time they anticipate and desire in moving toward their wished-for levels. More black managers anticipate quicker advancement and want to advance faster in reaching the same, if not higher, levels of management as those to which the whites aspire. The managers' differences in expected and desired times for promotion are illustrated graphically in Chart I.

The chart shows that 43 percent of the black managers and 28 percent of the white desire immediate advancement, but no black managers and only one white manager expect to be advanced immediately. Promotion is desired within at least one year by only 48 percent of the whites but by 72 percent of the blacks; and 35 percent of the blacks, as opposed to 23 percent of the whites, believe they actually will be advanced within the next year.

Large overall differences between the expected and desired times for advancement can create serious problems within firms, especially in conjunction with the more rigorous enforcement of equal employment laws. It was

TABLE 8–5   LEVEL OF MANAGEMENT THE MANAGERS WOULD LIKE TO ACHIEVE (in %)

Level	Black Managers ($N = 116$)	White Managers ($N = 156$)	White[a] Managers ($N = 156$)
Lower Level[b]	2	6	9
Middle Level	29	22	26
Upper Level	53	52	58
President	14	7	7
Stay at Present Level	2	13	0
Total	100	100	100

[a] This column includes the percentage of white managers who want to remain at their present levels.

[b] Even though all participants in this study were at least at the lower level of management, those who selected this level as their goal did so because they still have a number of steps within this level to which they could advance.

CHART 1 EXPECTED AND DESIRED TIMES FOR PROMOTION: BLACK AND
WHITE MANAGERS

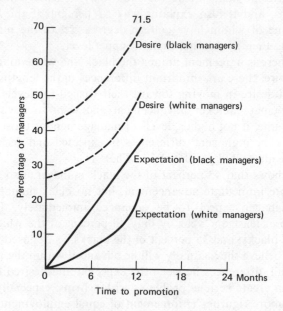

noted earlier (Chapter 3) that the present economic slowdown and overstaffing at middle and upper levels have contributed to the disenchantment of
both black and white managers with their progress. Emphasis on affirmative action happened to coincide with the economic slowdown and the consequent discovery of overstaffing, and thus many white managers grumble
that they are not being promoted because the promotions are being given to
the blacks. At the same time, many blacks who expected to be promoted attribute their lack of progress only to racial discrimination within their
particular firms. Such variance of outlooks, if not dealt with properly, can
lead to direct confrontation; some possible remedies will be offered in the
final chapter.

From the data so far presented, it has been seen that the black managers
place more emphasis on high income and chances for advancement than do
the whites, and also that the blacks would like to be promoted sooner and to
slightly higher positions. These findings contradict the stereotypical white
belief that blacks lack ambition, but it is important to delve further into the
possible reasons for the similarity of black and white goals and the greater
ambition of the blacks.

As Chapter 2 pointed out, many studies have shown that middle class people have higher occupational aspirations than lower class people, primarily because of more parental counseling and encouragement (see, for instance, Ginzberg et al., 1951, p. 78; Bendix and Lipset, 1962; Crochett, Jr., 1966, pp. 280–309). Over 60 percent of the white managers come from middle and upper class backgrounds, and they seem to follow the trends found by such studies. But even though over 60 percent of the black managers come from working class backgrounds, their occupational goals are just as high as, or higher than, the whites. What is the explanation for this?

To answer this question, it is first necessary to review the managers' backgrounds. Those white managers whose fathers and/or mothers were highly educated and those white managers whose fathers held professional and/or managerial positions have higher aspirations than those whites whose parents did not have such achievements. For instance, of those white managers whose fathers had at least a Bachelor degree, 84 percent aspire to be or already are at the upper level, compared to only 57 percent of those managers with the same aspirations whose fathers had only a high school diploma or less.

With the black managers the pattern is not so clearcut. Sixty-five percent of the black managers whose fathers had only a high school diploma or less and 68 percent whose fathers had at least a Bachelor degree aspire to become upper level managers. The explanation seems to be that even though many blacks' parents were not of the middle class they still inculcated similar values and held just as strong work ethics as the white parents, if not stronger (for a corroboration of this among welfare and poor families, mentioned earlier, see Goodwin, 1972). As much as whites, black parents have expected and encouraged their children to get an education, work hard, and make something of themselves, as several managers have attested in previous chapters. What has been lacking is the opportunity for the blacks to act on these values.

Another probable influence on the black managers' goals and aspirations is their perception of how far blacks can go in their companies. If a black manager believes the highest a black can go in his or her firm is to the middle level of management, initial aspirations may be high but in time may become more realistic. Given the perceived impossibility of rising higher than middle management, a black manager's goals may be revised downward. Or a more drastic step may be taken and the black may leave the company entirely (see Wilensky and Lebeaux, 1965, p. 111).

In analyzing how far up the occupational ladder the black managers believe a black can go in their companies and the desired positions the black managers want to achieve, it is found that 63 percent of those black managers who plan to remain with their firms desire to achieve positions in the upper level of management. Half of them believe a black can make it to at least upper management positions; of the 35 percent who desire to achieve positions up to the middle level of management, only one-quarter believe blacks can make it to upper managerial levels. (See Appendix C, pages 259–278, for the frequency distribution and a detailed breakdown of the managers' reasons for how far a black can advance today in their particular companies.) From these figures it seems that some black managers might base their goals and aspirations at least in part on their impressions of how far a black can go in their companies. Of the 24 blacks who say they may leave their firms, 21 of them believe a black can go only as far as middle management, and 19 of these want to achieve upper level positions. (The managers who will leave their firms will be discussed later in this chapter).

Major Obstacles

Many of the black and white managers believe there are major obstacles preventing them from achieving their desired goals—56 percent and 47 percent, respectively. There are no large differences between those managers who believe there are obstacles and those managers who do not when the positions the managers eventually would like to achieve are correlated with whether they believe there are major obstacles preventing them from achieving those positions. Table 8-6 shows the various obstacles the managers see as hindering them from advancement.

The major obstacles, the managers feel, are generally factors other than those directly related to work experience and job knowledge. By far the most blacks believe their color will stand in their way. For instance, a black middle level manager at Cousins Manufacturing who is satisfied so far but rated his chances for reaching upper management as poor says the major hindrance is "the apathy and racist ultraconservatism of private institutions" such as his firm.

Although a female manager on the lower level at Triple C Bank is confident of her experience and qualifications, like many other black managers who single out no major obstacles, she nevertheless says, "Other things might hinder my progress," and it is clear that she means discrimination. In fact she is among the 67 percent of the black managers who want to achieve the upper ranks, but she is also among the half of this 67 percent who believe their firms will not allow qualified blacks to rise this high.

Lack of education is seen as a major problem by a large number of both blacks and whites. A white middle level manager at Triple C Bank formerly believed that his chances of rising to the upper level were excellent, but now

TABLE 8–6 MAJOR OBSTACLES TO THE MANAGERS' CHANCES FOR
ADVANCEMENT (in %)

Major Obstacles in the Managers' Opinions	Black Managers (N = 65)	White Managers (N = 73)
Race, i.e., being black	44	0
Lack of education	32	36
Great competition; only a few jobs at that level; only a few positions and those holding them are not about to retire	9	12
Sex, i.e., being female	7	4
Lack of seniority	7	1
Lack of specific technical, scientific, or professional skills; not being in the specific area to get the position	6	8
Age, i.e., too old	3	14
Lack of diverse experiences	3	11
Age, i.e., too young	1	3
Lack political influence	0	8
Other	14	21
Total[a]	126	118

[a] The total percentages are over 100 because some managers believe there are a number of major obstacles.

he feels that his lack of a college degree will stand in his way. A black lower level female manager at Ace Public Utility has some interesting comments about the hindrance presented by race and sex in contrast to that of little education. She rates her chances of reaching middle management as only fair and tells why: "I lack a college degree. If you had asked me three months ago what were the major obstacles, then I would have said that being a female and a black would go against you. Now they go for you, but that old degree is just as important as ever, especially for females and blacks."

A provocative counterpoint to this manager's comments are those from a white male manager at the same level with the same company. He too rates his chances of rising as fair but sees the obstacles quite differently from the woman: "Since women have been discriminated against in the past, now a numbers game is being played in their employment. It will probably be a little more than tokenism—just 'window dressing.' But I probably won't be promoted because they'll put a woman in instead."

In sum, the managers have differing reasons and views concerning the progress they expect and desire within their firms. These differences are sometimes connected to their race and the degree of advantage they have been accustomed to or deprived of. Such differences are well illustrated by two young managers, both the same age, 28, and both at the lower level. Mr. J., the young black, comes from Texas, where he spent most of his life. He was raised on a small farm where he lived with his parents, both of whom had little education. He earned a Bachelor of Arts degree in History at Prairie View College in Texas. He is a Baptist but never attends church, considers himself a radical Democrat, and belongs to no outside organizations.

Mr. J. is not satisfied with his progress at his company primarily because he feels he has not been given the opportunity to demonstrate his abilities. Although he desires promotion now, he realistically expects it no sooner than four months in the future. He intends to stay with his firm; but if he were to seek another position, a high income and chances for advancement would be more important to him than interesting work and work that gives a sense of accomplishment.

At his firm Mr. J. would like to reach middle management, but he believes the firm is not ready for blacks to become even middle managers, much less upper managers. He says: "It's foolish to aim too high. As I see it, the major obstacle I have to contend with is race." Mr. J.'s aspirations, like those of many other blacks, tend to be influenced by the company's racial climate and the consequent belief on his part that a black cannot go very far.

The young white manager, Mr. M., spent most of his life in Missouri, where his father was a middle level manager and his mother a housewife. He received a Bachelor of Arts degree and a Masters degree in psychology from University of Missouri. Mr. M. considers himself a liberal Republican and has no religious preferences and belongs to a few social clubs.

He has been with his firm as long as Mr. J., two years, but unlike his black counterpart is satisfied with his progress. His desires and expectations for promotion coincide and he feels he is right on schedule. Although he would like to leave his company but expects he will stay, his reason is not firm-connected. He would like to become a psychoanalyst in private practice, and the major obstacle he would face, he says, is the lack of a doctorate for this work. The most important job considerations to him, whether in corporations or in his own practice, are interest and the sense of accomplishment provided by the work.

These factors are quite different from the young black's priorities. There is much difference in the job-related values of these two young men, and they are reflections in large part of their particular racial groups. Now let us turn to an exploration of the work environments of the participating managers.

THE MANAGERS' WORK ENVIRONMENTS

In the introduction to Alfred J. Morrow's book, *The Failure of Success,* Chris Argyris wrote:

Problems are equally severe at management levels, where incompetent organizational structures create executive environments lacking in trust, openness, and risk-taking. The attitudes that flourish best in such environments are conformity and defensiveness, which often find expression in an organizational tendency to produce detailed information for unimportant problems and invalid information for important ones. This tendency ensures ineffective problem-solving, poor decision-making, and weak commitment to the decisions made (Argyris, 1972, pp. 3–4).

In the past 20 years psychologists and sociologists have stressed the importance of good working relationships, which are characterized by high trust, high supportiveness, and high interest between and among subordinates, peers, and superiors in solving problems which confront organizational members. Good working relationships are very important in improving and/or maintaining organizational efficiency, and arc cnhanced by the lack of role ambiguity (see, for instance, McGregor, 1960; Likert, 1961, 1967; Argyris, 1964).

More explicitly, if on the one hand a manager does not have a good working relationship with the immediate work group (subordinates, peers, and superiors), his or her organizational role will be ambiguous primarily because the lack of trust, support, and interest will lead to a lack of necessary information for the manager. On the other hand, if a manager is in an ambiguous role, lacking adequate information about his or her role and the extent of his or her responsibilities and information necessary to carry them out, this ambiguity will lead to poor working relationships and conflicts that in turn make for job dissatisfaction (see Caplan and French, 1972, p. 51). It was found by Bray et al. that men who had high job challenge were more likely to reach middle management than those who had low challenge (Bray et al., 1974, p. 20).

How Dissatisfied Are the Managers?

Because of the paramount importance of the individual's feelings about his or her work, the views of the managers in this study about their general job environment will be discussed with special emphasis on their job responsibilities, their power and authority in making and influencing decisions, and their relationships with superiors. The managers were given a total of 10 statements of a negative nature relating to these areas and others and common to work situations. They were asked to respond to each in terms of how frequently they were bothered by them. Table 8-7 lists the statements and the managers' responses.

As the table indicates, the black managers are generally bothered more by these elements in their work environment than the white managers. This is not surprising, but what is surprising is that even more black managers are *not* bothered, despite their extremely negative views of their companies' employment policies and racial atmospheres (as discussed in Chapters 5 and 6). Bray et al. gave a possible explanation for this apparent contradiction. They found that 82 percent of the managers in their study believed their jobs were challenging; however, a group of independent raters believed that only 38 percent of the managers had challenging jobs. Bray et al. concluded, therefore, that the seeming overestimation of job challenge on the part of the managers themselves was self-protective; that is, the managers' self-esteem would suffer if they admitted that their jobs were not challenging or otherwise fulfilling (Bray et al., pp. 70–76). The seeming paradox among our managers is now more understandable. Those who say they are not bothered by negative factors may well be trying to protect their self-esteem.

To obtain a more concise and consistent view of the managers' attitudes, an index was formed from the six most important statements in Table 8-7. These statements are indicated by asterisks in Table 8-7 and have to do with the following aspects of the work environment: uncertainty about the opinions and evaluations of one's superior, ambiguity regarding job responsibilities and limits, deficiencies in influence with superiors and authority to do his/her job, and conflicts over orders to be carried out and demands to be met for various superiors. Table 8-8 shows the black managers' responses and Table 8-9 the white managers' responses. If the manager said that he or she was never or rarely bothered by a particular negative work situation, a score of 0 was given for that statement. If the manager was bothered rather often or nearly all the time, a score of 1 was given for each of those responses. For purposes of comparison both tables indicate percentages by sex and managerial level.

The two tables show quite vividly that overall the black managers are bothered by more things in their work environments than the white managers. More than half the white managers are completely satisfied with their work environment (Table 8-9, first line), as compared to only approximately one-third of the black managers (Table 8-8, first line). Of those managers who are most bothered in their work (both Tables 8-8 and 8-9 last lines), more than twice the percentage of blacks as whites feel the strains of troublesome elements.

When the black and white managers are compared by different categories, the results are interesting. For instance the tables show that the

TABLE 8-7 WHAT BOTHERS THE MANAGERS IN THEIR WORK ENVIRONMENT ^{a} (in %)

Examples	Never		Rarely		Rather Often		Nearly All the Time	
	Black Managers (N = 116)	White Managers (N = 156)	Black Managers (N = 116)	White Managers (N = 156)	Black Managers (N = 116)	White Managers (N = 156)	Black Managers (N = 116)	White Managers (N = 156)
The possibility of losing your job (p ≤ .30)	53	63	42	34	5	3	0	0
* Not knowing what your superior thinks of you, how he or she evaluates your performance (p ≤ .05)	31	31	43	54	16	13	10	2
Feeling that you may not be liked and accepted by the people you work with (p ≤ .01)	51	32	42	66	5	2	2	0
Thinking that the amount of work you have to do may interfere	28	14	41	44	27	38	5	4

TABLE 8-7 (Continued)

Examples	Never		Rarely		Rather Often		Nearly All the Time	
	Black Managers (N = 116)	White Managers (N = 156)	Black Managers (N = 116)	White Managers (N = 156)	Black Managers (N = 116)	White Managers (N = 156)	Black Managers (N = 116)	White Managers (N = 156)
with how well it gets done (p ≤ .05)								
The fact that you can't get information needed to carry out your job (p ≤ .05)	31	30	41	53	23	16	5	1
* Being unclear on just what the scope and responsibilities of your job are (p ≤ .02)	33	30	44	59	20	10	3	1
* Feeling that you have too little authority to carry out the responsibilities assigned to you (p ≤ .01)	28	16	36	68	32	15	4	1

158

* Feeling unable to influence your immediate superior's decisions and actions that affect you (p ≤ .01)	21	11	56	74	17	14	6	1
* Feeling that you have to do things on the job that are against your better judgment (p ≤ .01)	22	27	48	62	23	10	7	1
* Thinking that you'll not be able to satisfy the conflicting demands of various people over you (p ≤ .01)	33	12	53	68	12	19	2	1

[a] An asterisk indicates statement used for indexes to form Tables 8–8 and 8–9.

TABLE 8–8   THE BLACK MANAGERS' OVERALL VIEWS OF THEIR WORK ENVIRON-
MENT (in %)

Overall Views	Black Men		Black Women	
	Lower (N = 60)	Middle (N = 33)	Lower (N = 22)	Middle (N = 1)
Not at all bothered (0)	38	38	29	0
Somewhat bothered (1–2)	43	36	39	0
Most bothered (3–6)	19	26	32	100
Total	100	100	100	100

women of both races are much more bothered by various negative aspects than are the men. Although the few white women over 30 in middle and upper management are among the most satisfied groups, the white lower level younger female managers are among the most dissatisfied.

A 28-year-old lower level white female manager is a case in point. She has a Bachelor of Arts degree in sociology from San Francisco State College and has been with her company for 6½ years as a position analyst. Although satisfied with her progress thus far, she nevertheless feels that being a woman has held her back and has affected the amount of influence she has with her supervisor and the authority she commands with others. She

TABLE 8–9   THE WHITE MANAGERS' OVERALL VIEWS OF THEIR WORK ENVIRON-
MENT (in %)

Overall Views	White Males			White Females		
	Lower (N = 33)	Middle (N = 72)	Upper (N = 28)	Lower (N = 16)	Middle (N = 5)	Upper (N = 2)
Not at all bothered (0)	50	55	58	44	60	100
Somewhat bothered (1–2)	40	39	39	13	40	0
Most bothered (3–6)	10	6	3	43	0	0
Total	100	100	100	100	100	100

also feels she must do things against her better judgment. She is very dissatisfied with her work environment, as indicated by her score of 6 (Table 8-9) on the index, the highest possible.

A similar situation is evident in the case of a young 29-year-old black woman at the same company, where she has been for one year. She holds a Bachelor of Arts degree in English from Berkeley and worked for other companies for five years before coming to her present firm, where she is now a senior writer. Of the possible high of 6 on the work environment index, she scored 5. She feels keenly that her problems are not only related to her race but to her sex as well.

When managerial level among the managers is compared, it is seen that there are more similarities between the black and white lower level managers than between the black and white middle level managers. It seems that as whites move up the executive ladder, their job satisfaction increases, an observation supported by numerous past studies (see Gurin et al., 1960; Porter, 1961, 1962; Vroom, 1964, 1965; R. Campbell, 1973). But the blacks moving up are bothered more as they rise.

As most whites achieve higher managerial positions, they receive administrative/supervisory and decision-making positions with more responsibility and authority than they had at the lower positions. But most blacks who reach middle management are placed in nonadministrative/supervisory positions with no decision-making authority and with little or no responsibility. For example, 39 percent of the black middle level managers and only 8 percent of the white are frequently bothered by ambiguity about the scope and responsibilities of their jobs, and 50 percent of the blacks compared to 13 percent of the whites feel the stress of having too little authority to carry out their assigned responsibilities.

A striking illustration of the differences in attitudes and actual job responsibilities between the black and white managers is found with two middle level managers from the same company. They are about the same age, the white 32 and the black 34. The white manager has Bachelor of Arts and Master of Arts degrees in political science from the University of Southern California. He has been with the company six years and is now an industrial relations supervisor. On the index he responded that he was never or rarely bothered with regard to *all* of the statements. He supervises 15 people and controls a budget of $150,000.

The black manager has Bachelor of Arts and Master of Arts degrees in sociology from San Francisco State College. He was an administrator in various universities and for the Urban League before joining this company, where he has been for four years. In his present position he is involved in management training, evaluation, and development. He has no subordinates and controls no budget. On the index he scored 5 out of a possible 6, an indication that he is very bothered by many things in his work environment. Uncertain about the extent of his responsibilities, he feels he has no power or authority to carry anything out. The situations of these two managers dramatize the differences in feelings and the jobs themselves between blacks and whites at two middle management staff levels.

Of the black managers alone certain job characteristics contribute to their degree of satisfaction. The blacks most bothered in their work situation are those in personnel and urban affairs, and next bothered are those in scientific, accounting, and computer science areas. The most satisfied managers are those who hold administrative/supervisory line positions. Generally, inherent in these jobs are more influence and decision-making powers than in the former types of positions.

One black manager in urban affairs told the reasons for his dissatisfaction. An AAP coordinator, he was with his firm only one-and-a-half years when his white boss was promoted and the black was elevated to his post as the corporate AAP coordinator. The black had been a member of the U.S. Army and had retired as a colonel, but many times during his first six months as corporate APP coordinator, white managers who would normally consult the person in his position would first consult his boss to seek a solution to a particular problem. Other whites would first ask his boss whether it would be all right to confer with the black! Even though such overt racist actions ceased, the overtones linger and the black coordinator still feels that his power and authority are limited.

Among the black lower and middle level managers, much more dissatisfaction exists for those who have been with their firms less than four years than those at their firms for longer periods. This creates a very serious situation. The black managers with little service, who are educated and ambitious, are the ones the firms must depend on to fulfill their Affirmative Action Programs at the middle and upper levels. Dissatisfied with their work environment, the managers will become even more disgruntled and either will not perform their jobs to the best of their abilities or will simply leave the companies. In such circumstances the firms will not be able to achieve any affirmative action goals beyond the lowest level of management.

When the responses on the six statements comprising the index are averaged for each particular company, some interesting comparisons become evident. The biggest difference between the black and white managers occurs in the two companies with the weakest Affirmative Action Programs, Triple C Bank and Deuce Public Utility. The white managers in these two companies are the least bothered by their work environment and the black managers are among the most bothered.

In Triple A Bank the blacks and whites on the average have similar feelings. In Ace Public Utility the white managers are the most dissatisfied group of whites, a possible reflection of the greater conflict that often accompanies stronger affirmative action. The smallest difference between the black and white managers is also in Ace Public Utility. A large percentage of both races is bothered by certain negative aspects. It is possible that the company's overall management style is basically unsatisfactory and is a style that makes both black and white managers unhappy about their work environment.

How Satisfied Are the Managers?

In addition to finding out the managers' degree of dissatisfaction with their job environment, it is equally important to find out how satisfied they are, especially in relation to their work groups, the type of work they are doing, their salaries, and their companies in general. Such an inquiry will provide the balance needed to complete the picture of the managers' feelings about their work. The managers were asked to indicate their satisfaction by responding to several statements about the specific areas just enumerated. The results are shown in Table 8-10.

If one considers the black managers' dissatisfaction with their companies' employment policies (Chapter 5), it is quite surprising that such a relatively low percentage are dissatisfied with their job situations. However Bray's explanations about self-esteem not allowing many managers to indicate their dissatisfaction apply here.

As a means of looking further into the managers' responses, once again indexes by race, sex, and managerial level were formed. These indexes included the four previous statements and also the statement on views about progress. If the managers answered that they were "completely" or "very satisfied" on the four statements and answered "yes" on the progress statement, they received a score of 0. If they answered "not very," "not at all satisfied," or "no," they received a score of 1. The high score of 5 would indicate low satisfaction or none at all with every element of a manager's job situation. Tables 8-11 and 8-12 show the results.

There are greater differences between the races on these factors than on the bothersome factors in their work environment. More than double the percentage of white managers as opposed to black are completely satisfied with their progress, workgroup, type of work, salary and company in general. The attitudes of the men and women are more similar in these areas than in the work environment area. By educational level the most educated whites are the most satisfied and the most educated blacks are least satisfied. The educated white manager can look forward to rewards for his or her education in better opportunities, types of work, advancement, and salaries, much more so than the uneducated whites. But the educated black manager can generally

TABLE 8-10 THE MANAGERS' SATISFACTION WITH SELECTED ITEMS (in %)

Selected Items	Completely Satisfied		Very Satisfied		Not Very Satisfied		Not at All Satisfied	
	Black Managers (N = 116)	White Managers (N = 156)	Black Managers (N = 116)	White Managers (N = 156)	Black Managers (N = 116)	White Managers (N = 156)	Black Managers (N = 116)	White Managers (N = 156)
Are you satisfied—								
With the group you work with?	14	13	56	80	30	7	0	0
With the type of work you do?	22	33	60	59	17	7	1	1
With your salary?	7	16	35	59	47	23	12	3
With your company in general?	12	24	57	68	26	8	5	0

TABLE 8–11   THE BLACK MANAGERS' OVERALL SATISFACTION WITH THEIR JOB
SITUATION (in %)

	Black Men		Black Women	
Overall Views	Lower ($N = 60$)	Middle ($N = 33$)	Lower ($N = 22$)	Middle ($N = 1$)
Completely satisfied (0)	23	36	23	0
Satisfied (1 to 2)	45	36	53	0
Not very satisfied (3 to 5)	32	28	24	100
Total	100	100	100	100

expect much less in a total job situation than the uneducated white, and even
less than the educated white.

When the black managers' feelings are looked at by length of service,
there is further corroboration. The highest percentage of dissatisfaction occurs among those at the lower and middle levels who have four or fewer
years of service, a finding similar to length of time and dissatisfaction
regarding work environment. For instance of the black males in lower

TABLE 8–12   THE WHITE MANAGERS' OVERALL SATISFACTION WITH THEIR JOB
SITUATION (in %)

	White Men			White Women		
Overall Views	Lower ($N = 33$)	Middle ($N = 72$)	Upper ($N = 28$)	Lower ($N = 16$)	Middle ($N = 5$)	Upper ($N = 2$)
Completely satisfied (0)	39	55	93	50	100	50
Satisfied (1 to 2)	45	42	7	31	0	50
Not very satisfied (3 to 5)	16	3	0	19	0	0
Total	100	100	100	100	100	100

management who are most dissatisfied, 59 percent have been with their firms less than four years; of the middle level black male managers, the 63 percent who are most dissatisfied have worked in their firms less than four years (similar findings are reported in the Labor Department study [Freeman and Fields, 1972]).

When the degree of managerial satisfaction was related to company in the previous section, it was found that Triple A Bank has the most satisfied black managers. This is true also for overall job satisfaction. The second most satisfied group of black managers comes from Ace Public Utility, and the most dissatisfied black group from the two sister companies, Cousins and Aunts Manufacturing. Eighty percent of the blacks in these two firms have at least a Bachelor degree and many hold advanced degrees. These managers are also comparatively young. In addition, the managers in the bank and the utility company are more likely to be in administrative/supervisory positions, and those in the manufacturing firms are primarily in technical, professional, and scientific positions. This adds further support to the finding that the managers most unhappy with their corporate experiences are the young educated blacks in staff positions.

Who Will Leave and Who Will Stay

With such findings, it seems evident which of the managers intend to leave their firms, and the managers' responses to a question on this subject bear out the assumption that it is the young educated blacks who are the most likely to leave. All the managers were asked: If things go according to your greatest expectations, will you stay with your firm?

It is significant that 21 percent of the black managers on both the lower and middle level say they would not stay, even if the conditions were ideal, primarily because they do not believe they will ever be able to fulfill their greatest expectations in their present firms. (In the Labor Department study, which also found that young educated blacks were most likely to leave, the percentage was much higher, 45 percent [Freeman and Fields, 1972].) In contrast only 5 percent of the white lower and middle level managers indicate an inclination to leave. For both races the percentages of men and women who intend to leave are about the same.

Of the six large companies Ace Public Utility has the lowest percentage of black managers who say they will leave—8 percent. However many of the managers from this company qualify their responses by adding that they will give the company's relatively new Affirmative Action Program a chance to work. The highest percentages of managers who would leave are in Triple C Bank, Deuce Public Utility, and Aunts and Cousins Manufacturing, in which about 25 percent of the black managers say they will not consider staying.

Among the black managers the parallels are similar to those found in the previous sections. Those with four or fewer years of service are less likely to stay with their companies than those with more than four years, 31 percent as compared to 13 percent. Of the managers who intend to leave 41 percent are bothered by at least three of the six work environment situations on which Tables 8-8 and 8-9 are based, compared to 17 percent of those managers who will stay.

In addition, of the black managers less likely to stay, 75 percent have at least a Bachelor degree. Of these, 21 percent want to be middle managers, 33 percent upper managers, and 46 percent presidents. Two-thirds of them indicate that they will not remain in part because they are dissatisfied with their progress. Obviously these managers have much higher goals and aspirations than the less educated black managers.

Thus there seems to be a relationship between the managers' satisfaction with their progress and work environment and whether they will stay with their firms. However there seems to be a much stronger relationship between the managers' views of fairness of their companies' employment policies toward blacks and whether or not they will leave their firms. For instance none of the black managers who intend to leave their firms answered three or fewer of the questions on fairness negatively, whereas 20 percent of the blacks who intend to stay did answer negatively. Of the blacks who will leave 92 percent answered at least six of the seven questions on fairness negatively, compared to 53 percent of those who will stay (see also Chapter 5, Table 5-4). This means that the blacks consider equal opportunity more important in the overall scheme of things than troublesome factors that are a part of individual jobs.

Let us look at two representative blacks, one a man and one a woman, both of whom belong to the most dissatisfied groups and intend to leave their firms. The man is young and well educated. He is 28 years old and in the lower level of management. He comes from Chicago, where most of his life was spent. From a middle class home, where his father was a minister and his mother a social worker, he went on to earn a Bachelor of Science degree in economics from Ohio University. He belongs to the Church of Christ and attends church once a week. Politically he is a liberal Democrat and belongs to no organizations.

Before entering Triple C Bank, he had four years' work experience with a Chicago bank. Told by a friend that his present company was looking for blacks, he accepted a position as an operations trainee and stayed in that post for 1½ years. Then he became a pro-assistant cashier and six months later an assistant cashier. He was at this job for one year before promotion to management.

Feeling that he is overqualified for the position he now holds, he does not believe he is being promoted as fast as he deserves, which in his view should have been last year. He thinks his company's so-called equal employment opportunities are very poor: "Our company policies are pure public relations. There's a quota system which keeps the few blacks who are hired at the low levels." In his own situation he is extremely dissatisfied, scoring 6 on the work environment index. On overall job satisfaction he is also unhappy but less so—with a score of 4, he is satisfied only with the type of work he does.

He aspires to be president but feels that blacks will be allowed only as far as middle management. Because of this and his dissatisfaction with almost every aspect of his job and company, he intends to leave and is at present considering several job opportunities.

The black woman is equally dissatisfied with her situation, if not more so. She is 41 years old. She is the only black woman at the middle level in this study. Her father owned a black newspaper in Tennessee, where she was raised, and her mother was a housewife. This manager lived in many parts of the country before coming to California.

She is of the Unitarian faith and attends church a few times a year. She considers herself a liberal Democrat and belongs to civil rights, professional, and civic organizations. Highly educated, she holds a Bachelor of Arts degree in mathematics and chemistry from Knoxville University and a Master of Science degree in library science from Western Reserve University.

Before being recruited by her company four years ago, she had 17 years of experience in academic and government service. Because of this background, she believes her capabilities are not being utilized and is dissatisfied with her progress. She feels even better qualified than her boss and says she should be promoted now but also believes that she never will be. Her views are strong about the company's lack of action: "The company isn't doing a thing for black females. But it's not just us. No black will ever be able to go very far in this place." Like the young black man, she is thoroughly dissatisfied with her work environment and general career in this company. She intends to leave the firm and is looking forward to accepting the position of director at a managerial technical information center.

In summary, although these two black managers are extremely dissatisfied with their progress, work environments and overall job situations, most of the other black managers are not as dissatisfied as one might expect from their negative views about the fairness of their companies' employment policies. However, it is almost certain that dissatisfaction among black managers will increase because most of the firms in this study are not committed to equal employment opportunities. Although 67 percent of the black managers who intend to remain with their firms want to achieve at least upper management positions, only 34 percent believe that blacks can really achieve this level, primarily because of racial discrimination.

As we have seen, the younger, more educated black managers, especially women, are the most dissatisfied on all fronts: advancement bothersome factors in the work environment, type of work, work group, salary, and company in general. As a number of studies have shown, decisions to remain with a company are based primarily on perceived opportunities for self-development, personal growth, and challenging assignments (see Friedlander and Walton, 1964). The young black managers evidently see little or no opportunities in these areas. Other blacks, too, to lesser extents, feel these deficiencies.

Corporations should not place black managers—or any qualified ambitious managers, for that matter—in unimportant, uninteresting, low-paying jobs with little chance for advancement. This will lead only to dissatisfaction, and the managers will either become problem employees or leave their firms altogether. As R. Campbell noted: "Mobility is the mark of success for the new breed of manager—if advancement is slow, he or she should and will seek greener pastures (R. Campbell, 1973; see also Jennings, 1967; Albrook, 1968).

The most important implication of the findings in this chapter is in terms of equal employment opportunities. Those young educated black managers whom many firms will have to depend on to become middle and upper level managers will become increasingly dissatisfied with their general job situations and limited opportunities. And they will simply not stay. None of the firms are at present totally committed to affirmative action. They will be unable to establish a pool of black managers from which to select those to promote to higher managerial levels. This situation will provoke further problems unless the firms begin to make commitments—and to take them seriously—by becoming true equal opportunity employers.

CHAPTER NINE

Minority Managers in A Majority Setting

That corporations can create strong pressures among all employees to conform to bureaucratic cultures and the enterprise way of life is plain. That these pressures to conform are often offset by the loyalties and values employees bring to the work place from outside is equally plain. Our modern social order presents a paradox for the individual, as has been noted in a study on assimilation of Jewish and Catholic professionals in Protestant companies by H. L. Wilensky and J. Ladinsky. On the one hand, modern bureaucratic organizations create much occupational specialization and social heterogeneity, but on the other, these organizations draw people into the national mainstream and away from their racial, ethnic, religious, and local ties (Wilensky and Ladinsky, 1967). This chapter explores the effects of the modern white bureaucratic organization on the black managers, especially in terms of their relationship to the black community.

Wilensky and Ladinsky attempted to arrive at general propositions about the structural assimilation of religious minorities (Jews and Catholics) into WASP dominated organizations, concluding that for the "new men in higher circles, occupation will not merely be a way of life; it will be the death of the religious community" (Wilensky and Ladinsky, 1967, pp. 558–59). However, they realized that structural assimilation of different ethnic and racial groups varies greatly and that, because of blacks' unique situation, structural assimilation is problematic (Wilensky and Ladinsky, pp. 560–61).

THE UNIQUE SITUATION OF BLACKS

To grasp the black managers' situation in a majority setting, one must begin with the emergence of a new mood in the 1960s. These were the years when the Black Power and Black Separatist movements gained great momentum and popularity. It was at this time, after 100 years of attempting to integrate into white society with little success, that many blacks decided integration was not achievable or even desirable in the present or foreseeable future, and the separatist movements flowered.

At the same time, some corporations began to make more than token efforts toward integration. They began to hire blacks for positions they had so long been totally excluded from, those at the professional and managerial levels.

These two simultaneous developments created a poignant dilemma for black people. Just as they were attempting to act independently outside of the mainstream they were being invited into it. Some were finally obtaining an opportunity to participate in the corporate world. But those who did were denounced by other blacks for taking advantage of the new opportunities.

Many Black Power advocates and Black Separatists have consistently maintained that for black people to work in corporations undermines the black movement's aim of developing viable black economic institutions. They say that corporations physically and psychologically remove black people from their communities, and the black communities are then deprived of the black executives' expertise and technical skills that are so vitally needed for black economic development.

The black who does contribute his skills to the white corporate world faces an extremely difficult test. Although anyone who enters an organization must conform to its norms to some degree, the conflicts of loyalty are sharpened for the black. E. C. Hughes has described this dilemma with accuracy:

If he accepts the role of the Negro to the extent of appearing content with less than full equality and intimacy with his white colleagues, for the sake of such security and advantage as can be so got, he himself and others may accuse him of sacrificing his race. Given the tendency of whites to say that any Negro who rises to a special position is an exception, there is a strong temptation for such a Negro to seek advantage by fostering the idea that he is unlike others of his race (E. C. Hughes, 1958, p. 113).

In this study one of the white middle level managers speaks for many white managers in expressing concern over the black managers' potentially divided loyalties:

They demonstrate an extremely humanistic outlook—they are keenly aware of the plight of their subordinates, almost too aware sometimes. There seems to be a deep conflict between the black managers' relationship to their own communities, and everything that means, and their loyalties to their companies. In the end these two pulls could take away from their overall effectiveness.

It has been noted by several sociologists that the likelihood to assimilate is greater in proportion to the degree of negative ethnic reactions experienced (see Beattie, 1970). The more an ethnic group is looked down upon, the well-known black psychiatrist Alvin F. Poussaint has observed, the more the members are apt to try to assimilate into the majority setting (Poussaint, 1968, pp. 94, 96). Because of the natural conforming forces of bureaucracies and the psychological oppression blacks have lived under in this country, many people, both black and white, believe that blacks who become members of the corporate world will leave the black communities and attempt to assimilate completely into the dominant white society.

This will be true of only a very small fraction of black managers. Blacks can never completely assimilate into white society because they will never be allowed to forget they are black first and American citizens second. Religious and ethnic origins can, in most cases, be easily hidden or disguised, but color cannot. It is not only black "visibility" that leads to greater discrimination against blacks but history also. No other minority group now settled in America has a 400-year history of racial oppression that has continued to this day, and that is rooted in the institution of slavery. Such a history has brought about psychological problems in black-white relationships that are much more serious and deep-seated than psychological problems between white ethnic groups. Furthermore, despite centuries of physical and psychological oppression, blacks have been able to develop positive attitudes about themselves and a growing sense of commitment to other black people. They realize that as long as any of their black brothers and sisters are oppressed they too will be oppressed.

Even if some blacks were to desire complete assimilation into white society, it is highly unlikely that they could assimilate, and not only because of their color. The vast majority of the black managers hold jobs in which they deal with the black community and/or black employees. Assuming that white people were to let blacks wishing to assimilate fool themselves—which is hardly likely considering white racial attitudes and the racial atmospheres in the firms—the black community and other black workers would not allow those assimilative blacks to forget their origins.

There are additional factors that make assimilation very improbable. Black managers generally work in corporations located in cities with large black populations. And the blacks tend to live in all-black areas or, more typically, in integrated neighborhoods with large black populations. Assimilative tendencies are greatly reduced if members of a particular ethnic group live in the same or close neighborhoods, as a study of French assimilation in Canada pointed out (Beattie, 1970). And finally, the last potentially influential factor, the federal government, seems to be doing little to foster black assimilation into white society, especially in residential desegregation.

For all these reasons one can hardly expect blacks to repeat the cycle of social mobility and assimilation that has become the usual pattern for most other ethnic groups in this country. Although there are some integrationist tendencies among many of them, only a very small number of the blacks in our study seem to want complete integration and assimilation into white society.

NON-ASSIMILATION: EVIDENCE FROM THE MANAGERS

Much material has been presented in earlier chapters to support the overall attitude of nonassimilation on the managers' parts, but in past chapters the focus has been on other topics. Here we shall present the relevant managerial responses together in terms of their applicability to the question of assimilation.

Where a person chooses to live can be an indication of the kinds of people he or she wishes to associate with. It was found in Chapter 2 that 91 percent of the black managers live in neighborhoods where other blacks live and 66 percent in areas where blacks make up 46 percent or more of the residents. There seems to be no divergence among the groups of managers on this issue. That is, the older, college educated, middle level black managers who make higher salaries and who have been with their firms for long periods of time are no further removed from the black community than the younger, less educated, lower level managers who have been with their firms for a short time.

However, some differences are seen when it comes to non-work-related contacts with whites. For the managers as a whole 55 percent have very frequent or fairly frequent contacts with whites at social functions not related to work, and only 13 percent have no contact with whites at social functions. The younger, lower level black managers, especially the women, have the least amount of social interaction with whites. Also the younger, lower level managers are more apt to belong to all-black organizations than the older, middle level managers. And black women are more likely to belong to more racially homogeneous groups than the men.

A similar pattern holds on the managers' views of intermarriage. Again the younger blacks are more separatist, a trend reflected in the black population at large (see Chapter 2, the Gallup Poll results). Although until the late 1960s there was very little opposition to intermarriage throughout the black community, in our study 50 percent more of the black managers aged 30 or younger than those over 30 could hardly imagine themselves marrying a white person. The women are especially opposed: 74 percent, compared to only 27 percent of the men, could hardly imagine marriage to a white. The young blacks, especially women, hold strongly that interracial marriage means that a black has been psychologically oppressed and brainwashed by white America. In addition feelings about intermarriage are directly related to the amount of social contact with whites. Of the blacks who have very frequent social contact, 89 percent could imagine themselves marrying a white. Of those blacks with fairly frequent, not very frequent, or no contact at all, only 55 percent could imagine intermarriage for themselves.

Considering the fact that only one of the black managers is actually married to a white person, it seems clear that the black managers are not attempting to assimilate into white society through matrimony. The high percentages of responses for imagined marriage to a white does indicate that the black managers are going by individual attraction—color is unimportant. This same reasoning, that the black managers are not avoiding contact with whites simply because they are white, is the most valid explanation for the fact that the majority of the black managers have very or fairly frequent social contact with whites outside of work and many belong to integrated social and political groups. The Labor Department study findings were similar in this area, as well as in the fact that many of the black managers minimized nonbusiness associations with whites from the job; their white friends generally came from outside the corporate world (Freeman and Fields, 1972).

The managers' responses to several questions also give some indication of their views about assimilating into white society. When asked what advice they would give a black manager entering their firm, 38 percent say they would tell blacks to stand up for what they believe is right and be their own person. Do not conform, they say, to the general corporate view that the only way to be is "nonmilitant" and "agreeable with everything the whites say." Only two managers comment in what could be considered an "Uncle Tomish" way. They say blacks should forget their color and not be color conscious. (The black managers' advice to blacks entering business will be discussed more fully in Chapter 10).

Two questions previously discussed in Chapter 6 further show the managers' attitudes about assimilation. They were asked if they would consider the feelings of whites who might react with discomfort at having blacks in management positions. They were also asked how they, the blacks, would have responded to this situation 10 years ago. Twenty-six percent say that today they would tend to overlook negative white attitudes toward blacks and would have answered quite differently 10 years ago. They felt then that they were not conscious of themselves as black people; they were apathetic and tended to overlook the unjust racial situation in industry. And another 5 percent say they would have been much more influenced by negative white attitudes 10 years ago.

All these data strongly suggest that black managers, although they may live rather integrated lives and hold liberal integrationist views, are not attempting to bury their black identity under white trappings. Further evidence for this will be seen throughout this chapter. Even though these managers live in a more integrated manner, this is related primarily to their economic status, and it will be seen that their views are not very different from those of the general black population in America.

COMMUNITY RELATIONS: BLACK MANAGERS AND THE BLACK COMMUNITY

Given the integrationist attitudes of some black managers, and the fact that they have in some degree penetrated white society, it is of special interest to find out about their relations with their own communities. In this regard the managers were asked two questions:

1. With what segments of the black community do you have good communications?
2. With what segments of the black community do you have bad communications?

The managers were allowed to categorize elements of the black community in any manner they wished. As Tables 9-1 and 9-2 illustrate, most of the managers categorized either by class or political philosophy. In general about a third of the managers have good relations with their entire com-

TABLE 9–1   GOOD COMMUNICATIONS: BLACK MANAGERS AND THE BLACK COMMUNITY (in %)

Segments of Community	Black Managers ($N = 116$)
All segments	36
Moderates	33
Middle class	16
Lower class	7
All except militants and revolutionaries	4
Conservatives	3
Upper class	3
All except upper class	2
Militants	1
Revolutionaries and extremists	1
No segments	1
Other	4
Total[a]	111

[a] The total percentages in Tables 9–1 and 9–2 are over 100 because some managers indicated that they had good or bad communications with more than one segment.

TABLE 9–2 POOR COMMUNICATIONS: BLACK MANAGERS AND
THE BLACK COMMUNITY (in %)

Segments of Community	Black Managers (N = 116)
No segments	38
Militants	32
Revolutionaries and Extremists	17
Upper Class	11
Lower Class	4
Conservatives	3
Middle Class	2
All Except Militants and Revolutionaries	1
Other	5
Total	113

munity, and another third with the moderate segment. In terms of bad relations the segment that the highest proportion of managers has trouble with
is the militants.

There are differences between the male and female black managers when
sex is used as the control variable. Only 17 percent of the women, compared
to 41 percent of the men, indicate good communications with all segments
of the black community. More women, 70 percent, tend to believe they have
better communications with the moderates and middle class than men, 44
percent. This is surprising because, in general, blacks who identify with the
black moderate middle class are more assimilative in attitudes and behavior
than those who identify with all segments of the black community. However
there has already been evidence and there will be more that most black
women, although believing they get along well with the black moderate middle class, are not very assimilative in either attitudes or behavior. And so it
cannot be definitively asserted that blacks who identify with the moderate
middle class have more assimilative attitudes and behavior than those
blacks who identify with all segments of the black community.

There are, however, some other patterns that become evident. In general
the younger black male managers from all social backgrounds who live in
predominantly black areas are more likely to believe they have good communications with all segments of the black community than the older black
male managers who live in areas not primarily black. In addition, the less
conservative the managers are in their politics, the more they are apt to get
along with all segments of the black community. For example, the more

radical managers have better relations than the liberals, the liberals better than the moderates, and the moderates better than the conservatives. Similarly, the less religious the manager, the more likely he or she is to get along with the total black community. And Baptists get along better than members of the high-status Protestant religions, who generally come from the middle class and are conservative.

With regard to bad communications, there are few differences between the black men and women. However, as we might by now expect, the younger managers are more likely *not* to have bad relations with any segment of the black community than the older managers.

The managers have a number of explanations for the types of relations they have with the black community. In general, like any other group of people regardless of color, they have good communications with those people whom they have the most in common with, in beliefs, goals, and methods of achieving them. A lower level manager from Aunts Manufacturing illustrates this well when he says:

I get along with activists whether they are militant or moderate, middle class or lower class. I have friends from all groups, but I don't get along with the conservative black entrepreneur types and the fraternity and social club types because I don't accept a lot of their values—like trying to assimilate completely into white society and not really trying to help their own kind.

Tables 9-3 and 9-4 list the managers' reasons for their good and poor communications with various segments of the black community. It becomes clear from the tables that a majority of the black managers are moderate in their views and eschew violent philosophies and methods. One lower level manager from Triple C Bank comments: "I've got good communications with the moderates. I have friends in this group and I can talk with them. They accept my ideas even though they may not agree with me. But with the militants I've got bad communications. I don't know that many and I'm not exposed to them that often." One young black manager from Cousins Manufacturing, who has light skin, straight hair, and blue eyes, and could easily pass for white, tells why he gets along well with the moderates: "I get along with moderate, middle class blacks because I try to avoid types of situations where I would draw attention to myself and my family. The militants and I don't get along—they've abused me about my light skin and blue eyes."

Class differences are an important part of the quality of communications for some of the managers. A female manager from Ace Public Utility says: "I have good communications with all segments except the upper class. I can't stand their snobbishness and half-ass airs. They just can't relate to any other blacks." Another woman from the same company is equally candid:

TABLE 9–3   REASONS FOR BLACK MANAGERS' GOOD COMMU-
NICATIONS WITH THE BLACK COMMUNITY (in %)

Segments and Reasons	Black Managers (N = 116)
All segments: Respondent knows and associates with people from all segments; tries to learn from all.	28
Moderates: Most of the respondent's friends are from this background; can communicate and talk with them; they think along the same lines.	25
All segments: Blacks are all looking for the same thing—equality.	9
Middle and lower: Respondent comes from this background; therefore, understands their needs and desires.	7
Middle class: Most of respondent's friends are from this class; they have more in common.	6
Moderates: They have the best methods to achieve goals, freedom, and equality; they don't believe in violence or bloodshed.	6
All segments except militants, extremists, and revolutionaries: Respondent does not like violence.	4
Moderates: They just want what they deserve and work for.	2
Middle and conservative: They have nice paying jobs, they play golf, join clubs, and so on.	2
All segments except the upper class: Respondent is sympathetic to their goals and desires.	2
Other	9
Total	100

"I communicate fine with the middle class but it's the lower class I have trouble with. This is due to my own lack of drive to get to know different types of blacks. I'm an armchair revolutionary and lazy. I just don't know what's happening with the blacks who are exposed to poverty and bad living conditions."

To summarize, the majority of the managers are generally moderate in their views and get along best with the moderate segment of the black community, although there is a substantial minority, primarily the men, who believe they are able to communicate with all segments of the black community. But for the most part the managers cannot relate to revolutionary philosophies and violent tactics of the militants and revolutionaries.

However, it is noteworthy that the managers do not identify more than they do with the militants, in light of negative managerial views about existing opportunities for blacks in the corporate world. As just noted, the main

TABLE 9–4   REASONS FOR BLACK MANAGERS' POOR COMMU-
NICATIONS WITH THE BLACK COMMUNITY (in %)

Segments and Reasons	Black Managers ($N = 83$)
Militants, revolutionaries and extremists: Respondent does not believe in violent methods.	26
Militants: Respondent does not agree with their philosophy.	21
Upper class: Respondent believes that they have not done anything for blacks; they are snobs, callous, half-asses.	15
Militants: Respondent does not like their attitudes and treatment of other blacks who do not agree with them.	14
Militants: Respondent has not been exposed to them.	14
Militants, Revolutionaries, and Extremists: Respondent does not believe in black separatism.	8
Conservatives: Respondent does not agree with their attitude that everything is peaches and cream as long as you work hard.	5
Middle class: Respondent doesn't have much in common with the black bourgeoisie middle class.	3
Other	15
Total[a]	121

[a] The total percentage is over 100 because some managers have bad communications with more than one segment and gave more than one reason for this.

point of disagreement between moderates and militants is largely one of methods and rhetoric. They all share the belief that blacks have been unjustly treated in the corporate world—and everywhere else—because of the common enemy, racism.

ARE BLACKS PRESSING TOO HARD?

Because many of the managers are moderates and dislike violence, one might then expect them to hold the view that blacks are pressing their case too hard (see Chapter 6 for an earlier discussion of this question). This is not so. Almost all the managers, 96 percent, feel that blacks are not out of line, and their reasons are given in Table 9-5.

The managers believe that oppression of blacks has been going on far too long and that they have a right to press for their equal rights. As one manager from Triple C Bank predicts: "If we don't press we'll still have a token society and job discrimination will persist. Whites are satisfied as long as blacks don't push them and they're able to change things at their own pace." Many believe that blacks are not making enough of an effort, as an older middle level manager at Triple A Bank testifies: "I don't think blacks are pressing hard enough. Most blacks are still under the psychological hangups caused by racism and they won't stick their necks out. The younger blacks are aware of this, though, and I think they'll do something. I hope so."

Pressure on white society is necessary, many of the managers feel, for blacks to get what should be theirs; and according to one manager from Triple C Bank, the pressures must sometimes be extreme: "We must press for our rights. If a man shows you a house and you want to buy it and he won't sell it to you, then burn it down."

With such views on black efforts and white recalcitrance, one might assume that the managers would not consent to relocate, if their firm requested it, to geographical areas where discrimination is known to be more blatant, such as small white cities or towns. However the managers' views on this issue are enlightening.

TRANSFER TO A SMALL WHITE CITY OR TOWN

The managers' feelings about transfer out of more integrated urban areas are related to their responses to the contention, held especially by black nationalist groups, that corporations remove blacks both psychologically and physically from the black community. Eighty-nine percent of the black managers disagree with this statement and more than the majority, 56 percent, would move to a small white city or town. The individual comments of some of the managers indicate that physical removal is much less

TABLE 9–5 WHY BLACKS ARE NOT PRESSING THEIR CASE
TOO HARD (in %)

Reasons	Black Managers (N = 111)
White society will not change except under continuous pressure; if there is no pressure, there will be no change.	29
When people are pressing for civil and human rights, i.e., equality, they can't press too hard.	22
There has been relatively little positive change; thus, respondent does not believe that blacks are pressing hard enough.	19
Blacks are late in asserting their rightful position in this society which has been denied them too long.	14
Blacks who are qualified aren't making it; therefore, blacks aren't pressing too hard.	9
The militant blacks are pressing their case too hard, but in general most other blacks are not.	5
Blacks have a right to use pressure in order to achieve their fair share and equality in this country.	4
Respondent personally opposes violent tactics, but believes that they are helpful.	1
Blacks are pressing too hard when they use violent tactics.	1
Total[a]	104

[a] The total percentage is over 100 because of rounding errors.

important than psychological removal, and they maintain that this latter aspect is the crucial one. (See Table D-6, Appendix D, page 284, for the reasons the managers disagree that they are being psychologically and physically removed from the black community and the frequency distribution of the reasons.)

For instance, a female manager at Ace Public Utility says: "I'm still interested and a part of the community and I do my share. The militants talk but I prefer to go out and show whitey that I am together—my actions speak louder than the militants' words." Another woman, from Deuce

Public Utility, agrees and describes her attitude in terms of black assistance to other blacks: "When a black is hired he's going to do the job he's there for and he's not going to forget there are other qualified blacks. That he'll make apparent to the people he works for and with. The black won't forget his people—he only wants a job and compensation for it. He's not going to change his race."

Other managers emphasize the right of individual choice. A lower level manager from the same firm feels that he is not undermining the black movement but the reverse: "One day I'll be in a position to help some other blacks economically. I refuse to work outside the black community, so I'm not removed from it." And a female manager also from the same company makes an interesting observation: "It's not the corporations who are removing people, it's the Black Nationalists who are trying to move people away from the community. People must live together, wherever we want to. We should all have that right."

It is such attitudes that contribute to the managers' decisions to accept a transfer to all-white areas. Table 9-6 shows their responses by age group. Although there are no differences by sex or educational level, it will be seen that the young, lower level managers are least likely to accept a transfer. Acceptance is not affected by the managers' social class, how integrated their neighborhoods are, their communications with other groups, and their career aspirations. But geographical background does have some bearing. The black managers who grew up in the South would accept a transfer more readily than others. Probably these Southern managers feel that since they grew up in one of the most racist, segregated parts of the country, any other white setting would present no more of a challenge in living and working conditions.

The managers give varied reasons for accepting a transfer, and these are closely tied to their earlier disagreement with the claim of psychological and

TABLE 9–6 WOULD BLACK MANAGERS ACCEPT A TRANS-
FER TO A SMALL WHITE CITY OR TOWN? (in %)

	Black Managers' Ages		
Response	30 and Under ($N = 45$)	31–40 ($N = 53$)	Over 40 ($N = 18$)
Yes	48	59	67
No	52	41	33
Total	100	100	100

physical removal from the black community. As Table 9-7 shows, the managers have much faith in their own strength and capabilities. Almost half would go in order to educate whites. As a lower level woman manager from Ace Public Utility puts it: "I'd be able to make changes. I'd bring more blacks in and increase the standards to show them we could do it. A small white community doesn't frighten me. I could out-think them."

Promotion and increased job opportunity are also primary reasons for some of the managers. These reasons would influence a woman manager on the lower level at Triple C Bank, as well as the opportunity to educate white society: "I'd go if it were a promotion. If they gave me the opportunity, I could do the job well. It's surprising what happens when whites find out blacks don't just want to socialize with them. We could show them we just want the right to be equal. I'd welcome the opportunity so people could see that I'm qualified and a person."

The third most important reason for the managers is their own faith in their abilities, regardless of environment. A male manager from Triple C Bank asserts: "My pride is the fact why I believe I can succeed wherever I am, no matter what the population ratio. I never want to place a limitation on myself. I'd meet all pressures eagerly and enthusiastically." Such reasons as these do not support the idea that the managers are desirous of leaving the black community. Rather, they point to the pride and confidence the blacks possess that they can succeed in any type of environment.

On the other hand, many other managers see detriments to living and working in a small white city or town. It is usually the younger managers who are most opposed to such a move, and Table 9-8 lists their reasons. One manager remembers the treatment his father and brothers received in a small white town. They were refused positions at small plants because, as the personnel managers said, they "lacked the qualifications," although it was more probable that they were not the right color. Other managers feel strongly about staying in their own communities. As one manager from Triple A Bank says: "I would not go because of my family. I feel that blacks should not be isolated in an all-white community." And a manager from Ace Public Utility says simply: "I would not go because I want to be around my own people."

Such responses indicate that these managers believe racial discrimination would be so acute that they and their families would be adversely affected. These responses also indicate that many of the black managers do not see themselves being accepted by white society. For some managers this is good—they want to retain the individuality of their race in a challenging atmosphere. But for others, those who wish to assimilate, transfer to a small white city or town that presented racial obstacles could work against their desired goals of assimilation.

TABLE 9–7 WHY THE BLACK MANAGERS WOULD ACCEPT A
TRANSFER TO A SMALL WHITE CITY OR TOWN (in %)

Reasons	Black Managers ($N = 64$)
Would go in order to show whites that blacks are qualified and capable; to educate whites about blacks and change their stereotypes	42
Would go as long as it was a promotion and offered viable opportunities	24
Would go because feels he/she could function in any type of environment; would be able to overcome many obstacles	17
Respondent already operates in such an environment	8
Would not matter	8
Would go to any place except the South	5
Would go because believes pressures are the same anywhere in a white society	2
Total[a]	106

[a] The total percentage is over 100 because some managers gave more than one reason.

THE BEST PATH FOR BLACKS TO PURSUE

In light of the obstacles blacks face, wherever they may live and work, one could imagine them opting for a path of total separatism. But most of the black managers are, on the whole, moderate in their political views and liberal about interacting socially with whites. This is not to say that most black managers are for complete assimilation into white society. Even though in general the managers hold integrationist attitudes, interact frequently with whites, and believe that housing, jobs, schools, and public facilities should be desegregated, this by no means equals complete assimilation. The black managers are not at all trying to lose or hide their black identity or cultural ties.

Essentially, the black managers are espousing a middle ground that at once affirms cultural pluralism and opposes all forms of discrimination and forced segregation. They are for neither separatist nor assimilationist extremes. They are in favor of blacks forming strong social, political, and economic organizations and believe that every other minority has the same right to fight for its equality. In addition, they show a strong commitment to the work ethic and individual development. (See Table D-7, Appendix D, page 285, for the advice the managers would give other blacks for living a free and prosperous life in this society.)

Further evidence of these attitudes appears in the managers' views of the best course of action for blacks in this country, as shown in Table 9-9. Only 12 percent of all the black managers—13 men and 1 woman—believe that blacks should assimilate and integrate completely into white society. It is the older, better educated black male managers from the middle class, living in integrated neighborhoods and communicating well with the moderate, middle class blacks, who are much more inclined to believe in complete assimilation than the younger, less educated* blacks from working class families, who live in predominantly black areas and communicate well with all segments of the black community.

As a middle level manager from Aunts Manufacturing comments: "I

TABLE 9-8   WHY THE BLACK MANAGERS WOULD NOT ACCEPT A TRANSFER TO A SMALL WHITE CITY OR TOWN (in %)

Reasons	Black Managers ($N = 52$)
Would be too much pressure; would not be able to do a good job	38
Would be too much pressure for his/her family to put up with	38
Would not be able to grow within the company; opportunities would be limited	30
Would not go because wants to live near a black community; wants to stay here to help the black community	26
Does not like small white cities or towns	21
There are enough pressures here	4
Other	2
Total[a]	159

[a] The total percentage is over 100 because many of the managers gave more than one reason.

* "More educated" generally is taken as having advanced degrees, "less educated" as having a Bachelor degree or less.

TABLE 9–9   WHAT IS THE BEST PATH FOR BLACKS TO PUR-
SUE IN THIS COUNTRY? (in %)

Reasons	Black Managers ($N = 116$)
Form strong social, political, and economic organizations to pressure white society into assuring blacks equal opportunity and freedom in the larger society	76
Assimilate and integrate completely into white society	12
Form their own separate black nations	3
Withdraw into the urban areas and form separate all-black communities	2
Other	7
Total	100

don't believe you can go very far if you don't interact. We are in a multiracial society and we must live that part." A lower level manager from Triple A Bank sees integration as "inevitable":

The trend of everything is that way; it is inevitable. There will always be some intermingling, and I think it would be for the better to have it all broken down. I think forming strong organizations has been somewhat a failure—you can pressure white society until you are blue in the face. The black community doesn't have a lot of money so there can be no real pressure.

Only 5 percent—five men and one woman—want to separate completely. One female manager from Ace Public Utility gives her reason for this response: "Blacks have the responsibility of taking care of their own kind. We must pressure blacks and not whites. We have to use our own resources and get our thing together." But the overwhelming majority, 74 percent of the men and 83 percent of the women, believe that blacks should form strong social, political, and economic organizations as the most effective way to bring about social change. (See Table D-8, Appendix D, page 286, for the reasons the black managers selected this as the best choice.) One manager sees this path as unquestionably the strongest one: "By organizing we are not isolating ourselves and letting whites corral us. We are being forceful." Another, from Cousins Manufacturing, says: "We must start by forming strong organizations and then go on to integrate into white society. If you deal with white society from a power position, you will finally become integrated." It is interesting that among these managers, who want strong social, political, and economic organizations, 10 percent see as the ultimate social goal a merger of black and white culture, with total integration on both sides and an amalgam springing from the best of both cultures. Such a goal is close to utopian in terms of the elimination of any kind of racial discrimination and friction.

THE BLACK MANAGERS' OVERALL ASSIMILATION

To get a clearer, more precise view of the assimilative views and actions of the black managers, two overall indexes were drawn up. The first assesses the degree of managers' assimilative attitudes, and the second the degree of their assimilative behaviors. Each index was made up of responses to several questions and statements that were weighted appropriately. Thus each manager received a specific score for his or her composite of answers. For example if managers strongly disagreed with the statement, "I could hardly imagine myself marrying a white person," they received a score of 0, if they disagreed a score of 1, if they agreed a score of 2, and if they strongly agreed a score of 3.

The Assimilative Attitude Index

The statement and two questions that made up the assimilative attitude index are as follows:

1. I could hardly imagine myself marrying a white person.
2. What is the best path for blacks as a group to pursue in this country?
3. Would you accept a transfer to a plant located in a small white city or town?

Table 9-10 shows the black managers' assimilative attitudes by age and sex.

From this table several conclusions can be drawn. In all age groups the black men have more assimilative attitudes than the black women. The older men hold stronger assimilative views than do the younger men. Age does not seem to make a difference with the women—those of all ages are quite similar in their assimilative attitudes.

Background has a bearing on the degree of assimilation of some of these groups. Although the social backgrounds of the women do not give any indication of how assimilative their attitudes might be, backgrounds of the men do: Those from the working class are less likely to hold extreme assimilative attitudes than those from the middle class. Where the managers grew up does not appear relevant, but where they now live does. The black managers who now live in predominantly black areas, with a black popula-

TABLE 9–10   THE BLACK MANAGERS' OVERALL ASSIMILATIVE ATTITUDE INDEX (in %)

	Age			
	30 and Under		Over 30	
Assimilative Attitudes	Black Men ($N = 32$)	Black Women ($N = 13$)	Black Men ($N = 61$)	Black Women ($N = 10$)
Most assimilative (3 to 5)	41	15	54	20
Moderately assimilative (6 to 8)	50	70	41	70
Least assimilative (9 to 11)	9	15	5	10
Total	100	100	100	100

tion of 50 percent or more, have fewer assimilative attitudes than those living in predominantly white areas.

Other factors too have some relationship to the degree of assimilation the managers believe in. The men in middle management have more assimilative attitudes than the men of the same age group in lower management. The managers who have the least assimilative attitudes are the most critical of their companies' employment policies. Furthermore the most ambitious managers do not necessarily have the most assimilative attitudes. One might expect them to overconform so as to be accepted into the white power structure, but the data show that just the opposite is true. Also the managers with less assimilative attitudes are those who have good communications with all segments of the black community and who are the least likely to be called "Uncle Toms" (to be discussed later in this chapter).

Thus the managers with the most assimilative attitudes tend to be the older, middle level blacks from middle class backgrounds, who live in predominantly white areas. It is possible to conclude from this that as blacks get older and rise in the hierarchy, their views will become more assimilative. However this would be a misleading generalization because too many of the younger black managers have been brought up in an era of black awareness and pride (and some of the older black managers have begun to rethink the values of integration and assimilation). It is not likely that they will lose their strong identity with blackness and their increased understanding of the injustices of society as they advance in the business world.

The Assimilative Behavior Index

Four questions went into the assimilative behavior index:

1.   How frequently do you have contact with whites at social functions not related to work?
2.   Do blacks live in your neighborhood?
3.   About what percentage of blacks live in your neighborhood?
4.   To what types of social organizations do you belong (all-black or integrated)?

Scoring procedures similar to those for the assimilative attitude index were used and the results, delineated by age and sex, appear in Table 9-11.

The most assimilative behavior occurs in the black men over 30 and the least in the black women over 30. When the two indexes are compared, it is clear that the black men have more similarities in assimilative behaviors than attitudes, but it is just the opposite for the black women. The personal characteristics that describe managers with the most assimilative behaviors are the same as for those with the most assimilative attitudes.

As previously suggested, the relationship between assimilative attitudes

TABLE 9–11   THE BLACK MANAGERS' OVERALL ASSIMILATIVE BEHAVIOR INDEX (in %)

	Age			
	30 and Under		Over 30	
Assimilative Behaviors	Black Men ($N = 32$)	Black Women ($N = 13$)	Black Men ($N = 61$)	Black Women ($N = 10$)
Most assimilative (3 to 8)	41	31	48	20
Moderately assimilative (8 to 12)	43	54	41	40
Least assimilative (12 to 18)	16	15	11	40
Total	100	100	100	100

and behaviors is far from perfect, as Table 9-12 shows. Although many black managers have nonassimilative attitudes, they do have assimilative behaviors; many of those with nonassimilative behaviors have assimilative attitudes. Thus broad generalizations as to blacks and assimilation must be cautioned against.

In reviewing the characteristics of the black managers who fall into the extreme groups—that is, the most and least assimilative in attitudes and behaviors—one finds that the older blacks have the most assimilative tendencies. They have achieved middle management positions and generally hold staff jobs in which they have very frequent contact with whites, especially at corporate headquarters. It is because of their ages, family background and positions in the white corporations, and the fact that they were brought up in an era where black pride and identity were minimized and integration was the goal of the black community, that these managers hold the most assimilative attitudes and behaviors.

The younger blacks from the lower class, who are at the lower level but moving rapidly within the white corporations although in almost exclusively black settings, have the least assimilative attitudes and behaviors. Again this can be attributed to their ages and positions in the firms. Although the likelihood is not great that they will change radically, it remains to be seen if they will continue to possess the same nonassimilative attitudes and behaviors as they move further up the corporate ladder and begin to find themselves in the predominantly white work atmosphere.

THE ACCUSATION OF "UNCLE TOM" AND "SELLOUT"

There are some blacks who feel that a black who works in a white setting, among predominantly white associates, is a traitor or "sellout" to the black

TABLE 9–12   THE RELATIONSHIP BETWEEN THE BLACK MANAGERS' ASSIMILA-
TIVE ATTITUDES AND BEHAVIORS (in %)

	Assimilative Behaviors					
	Most		Moderately		Least	
Assimilative Attitudes	Black Men	Black Women	Black Men	Black Women	Black Men	Black Women
Most assimilative	52	0	35	50	13	50
Moderately assimilative	44	31	46	50	10	19
Least assimilative	0	33	67	33	33	33

movement. As noted earlier, the Black Nationalists and militants especially level this accusation at blacks in the business world. One older middle level manager from Cousins Manufacturing relates: "I am called names on any occasion when I don't agree with the militant segment of the community."

But on the whole, not many of the managers have experienced this problem. Only 9 percent of the women and 28 percent of the men reported that they have been called "Uncle Toms" or "sellouts." Also 30 percent of the managers with the most integrationist attitudes and only 13 percent of those with the least are called such names. Oddly, the degree of segregation in the managers' neighborhoods has no bearing on whether they are called these names. A lower level manager from Aunts Manufacturing recalls: "I used to live in [a heavily black neighborhood], but after I was ripped off I moved to a mainly white middle class area. While I was living in the black community I was never called an "Uncle Tom," but since I moved, when I go back people are friendly, but some of them call me an "Uncle Tom" in a joking manner."

However, where the managers work and the type of work they do has a significant bearing. For example, 50 percent of the managers who have been called "Uncle Toms" come from the two banks. It was pointed out earlier that most of the black bankers are placed in branches located in black communities. As a result, many of the managers experience name-calling when they do their job conscientiously by letting a poor employee go or not approving a loan or a check. A lower level manager at Triple A Bank remembers: "I was called an 'Uncle Tom' when I fired a black who wasn't doing his job properly." A fellow manager at the bank says: "I've been called those names especially when I haven't approved a loan for a black customer."

Two managers at Triple C Bank have had similar experiences. One explains:

Many blacks don't understand why I am working in the system. I do it because I want to get aid for my brothers and I'm a representation that there are job opportunities in the bank for blacks. But I get cursed out and accused of looking, dressing, and talking like whites and not understanding the black problem.

His colleague tells of unwanted attention from whites as well as blacks: "I'm always questioned about being an 'Uncle Tom.' Sometimes a white will ask me too. White women particularly have asked me about it."

Thus the black managers who work in service-oriented jobs such as banking and who hold integrationist views are quite likely to be called such names as "Uncle Tom" or "sellout." The effect of such name-calling on their job performance was not explored in this study, but a situation in which they are continuously called names and at the same time are under pressure to conform to their companies' standards could result in serious conflicts in the black managers' identities, and their work performance could suffer. In any case to be called in effect a traitor to one's race certainly does not improve anyone's morale.

The feelings, attitudes, and actions of the black managers as they work in the setting of the white majority can better be understood by several profiles of black managers that illustrate the varying points of view that have been found within our sample of participating managers. We will present four managers whose personal characteristics and views represent the range of assimilative and nonassimilative attitudes and behaviors of blacks in a white environment.

The first manager is a young, mobile 29-year-old black man, who is fairly but not very assimilative in his attitudes and behaviors. He works as a bank branch manager in a primarily black community. He reached this position in only 4½ years, a very short time considering that the average period it usually takes to become a bank manager is much longer.

His personal background includes a boyhood in Missouri, where his father owned a hardware store. Neither of his parents had more than a high school education. He has lived most of his adult life in California, having earned a Bachelor degree in business administration from Golden Gate College, San Francisco. He now resides with his wife in a neighborhood that is 70 percent black.

This manager is a nominal Baptist but never goes to church. He considers himself a moderate Democrat and belongs to numerous community, civic, and business organizations. He also is quite active in a variety of organizations—the NAACP, the Urban League, ACLU, and a small black social club. Because of his participation in so many diverse activities, he has frequent contact with whites outside of work and has white friends. Partly as a result of his white contacts, he feels he could marry a white woman.

Moderate blacks are the members of the black community he feels most comfortable with: "These are the blacks who desire the financial assistance and advice I can give them. The militants I don't get along with. They don't relate to me and they feel I've conformed to the white establishment." It is the militants, he says, who have called him "Uncle Tom" and "traitor" when he has had to refuse loan or check approval. But he also has a strong sense of black identity and feels that blacks are not pressing their case too hard: "You must pressure whites. If you don't, and don't demand your rights, you'll receive nothing."

The best way to accomplish black equality, he feels, is to work parallel to the established system by forming strong black social, political, and economic organizations. In line with this attitude, he disagrees that blacks are being removed psychologically and physically from the black community and his reasoning is quite practical and logical: "We can gain the necessary skills to develop a viable black economy through experience in white corporations. Let's face it—there aren't too many black financial institutions."

He is also extremely realistic about racial attitudes in a small white city or town and would not accept a transfer to one: "Society's attitudes have not changed. I'd have to put up with too much pressure in and outside of work to be able to do an effective job." Thus he sees social change in terms of developing strong, individual black economic, political, and social institutions: "We should keep our traditions and characteristics. The only way we will be accepted on our own terms is from a position of power."

Another black manager, similar to this one in age, nevertheless illustrates the extremely nonassimilative position of some of the younger blacks. He is 28 years old and a lower level manager. He has been in the corporate world 2½ years. All of his life has been spent in California, and he received a Bachelor degree in finance from the University of California, Berkeley. Both his parents had eight years of schooling; his father was a mechanic and his mother a housewife. This manager is married and lives in San Francisco in a 95 percent black neighborhood.

He has no religious preferences and attends church a few times a year. He considers himself a liberal Democrat. Unlike the previous manager, he belongs to no organizations and has very little contact with whites: "I am not easy in dealing with most whites. I dislike always having to explain myself." Not surprisingly, he is quite adamant about not considering marriage to a white and would not consent to moving to a small white city or town because, he says, "I have no common ground with the whites except having to work in the same company."

He believes he has good communications with all segments of the black community: "I have friends from all segments. We're all working toward the same thing but in different ways." He feels blacks need to press their case even harder than at present to gain ground: "This is a sit down, do nothing nation. Capitalism can't solve problems quickly. It's only severe crisis that provokes movement and change."

Like the previous manager, he does not credit the white corporations with removing blacks from their community and feels that they can learn best in white institutions: "Corporations don't remove blacks. It's the blacks' own choice. The only way we can get experience is from the white business world and then take it back to the community." With this experience he would not work within the existing society but would advocate forming a separate black nation: "Throughout history there's been racial bigotry and it will continue. You're not born with it but as long as you're part of the established society you're trapped by it. A new nation, on our own terms, is the best alternative."

Less extreme, although still quite nonassimilative, are the majority of black women, as exemplified by a 41-year-old female manager. Even though she has a degree in business administration from Prairie View College, she started as a stenographer and after 13½ years is only in lower management. It took her seven years to reach her present position.

Her parents had minimal schooling, and her father was a self-employed painter in Texas, where she spent most of her life. She is a Baptist, attends church once or twice a month, and now lives in an 85 percent black neighborhood. A moderate Democrat, she belongs to a number of all-black social clubs and the NAACP. Outside work she has little contact with whites, with only a few neighborhood friends and some encounters at parties. Marriage with a white man is hardly imaginable to her. She would refuse transfer to a small white town because she feels that as a black she would not be accepted.

So far as communications with the black community are concerned, she has the best with the moderates because most of her friends are from the moderate middle class. She gets along least well with the militants, disagreeing with their extreme and violent tactics. However she has never been called an "Uncle Tom" or "sellout."

She emphasizes the need for blacks to be equal and thinks they are not pressing too hard to achieve this: "We must make whites aware that things must change in jobs, housing, everything. Things must become equal." Psychological and physical estrangement from the black community are not likely, she feels, for blacks who work in the white establishment: "Blacks just want a job and compensation. They won't change their race. They won't forget their people." To her the best way to attain equality is through strong social, political, and economic organizations. In her view blacks only want to be left alone to pursue their own goals: "Blacks don't want to assimilate completely or separate completely. They just want to be able to live a free and equal life."

Much more conservative than this woman, and the most assimilative of all these managers, is a 49-year-old middle level male bank manager. He has a Bachelor of Arts degree in political science from the University of California, Berkeley, and a Masters in Business Administration from Golden Gate College. Before joining the bank he had a number of years experience in government and in a black-owned company. Now he manages a branch in a black area.

He spent most of his life in Utah and California and comes from a family in which his father, who had a high school education, was a civil service supervisor. His mother, a housewife, had two years of college. This manager is married and resides in an almost completely white area of San Francisco. He is a Methodist and attends church a few times a year. Like two of the other managers he considers himself a moderate Democrat. He belongs to several business and civic groups, all of which have white members, and he has very frequent contact with whites at parties and social functions. A number of his friends are white and he could easily imagine himself marrying a white woman.

Similar to two of the other representative managers, he gets along best with moderates because: "They are not militant or revolutionary. The tactics of the militants I don't agree with." But he recognizes that blacks must use pressure or they will not get anything. At the same time, he believes the white business world does not interfere with blacks' allegiance to their own community, and he would, if asked, move to a small white town. He summarizes these beliefs by saying: "I can function in any atmosphere. I don't believe in black or white anything." Not surprisingly, and in contrast to all of the other managers profiled, he believes that the best path for blacks is to assimilate and integrate completely into white society: "This is the only way it will ever work."

This manager is an example of the trend found in this chapter that the older, middle level black men, usually from the middle class, have more assimilative attitudes and behavior than the other groups of black managers. This could possibly indicate that as black managers move up the corporative ladder they will become more integrationist. The degree to which this will happen will depend on many things: the types of jobs blacks hold, the opportunities they are afforded for advancement in the business world, the racial attitudes of white America in general, and the government's action on integration in the areas of housing, schooling, and employment.

In general the black managers in this study are moderate in their racial views. They seem to be more assimilative in attitudes and behavior than the general black population, even though it has been found that the vast majority favor desegregation and, as Campbell has noted, "the number of people of both races who count their friends exclusively within their own race has declined" (A. Campbell, 1971, pp. 134, 146).

The managers in the present study tend to live in more integrated neighborhoods and have more overall contact with whites than the black population at large. This is due to the managers' unique positions within the white corporate structure and is in a sense an artificial measure of integration. True integration will be the result of blacks working in areas not related to the black consumer market and black employees, of white society accepting blacks as neighbors, colleagues, and friends, and of the government pushing for equality of opportunity. Then the attractions of separatism will be less tempting, and blacks and whites will be able to participate in meaningful integration.

CHAPTER TEN

Some Conclusions and Suggestions

The detailed analysis this book has presented of black managers in white corporations reveals unmistakably that there is a long way to go before equality between the races is achieved in the business world. In this chapter we will discuss the primary factor hindering black managers from fully participating in the corporate world—racism. A greater understanding of this phenomenon will serve as a background for concrete suggestions made by the participating managers themselves for improving the present situation of black managers both in the corporate world and in their own firms, with special reference to their companies' promotion policies. I will also offer my own views on what must and should be done for corporations to provide and insure equal employment opportunities.

THE MAJOR PROBLEM: RACISM

This study has demonstrated unequivocally that the major problem confronting blacks in their employment in corporations is racism. Most white managers believe racial discrimination exists generally within the corporate world, but many are reluctant to admit to its existence within their own companies or are virtually blind to it. Corporate racism, as well as individual racism, has become much more refined than in the past. Generally it is no longer overt and unsophisticated, demonstrated, for instance, by companies simply not hiring or promoting blacks because of their color. Rather racism has become much more covert and sophisticated with many more subtle and complex attitudinal and institutional components.

In discussing this change Robert Blauner has suggested a new term for the racism existing today and has pointed out:

> ... it is still difficult for most whites to accept the unpleasant fact that America still remains a racist society. Such an awareness is further obscured by the fact that the more sophisticated, subtle, and indirect forms, which might better be termed *neoracism*, tend to replace the traditional, open forms that were most highly elaborated in the old South (Blauner, 1972, p. 141, emphasis added).

Racism of any kind is against the law. Many government laws have made illegal all rules and regulations excluding blacks solely on the basis of color. The government has issued its own further checks. Some require employment tests to be validated before being used. Others require that reasons for not hiring or promoting be based on "objective" criteria that must be directly related to the position under consideration. Still others make it mandatory for institutions to take affirmative action to increase the number of blacks in their employ.

Unfortunately, however, such government regulations leave gaping loopholes. The regulations requiring "objective" qualification criteria are extremely general and are effective primarily for entry-level positions. There is a great amount of leeway for individual interpretation of what "objective" criteria consist of for positions above the entry level. Also there has been no real government enforcement. Affirmative action by corporations is to be made in "good faith," a term that can easily be interpreted by decision-making white individuals in the vaguest possible terms, if not outrightly ignored.

Two Important Forms

Because of such vagueness and because this is a racist society operated almost exclusively by and for white people, I suggest that two important forms of racism are operating, too often simultaneously, to exclude blacks from participating fully in society's institutions. These are neoracism, as defined by Blauner, which pertains particularly to individual white attitudes; and institutional racism, which pertains to exclusionary procedures, rules, and regulations. Although institutional racism can be an instrument for neoracism in the individual interpretation of rules and regulations, most often such rules were formulated without the specific intention of excluding blacks. It is simply that in our white-oriented society, most institutionalized procedures and rules have been made with whites in mind, especially white males. This has also resulted in the almost total barring of blacks from equal and full participation in the society in which they are nominally full citizens.

Throughout this study we have seen ample evidence of both forms of racism, although we have concentrated on individual attitudes and their effects on the black managers. A number of writers in the sociological field have recently pointed out the need for more emphasis on the examination of institutional racism. In one such study Harold M. Baron delineated how this form of racism can work:

. . . the individual generally does not have to exercise a choice to operate in a racist manner. The rules and procedures of the large organizations have already prestructured the choice. The individual only has to conform to the operating norms of the organization and the institution will do the discriminating for him (Baron, 1969, pp. 142–43).

Writing along similar lines, Robert Blauner argued that individual white racist attitudes are not the most important factor in denying blacks equal opportunities. Although opinion polls and attitude surveys have shown decreasing white racist attitudes, at the same time there has been a continued deepening of racial crisis and conflict. Blauner noted wryly that as sociologists were using the polls and surveys to show the decrease of racial tension, the well-known riots of the 1960s occurred and secret extremist groups began to organize (Blauner, 1972, pp. 8–9).

The explanation, said Blauner, lies within the institutions, and he observed:

The processes that maintain domination—control of whites over non-whites—are built into the major social institutions. These institutions either exclude or restrict the participation of racial groups by procedures that have become conventional, part of the bureaucratic system of rules and regulations. Thus there is little need for [individual] prejudice as a motivating force. . . . (Blauner, 1972, p. 8, 9)

Blauner cogently analyzed the insidiousness of such a racist structure by describing its effects on well-meaning individuals and how they inadvertently perpetuate the unjust system:

The [people] of goodwill and tolerance who identify racism with prejudice can therefore exempt themselves from responsibility and involvement in our system of racial injustice and inequality by taking comfort in their own "favorable" attitudes toward minority groups. . . . The error in this point of view is revealed by the fact that such [individuals] of goodwill and tolerance help maintain the racism of American society and in some cases even profit from it (Blauner, 1972, pp. 10, 9).

In their study of institutional racism primarily at the University of Santa Barbara, H. Molotch and L. Wolf concentrated on the day-to-day routines of the university, which intentionally or unintentionally excluded blacks and other minorities. Molotch and Wolf placed a great deal of emphasis on the inability of minorities to meet certain white, middle class requirements that are considered necessary for entrance into the academic community at various levels. They also emphasized the conventional recruitment procedures that have unintentionally excluded larger numbers of minorities. Their study leaves one with the uneasy feeling that all minorities need special consideration and that all that has to be changed to insure blacks equal opportunities are the conventional procedures, rules, and regulations. They placed very little importance on the role white racist attitudes play in the exclusion of blacks (Molotch and Wolf, 1972).

The position of these researchers, as well as the others previously quoted, was aptly summarized by Hardy Frye, assistant professor of sociology at Sacramento State College, in a conversation with me: "The white people's attitudes are not important. The primary factors of importance are the institutional structures which exclude blacks. You can't change the attitudes of whites, but you can change the structures."

Certainly it is true that conventional procedures, rules, and regulations are serious and important barriers to blacks in attaining equal opportunities in the corporate world and equal participation in societal institutions generally. It is also true that some blacks, just like some whites, are unable to meet particular requirements for many positions within various societal institutions. It is equally true and important to emphasize that many blacks who are not deficient in meeting requirements and who are not hindered by conventional procedures are still excluded from full participation. Thus one cannot help but conclude that individual white racist attitudes, based on a neoracist ideology, are just as important as the various manifestations of institutional racism in keeping blacks back.

Varying Degrees at Different Levels

These forms of racism work in the corporate world at all levels, but it is my observation that the degree of importance and effectiveness in the exclusion of blacks varies among the levels of the corporate hierarchy. At the top are members of boards of directors. In one study on a group of university directors, which parallel corporate directors, sociologist Troy Duster found that because of their advanced ages, predominantly Protestant and business backgrounds, and high status, directors were a very conservative group. Duster also noted that individuals with such characteristics generally believe that people get what they deserve in this world and deserve what they get (Duster, 1971, p. 24). It would follow then that these corporate directors were convinced that blacks have not achieved high positions in the corporate world because they do not deserve it, a form of apparent logic that is in reality a form of neoracism.

The self-perpetuating characteristics of the boards of directors lead quite naturally to institutional racism. Institutional racism is reinforced by neoracist attitudes that state that because blacks have a different culture producing different social mores, personal mannerisms, styles of dress, and modes of speech, blacks could not possibly fit into the higher business circles or interact effectively at the high status social functions where so much business activity takes place. Thus the directorial group is an obvious embodiment of the theory that in order for organizations to function smoothly, especially at the upper managerial levels, a culturally homogeneous group must be maintained (as discussed at length in Chapter 5). The outcome of adherence to such a theory results in an enormous barrier to blacks.

However, the other neoracist attitude revolving around "qualifications" is just as harmful to blacks. Because there are no qualifications specified for the position of "director" in firms, lack of "qualified" blacks continues to be used to explain the absence of blacks at high levels, and neoracist ideology is left to operate unchecked.

Upper level managers, who are in fact approved by the board of directors, possess very similar attitudes and characteristics. Thus the forms of racism at this level for excluding blacks are similar to those at the board of directors level. The most usual, time-honored way to advance within a corporation has been the slow one of gradual rising from the lowest ranks to the higher managerial levels. The fact that until recently all but a few blacks have been barred from even the low levels of management means that this convention of promotion from within has become an effective means of institutional racism that keeps whites exclusively at the top.

In addition, when attempting to fill a position with someone from outside the organization, upper level managers seek candidates through friends and contacts. Because the vast majority of upper level managers are white, and because their friends and contacts are generally white—and they too probably have little contact with blacks—whites alone will generally be recommended for the open position. Again blacks are excluded from top management by another conventional procedure.

Even if such forms of institutional racism did not exclude blacks, they would nevertheless be barred from upper management, as they are from the board level, by two widespread forms of neoracism. As was the case with the directors, the most important type of racism that exists at upper levels is the neoracist ideology which says blacks are not socially compatible and therefore not acceptable colleagues. We have seen that many managers of both races in this study believe that blacks cannot achieve upper management positions in part because whites are not ready to accept them as social equals. Blacks would then be prevented from participating in many of the business decisions that take place in social activities.

Also at this level, the neoracist ideology that excludes blacks because they do not have the "proper qualifications" begins to play a more significant role than at the board level. No specific qualifications have ever been set down to elect members to a board, but at the upper levels of management many positions require certain definite skills and experiences. Thus the need becomes greater to develop a rationale for the virtually complete exclusion of blacks from high managerial positions, and this takes the form of a "lack of qualifications."

Considering the "lily white" nature of the upper levels of management, the various forms of racism that are so prevalent, and the tremendous power and influence the individuals at these levels possess, one would expect their racial attitudes and ideologies to permeate the entire institutional structures. To an extent they do, but the upper level neoracist ideology—particularly that blacks cannot interact with whites because of different cultural backgrounds and that blacks are socially unacceptable because social homogeneity must be preserved—becomes less important as one looks at the middle and lower levels of the managerial hierarchy. This is, primarily and simply, because outside social interaction assumes less significance the lower one is on the corporate ladder.

This is not to say that there is no neoracism or institutional racism at the lower levels. Institutional racism in the form of conventional rules, regulations, and procedures becomes correspondingly more important at these levels, especially because candidates must go through the prescribed channels to a greater extent. Neoracism comes into play here too—individuals with neoracist attitudes generally interpret institutional procedures to the detriment of blacks.

The form of neoracism that becomes most important here is not, as at the upper levels, related to social and cultural incompatibility, but to type of job. No longer is it assumed among many white managers that all blacks are incapable of performing any managerial job; rather the question now becomes one of qualification—who is the "most" or "best" qualified for what. It is the belief of many whites that blacks can perform only certain types of managerial jobs directly connected to the black consumer market or black personnel.

Stress is now also placed on overqualification. Many corporations have accepted the fact that blacks can no longer be totally barred from management, but they still make it harder for blacks than whites to enter the managerial ranks. If blacks must be brought in at all, the rationale goes, they must be more qualified to merit the same positions that would normally be filled by only average white men. As Chapter 5 showed, 92 percent of the white managers believe that blacks receive fair and equal treatment in their firms, but 53 percent of these white managers believe that blacks must be better than whites to get ahead and/or that the firms are more careful in promoting blacks because they want to be certain the blacks will succeed.

It must also be stressed that neoracism not only affects blacks' abilities to be hired and promoted but, once hired, their abilities to do the job well. As was noted earlier, a qualified black can fail in a job assignment because of white reluctance to treat him or her equally. White superiors, peers, and subordinates consciously or unconsciously may refuse to cooperate in the many ways necessary for a black co-worker to successfully accomplish any assignment.

Both institutional racism and neoracism, then, are strong components in keeping blacks out of corporate management. The facts that only 9 percent of the participating white managers expressed no negative racial attitudes and that the vast majority of both the black and white managers are aware of negative racial atmospheres within their companies indicate the gravity of the situation. Furthermore the regression analysis in Chapter 5 clearly showed that various forms of institutional racism and neoracism have been translated unmistakably into discriminatory behavior against blacks.

In sum, blacks in corporations are being confronted less by overt, unsophisticated racist attitudes and actions than by the more indirect and insidious forms of institutional racism and neoracism. Although the emphasis on one or another of these forms varies at the different levels of management, they all have the same effect, particularly at the middle and upper levels of management—the almost total exclusion of blacks. Very few of the firms participating in this study have taken any concrete steps to eliminate racism and to assure blacks equal opportunities. This is the major task and problem facing the white firms with regard to black managers. Corporations must squarely confront the more subtle forms of corporate racism so that equal employment opportunities will become a reality and not simply a public relations catch phrase.

SUGGESTIONS FOR IMPROVEMENT: THE MANAGERS

A Strong Stand

The managers are aware in varying degrees of this problem, and throughout the interviews they were given the opportunity to express their opinions on what (if anything) should be done to assure blacks equal employment opportunities. A frequently given opinion of both black and white managers is that corporations should take public positions on civil rights. The blacks feel stronger than the whites on this point, of course, and are more vocal, as indicated by a black female manager from Ace Public Utility:

Corporations make decisions every day which influence social attitudes. They take public stands and try to influence attitudes on issues which they believe will help or harm their firms, but very few will take a strong public stand on civil rights. They don't realize that the progress of civil rights can have a helpful or harmful effect on their firms. Corporations are afraid of being the leaders in the business community's efforts for civil rights or they just don't want to take positive public stands on civil rights.

This manager's view is corroborated by a black middle level manager from Triple C Bank: "By discriminating against blacks, corporations are taking public positions regarding civil rights—they are taking a negative position." Concurrence by white managers is evident from this eloquent statement by a white upper manager at Ace Public Utility: "The corporate world must take rational and worthy stands on civil rights. Corporations are an integral and powerful force in society and they can no longer ignore social problems."

A central part of taking positive public stands is for the firms to set an example for other institutions by providing equal employment opportunities for blacks. The managers were asked for their opinions on what the "right thing" is for companies to do in the hiring and promoting of blacks. The managers had six choices and could choose more than one by listing them in order of importance. Table 10-1 shows the managers' first-choice responses. As can be seen, most black and many white managers believe definite steps are necessary by firms to improve the employment situation of blacks. It should be remembered that some white managers generally believe their own firms are already providing blacks with equal employment opportunities and that the fault lies with other firms. Thus these managers' responses usually pertain to what they believe other firms should do, not their own.

Despite this consideration the managers' overall responses are significant. The most frequent second and third choices, given by both blacks and whites, is the necessity of firms' giving careful attention to the promotion of qualified blacks (see Appendix C, pages 259–278, for the frequency distribution of the managers' second and third choices). That is, many managers believe firms should go beyond hiring and promoting strictly on the basis of qualifications. After the firms recruit and train black managers, they should expend more effort, the managers believe, in close attention to the promotion of qualified blacks.

TABLE 10-1 WHAT COMPANIES SHOULD DO TO PROVIDE BLACKS EQUAL OPPORTUNITIES: MOST IMPORTANT CHOICES (in %)

Right Thing to Do	Black Managers (N = 116)	White Managers (N = 156)
Make special recruiting and training efforts among blacks	50	44
Hire and promote strictly on the basis of qualification for the job ·	22	41
Give careful attention to the promotion of qualified blacks	12	11
Practice positive (reverse) discrimination	9	1
Do nothing	7	3
Other	0	0
Total	100	100

When the managers' first, second, and third choices (the latter two of which are shown in Appendix C, page 259) in the same category are combined for the three most important selections (the first three in Table 10-1), it is found that 81 percent of the black managers and 69 percent of the white believe that "doing the right thing" includes making special recruiting and training efforts among blacks. Fifty-eight percent of the black managers and 44 percent of the white believe careful attention should be given to the promotion of qualified blacks. And 45 percent of the blacks and 57 percent of the whites believe hiring and promoting should be done strictly on the basis of qualifications. In addition, very few of the managers, 25 percent of the black and 13 percent of the white, believe reverse discrimination should be practiced as part of the best employment procedures.

The managers were also asked for their own personal suggestions about what should be done to further reduce barriers to black managerial employment. Their responses are extremely varied, as indicated by Table 10-2. The suggestion made by the most black managers, 23 percent, is direct action by the companies—Affirmative Action Programs with specific standards, goals, and timetables. In about the same proportion 25 percent of the whites offer "no suggestions." Such responses may have prompted the pessimism of one black woman from Ace Public Utility: "There is no way to reduce barriers as long as the same kind of people run the corporations. We all know the corporations attract the same people—conservative white racists. . . ."

An upper level white manager from Aunts Manufacturing is more constructive and elaborates on the idea of full company commitment:

The most significant thing to do to reduce barriers is to get management to understand that the concepts involved in this change process of minority involvement encompass more than the hiring process. You can force industries to hire but it is more difficult to force them to promote. There has to be a complete understanding at every level of what the change means.

A concrete suggestion to implement such change, and one that would probably be quite effective if it were made standard procedure, is offered by a black lower level manager from Ace Public Utility: "White supervisors should be made responsible for their actions on the job. Their promotions and raises should be dependent on their ability to treat all people fairly." Another manager from Ace Public Utility, a white who represents the 9 percent suggesting greater interaction between the races as a possible remedy, says: "Whites should make a determined effort to interact more with blacks. And blacks in turn should be less sensitive about what whites say and do. The whites usually don't even know or understand what they are saying or doing." Sadly, one might note, very few whites are willing to examine their subconscious minds for racist tendencies.

TABLE 10-2 THE MANAGERS' SUGGESTIONS FOR REDUCING BARRIERS TO BLACK EMPLOYMENT (in %)

Suggestions	Black Managers ($N = 116$)	White Managers ($N = 156$)
Companies should adopt and enforce Affirmative Action Programs with specific goals, timetables, and standards	23	12
Whites should be educated and made more aware and sensitive; they should learn about black history, culture, and so on; they should have actual contact with a number of black people so their stereotype of blacks can be overcome	12	9
No suggestions	11	25
Establish and/or place more blacks into management training programs	11	11
Discipline the white racists, by weeding them out, firing them, and the like	11	1
Companies should improve the caliber of their recruiters, employ more black recruiters and improve their recruiting methods	7	6
An undeniable, known commitment from top management to other managers and to the community	7	4
There should be more interaction between blacks and whites so that both groups could begin to understand and respect each other more	5	9
Blacks should prepare themselves, i.e., get an education, training, skills, and so on	5	7
Blacks should not become complacent; they should continue to pressure firms from the inside and outside	5	0
Blacks themselves can be the most effective in eliminating barriers by doing outstanding jobs in their present positions	4	5
Blacks must have more positive attitudes toward themselves	3	3
Doesn't believe there are any barriers	1	5
Time will break down the barriers	1	2
Do not practice reverse discrimination	0	5
Corporations should become more involved in cooperating with and assisting educational institutions to educate blacks	0	5

TABLE 10–2 (*Continued*)

Suggestions	Black Managers (N = 116)	White Managers (N = 156)
It is the blacks' own fault that they haven't made it; their attitude is bad, i.e., they are lazy, don't want to work, and so on	0	2
Other	5	10
Total[a]	111	111

[a] The total percentages are over 100 because some managers gave several suggestions.

As the last part of Table 10-2 indicates, some managers, primarily the whites, persist in seeing no problems at all, or if they do, they attribute the problems to the blacks themselves. In a typical racist statement a white lower level manager from Ajax Manufacturing asserts: "There is nothing stopping the blacks. There's been a push to give them the opportunity to obtain a higher education. They got a shot in the arm from this. It's their own fault for not having the necessary education to get jobs. This is true for women, too."

Except for those who feel as this manager does, the vast majority believe that industry should take special steps to provide equal employment opportunities for blacks. The most serious block to the white managers' carrying out such steps is that they are likely to support affirmative action so long as it does not affect their own careers. For instance, it was pointed out in Chapter 3 that many of the black and white managers believe resistance to equal employment opportunities is greatest in those ranks where blacks compete with whites for jobs. Strong support by whites of affirmative action within their own firms is less than hopeful; as mentioned earlier, even though many whites agree that affirmative steps are necessary and go so far as to make constructive suggestions, they mean the advice to be taken by other firms and see no need for following it within their own.

Promotional Policies

The white managers, too, have their sources of dissatisfaction. It is not only blacks and women who have been treated unfairly in the hiring and promotion areas. This is because determining whom to hire or promote is at best subjective and ambiguous. It will be remembered from Chapter 5 that large percentages of both black and white managers feel there are unwritten company policies that realistically affect the companies' employment decisions. When the managers are asked about their firms' promotional policies, 85 percent of the blacks and 62 percent of the whites say they see the need for some type of change. Table 10-3 shows what the managers would do.

What is striking is that overall both races tend to see similar nonability mechanisms working in their companies' promotional systems. That is, the managers' primary concern is that selection and evaluation procedures become more specific and objective. However, the most frequently mentioned change cited by the black managers in this regard is de-emphasis of the seniority system. One of the most frequent changes the white managers would make is to emphasize the seniority system. A black lower level manager at Cousins Manufacturing, for instance, says: "The main current criterion here is one of seniority—hierarchy of positions. The next guy in line is entitled to the job regardless of qualifications. People should be promoted into positions of responsibility not after long years of service but on their potential."

Politics is an important factor that many of the managers would attempt

TABLE 10-3 CHANGES THE MANAGERS WOULD MAKE IN THEIR COMPANIES'
PROMOTIONAL POLICIES (in %)

Changes	Black Managers ($N = 116$)	White Managers ($N = 156$)
De-emphasize seniority	23	6
None	15	38
Do away with politics	15	7
Provide better information on promotional opportunities	14	8
Have more objective evaluation procedures	13	8
Do away with discrimination	13	1
Provide better identification and preparation of potential managers	8	12
Emphasize seniority	5	12
Give women more opportunities	3	2
Promote on merit and not because of being a woman	2	3
Other	4	8
Total[a]	115	105

[a] The total percentages are over 100 because the managers could indicate as many promotional changes as they would wish to make.

to eliminate. As a black lower level manager from Ace Public Utility observes: "The company should give more importance to an individual's performance and not to who you know." A white female manager at the same level with the same company agrees and sees sexual discrimination as well as politics at work: "The promotional policies should be based strictly on an individual's merit and ability. In the past they have been based on an individual's sex. I haven't observed a racial bias but my sample has been small. Political factors—what alliances you have—also play too large a part."

Doing away with racial discrimination is another of the black managers' goals. A black lower level manager also from Ace Public Utility says: "Now too often too many people get screened out because of their ethnic background, hair styles, or dress. I would certainly select more objective evaluation criteria." And finally, a black lower level female manager at the same company suggests a method to abort such discrimination: "The evaluation program should include written and oral examinations and interviews by people other than the individual's immediate superior. Those who evaluate should be at levels above the level of the person they are evaluating."

The guidelines to be suggested shortly will deal with many complaints all of the managers have, regardless of race, sex, or any other subjective factor. First it will be interesting to see what advice the black managers would give young blacks about to enter the business world.

Advice to Young Blacks

Based on many of the black managers' previous responses, it is questionable whether they would encourage a younger black to enter the business world at all. But almost all the managers, 96 percent, say they would definitely advise young blacks just out of school or college to seek out the business world. This response is certainly surprising since the vast majority of the black managers also believe that both the corporate world and their own firms provide only limited opportunities for blacks in mainly hostile, frustrating atmospheres.

The primary reason behind this seeming inconsistency is that most of the black managers believe that the business world is no better and no worse than any other institution in this society—racism exists everywhere else too. Thus young blacks have no worse opportunities in business than they do in the government or academia.

When the managers were asked what specific advice they would give the young blacks to help them to achieve high managerial positions, many of their answers were based on the realization that blacks must be better qualified than whites to get ahead in the corporate world. Contrary to white belief, not one manager suggested that younger blacks should try to get things just because they are black. Rather, the managers encouraged young blacks with the following words: pursue the best possible education, develop your skills, do your job well, work hard, keep abreast of your job and always strive for more, set goals, and don't let people deal with you unfairly. (See Appendix C, pages 259–278, for the details of advice the black managers would give young blacks to help them to achieve high managerial positions.)

This advice is inspiring and in fact sounds like the kind of encouragement anyone would give to a young person just starting out. But these words are much more idealistic than what the managers would say to young blacks about to enter their own firms. Here the managers have experienced the harsher realities, and the most frequently mentioned advice is: "Stand up for what you believe is right—be your own person." Such advice is also an attempt to counteract the idea of adherence to company "standards," which is often a racist codeword, as Chapter 5 noted, for conformity to white standards of appearance values and attitudes. Many blacks correctly interpret such demands for conformity as the demand for blacks to become "yes niggers."

The black managers offer as their second most frequent piece of advice: "Be aware of corporate politics. Be cautious, and learn to use politics to your own advantage." This advice is consistent with the black managers' own experiences, in which corporate politics have played a very important role in both hiring and promoting.

Thus the advice the black managers would give to young blacks entering the business world and their own firms reflects on the whole the continuing struggle of blacks in industry to achieve what they know they are capable of without compromising themselves completely. They must make sure they are more qualified than whites; make few, if any, mistakes; be skilled in corporate politics; and with all this, maintain their integrity as blacks and as individuals.

GUIDELINES FOR IMPROVEMENT: PERSONAL OBSERVATIONS

For the majority of blacks or even whites entering the business world today to meet all these requirements is well-nigh impossible. Clearly, concrete, cooperative steps must be taken in all parts of the corporate world to provide blacks, as well as every other group of employees, with equal employment opportunities. There are a number of things that can be done, in my view, by each group within industry, by the white executives and officials, by corporations as a whole, and by the blacks, separately and collectively.

What Whites Must Do

First of all, white executives and officials must recognize unflinchingly that racism exists within corporations at all managerial levels. Because racism is so deeply embedded, special efforts must be made to insure equal employment opportunities. Such special efforts do not constitute systematic favoritism or preferential treatment, a charge that so many whites have leveled against many affirmative action efforts. Such accusations may be answered by the forthright words of Carl Rowan in his article, "A Defense of Job Quotas":

It is going to come as a wry shock to millions of hungry, miserable black Americans that they have been getting so many of the goodies of American life that the white majority feels discriminated against.

Honest officials have simply noted that the bureaucracy does not respond to general orders to end discrimination. You have to spell out a "goal." Only then will personnel departments cut out the nonsense where a black college graduate is adjudged scarcely capable of cleaning spitoons (C. Rowan, 1972, p. 9).

It is essential for white executives to realize that special efforts are not reverse racism but necessary steps for firms to achieve real nondiscriminatory policies.

To hold that unfair practices will be eliminated simply by eliminating overt discrimination, a position held by many liberals, is not going far enough. As Robert Blauner points out, this position assumes erroneously that blacks will automatically gain equitable opportunities if discrimination is ended. But this is not so—much of the racial exclusion now evident is "the present-day reflection or residue of past racial discrimination . . ." (Blauner, 1972, pp. 278–279) and therefore specific efforts must be made to actively reverse inequality.

The purpose of what is called preferential treatment, says Blauner, is not so that "non-whites will be in the position of dominance," but so that true equality may be achieved. He also observes, with regard to the opponents of preferential treatment, that ". . . the cry of reverse racism is . . . more and more raised by conservatives . . . who have never raised a finger in the past about the society's predominant white racism" (Blauner, 1972, pp. 278–79; see also Silberman, 1964, p. 241).

Such white resentment toward the necessary special steps for equal employment opportunities will only lead to greater tensions between the races, which in turn will eventually and with even greater difficulty have to be overcome. The longer these steps are put off, the greater the costs and the harder the task. Personal and social trauma are inevitable as part of such a far-reaching change as that from racist, inequitable systems to fair ones. The cries of preferential treatment and reverse discrimination stem from fear, fear on the part of white men that their privileged positions are being threatened.

What Firms Must Do

This fear must be recognized for what it is, but it can no longer stand in the way of concrete, positive steps by the corporations as a whole. The first step a company should take to assure that blacks receive equal opportunities is to establish goals and timetables for all departments, divisions, and sections within the entire firm. These goals and timetables should not only be directed toward making the overall number of blacks in the company representative of the population at large, but also toward placing representative numbers of blacks in *all* levels of the firm's hierarchy and job areas.

To reach such population and employee parity, corporations must be willing to implement actions that seem like reverse discrimination; however, such actions are merely compensatory until parity is achieved. This is the purpose of affirmative action. Once parity is achieved, the apparent preferential treatment of an affirmative action effort can then be replaced by actual *equal* opportunity.

As a company develops its goals and timetables, it should begin to take three concurrent and equally important steps:

1. Develop the organizational structure necessary to insure compliance with the programs.
2. Recruit and train black managers for *all* levels of management.
3. Institute a reward system—promotions and salary increases to those managers who are meeting their equal employment goals, and demotions and dismissals to those who are not.

The last of these steps may raise opposition as being unprecedented and even incendiary. But when it is recalled that goals and timetables are set for many other managerial activities, and managers are rewarded or not in the same ways as those suggested, the application of such a reward system to equal employment opportunity goals should be seen as a routine part of the corporate system. In fact the sooner companies begin really to practice equality in employment, the less time and money they will spend in answering discrimination charges, and the more they will be able to devote their energies to the real business of business—providing a service or a product and making a profit.

The types of actions we have been suggesting, of course, come under the general title of Affirmative Action Programs, which were discussed at length in Chapter 3. But there is more to effective operation of a company and satisfaction of all its employees than just a strong AAP effort. An integral part of equal employment opportunity is a comprehensive management program, with certain specific and objective components. Such a program, in conjunction with a forceful AAP, will greatly assist firms in combatting the fear among their white managers of black competition and the concern among black managers of inequitable treatment.

The Optimum Management Program

There are three main aspects of this program, which was developed by me and several of my former colleagues at American Telephone and Telegraph, from much observation of firms and their problems and many conferences with employees at all levels.* The first aspect is *job enrichment,* the goal of which is for all employees to have more satisfying, rewarding, and growth-promoting jobs. The second is *joint target setting,* which means management by well-defined and agreed-upon targets (goals). And the third aspect is that of *objective employee assessment* through the realistic evaluation of employee potentials and abilities not only by bosses but in assessment centers. Many firms already make use of these concepts, but they are used selectively, not throughout an entire organization, and are not implemented in any systematic, integrated manner.

The well-integrated, smoothly working management program will first be described in a brief overview. All jobs, where practical, would be analyzed to make certain that they are "whole" jobs or work modules with specific, well-defined responsibilities, and that the individuals assigned to the jobs have the necessary decision-making powers and feedback to perform them successfully. The design of whole jobs (work modules) can be a mutual task between bosses and subordinates.

Once the work modules are designed, the bosses and subordinates should mutually develop and agree on the major targets (goals) and how these targets are to be measured. Subordinates' performances would then be judged on how well they do in meeting the targets and not on subjective criteria such as race, sex, dress, or particular personality characteristics.

The bosses should be trained in job enrichment methodologies, joint target setting guidelines, and validated potential assessment techniques, which would assist them in developing jobs and in evaluating their subordinates' performances and potentials. All managers should attend assessment centers that would evaluate their managerial potential. This way a check could be made on their bosses' evaluations of their potentials for ad-

---

* At present, a number of Bell System companies are using this program, which is in the process of being evaluated. It is too soon to draw final conclusions, but the initial observations and data suggest that the program is working quite well.

vancement. More systematic career planning could then be carried out, based on reliable assessment results.

This is the generalized view of how a successful management program would work. Each of the three major components is equally important, and for a better understanding of them, it is necessary to look more closely at their theoretical bases and practical implementations.

Job Enrichment

One of the major principles of job enrichment is that the job be a module, that is, a complete piece of work with an identifiable beginning and end, a total entity that can be handled successfully by a single individual. For each module specific responsibilities should be stated in broad terms with specific tasks listed under each responsibility. It has been noted by Robert Ford that most job modules can be improved, in terms of both "horizontal" and "vertical" loading:

Responsibilities or tasks that exist elsewhere in the shop or in some other shop need to be combined with the job under review. This horizontal loading is necessary until the base of the job is right. . . . [E]specially in management positions, many responsibilities can be moved to lower grade levels, usually to the advantage of every job involved. This vertical loading is especially important in mature organizations (Ford, 1973, pp. 96–99; see also Blauner, 1964; Vroom, 1964; Herzberg, 1966; Ford, 1969; Foulkes, 1969).

Another important component of a good job, as Ford and others have pointed out, is that the job be fitted to the subordinate, and not the subordinate to the job. An integral part of this is for subordinates to have enough decision-making power and autonomy to carry out their responsibilities—to set their own priorities and do their job the way they see fit.

Finally, in a good job the subordinate must receive frequent, relevant, clear, and direct feedback about his or her performance. Such feedback, as Ford observes, is essential for both the smooth working of the module and the increased motivation of the employee: "People have a great capacity for midflight correction when they know where they stand. . . . When the module is right you get feedback 'for free'; it comes directly from the customer/client/task. During the learning period, however, the supervisor or teacher should provide the feedback" (Ford, 1973, p. 101). Ford also makes the important connection between the good work module and employee attitudes: "When the work is right, employee attitudes are right. That is the job enrichment strategy—get the work right" (Ford, 1973, p. 106).

There is one drawback, however, to Ford's overall conception, and it is that he seems to see the boss or supervisor as doing all the deciding on work module, control of it, and feedback. Job enrichment can rarely be optimized by one-sided decisions. The subordinate must feel a part of the entire process if he or she is to be totally committed to the job. This is where job enrichment and joint target setting come together.

It is obvious that new employees will not be able to contribute much at first to decisions about their job design and initial responsibilities, means of measurements, and job targets. But bosses should nevertheless, at the initial meeting, begin to introduce the procedures of joint target setting, or, as it is also known, management by objectives.

Joint Target Setting

Joint target setting or management by objectives is a continuous process whereby bosses and subordinates periodically define and agree on the subordinates' responsibilities, the means of measuring them, results to be obtained and/or the target levels of performance in each area. They use the agreed-upon targets as guides for reaching organizational goals and for assessing the subordinates' contributions to the attainment of the goals. (See, for example, Drucker, 1954, 1964; McGregor, 1960; Likert, 1961; Blake and Mouton, 1964; C. Hughes, 1965; Herzberg, 1966; Odiorne, 1969; J. P. Campbell et al., 1970.)

The advantages of the cooperative and reciprocal nature of management by objectives are many. For one thing a clear understanding will be reached between boss and subordinate about the subordinate's exact responsibilities, means of measurement, and target levels of performance. For another the subordinate will develop a strong commitment to completing the job successfully and on schedule—this is control through commitment. The subordinate will also know how well he or she is performing at all times, and the boss will have some objective criteria on which to evaluate the subordinate's performance. If necessary, the subordinate will be able to challenge the boss's evaluation of his or her performance, based on the same objective criteria. And finally, if a subordinate is not promoted or is terminated and files a discriminatory complaint against the company, the company and subordinate will have objectively documented proof with which to argue their cases.

Aptitudes and potentials for both present and possible future jobs play an important part in the total optimum management program, as do the objective evaluations of such potentials. The use of assessment procedures and centers can be invaluable here.

Assessment

One of the leading experts on assessment, Douglas Bray, although writing about women specifically, has made some observations that have great relevance to the full utilization of all minority groups:

... effective change requires both motivation and method. Motivation to provide greater opportunity for women there is in abundance, not only in legislation and unrest among female employees, but in management's growing awareness of the tremendous hidden waste incurred in the failure to let women use their full potential. Method, however, is something else. Good intentions alone won't go far to correct imbalances and injustices that have been years in the making. Programs and techniques are needed (Bray, 1971, p. 30).

It is not only women and other minorities who are affected, Bray points out. Even white men, who encounter no discriminatory resistance because of race or sex, are quite frequently not properly utilized because of internal organizational barriers, such as unrecognized potential, reluctance of department heads to accept recommended transferees, and candidates' lack of relevant experience, all of which inhibit the free movement of employees between departments.

If it is this hard for white men to move, it is even harder for women and minorities. Bray foresees great difficulty in convincing managers that women have the ability to perform those jobs traditionally associated with white men. And, one might add, for blacks it will be even more difficult to persuade white managers that blacks can perform jobs not specifically related to the black consumer market or black employees—that blacks can do "white" jobs.

Potential is a critical factor here and presents somewhat of a double-bind situation. Women and other minorities most often hold jobs that do not by any means make use of their full potential. Their bosses may then be extremely reluctant to promote them because they have not demonstrated the greater abilities needed for a more challenging job, but their present job does not call for the demonstration of further capabilities. An effective way to break this wasteful cycle is suggested by Bray: What is needed to convince bosses that women (and minorities) do possess the necessary qualifications for the more challenging position is solid evidence (Bray, 1971, p. 31).

This is where assessment centers come in. At these centers managers and potential managers deal with standardized work performance situations, simulated exercises that allow the assessment center staff to evaluate the individual's managerial abilities and potentials. Through a number of methods the staff is able to evaluate such important managerial dimensions and characteristics as leadership, flexibility, communications skills, planning and organizational abilities, scholastic aptitude, decisiveness, and motivation. (See Bray, 1964; Bray and Grant, 1966, 1969; Bray and R. J. Campbell, 1967, 1968; Wernimont and J. P. Campbell, 1968; Byham and Thornton, 1970; Dodd, 1971; Moses, 1971.)

There are several impressive advantages to assessment centers, especially in terms of the crucial factor of objectivity. A number of these advantages have been noted by William C. Byham, and they are worth quoting in their entirety:

The exercises used are designed to bring out the specific skills and aptitudes needed in the position(s) for which a group of candidates is being assessed.

Since the exercises are standardized, assessors evaluate the candidates under relatively constant conditions and thus are able to make valid comparative judgments.

The assessors usually do not know the candidates personally; so, being emotionally disengaged, they are unbiased.

The assessors are shielded from the many interruptions of normal working conditions and can pay full attention to the candidates' behavior in the exercises.

The procedures focus their attention on the primary kinds of behavior they ought to observe in evaluating a promotion candidate.

They [the assessors] have been trained to observe and evaluate these kinds of behavior (Byham, 1970, p. 151).

Another advantage, which Byham does not mention, is that evaluations are more likely to be objective when more than one assessor is involved. It is also very important, if assessment centers are going to evaluate minorities and women, that their staffs include members of these groups. This will help insure that racist and sexist attitudes do not interfere with a fair evaluation. Furthermore, the assessors should be aware of possible racist and sexist attitudes among a given group of assessees. Negative attitudes are easily transmitted and may hinder women or other minority group members from demonstrating their true abilities. This is not to say that assessment centers will solve all the problems of giving women and minorities equal opportunities, but I believe, with Bray, that the centers would go a long way in righting the balance in the shortest possible time.

Not only will it be immeasurably helpful to send managers to assessment centers for evaluation, but it will also benefit the company for all managers to be taught assessment techniques. This will accomplish two things: to assist the manager in objectively evaluating his or her own subordinates' potentials and to assist both manager and subordinate in developing work modules and setting targets that would allow the measurement of additional supervisory skills.

If firms make a concerted effort to develop the optimum management program discussed here, many of the fears of both black and white managers will disappear. But white managers will still find it very difficult to deal with blacks in the spirit of good will and mutuality that is necessary for agreement on the implementation of job enrichment and joint target setting. Thus the management program alone will not afford blacks true equal employment opportunities. What is needed is a combination: a strong and objective management program with all the components just discussed *and* a well-developed Affirmative Action Program with effective compliance procedures. Then the changes will increase for blacks and all minorities to become equal in reality.

What Blacks Must Do

Nevertheless, black managers and blacks in general must face the sad and proven fact that they cannot depend exclusively on the government or any other agency or force to assure them equal opportunities. In the end it is up to the blacks themselves. Frederick Douglass knew this truth, still pertinent today over a century later. In 1849 he wrote:

Power concedes nothing without a demand. It never did and it never will. Find out just what people will submit to and you have found out the exact amount of injustice and wrong which will be imposed on them; and these will continue till they have resisted either with words or blows or with both. The limits of tyrants are prescribed by the endurance of those whom they suppress (Douglass, 1970, p. 15).

Blacks in corporations must continuously stand up for their own rights to be treated fairly. They must also assist other blacks to do the same. Beyond that, the black population in general has more power, of an economic nature, than most realize. Clifford Alexander observed: "Blacks have a tremendous purchasing power, variously estimated from $21 to $40 billion, that they spend on a large number of products. This, of course, could make or break certain kinds of products" (Alexander, 1968, p. 7). In today's economy the estimates would probably be even higher. It may be time to use this power, usually the only kind that the business world will listen to. It may be time to seriously consider and act on the boycott techniques used by the Rev. Jesse Jackson of wide varieties of products normally used by large proportions of blacks. It may be that only such action will force the hand of white corporations to provide blacks with equal employment opportunities.

What blacks must remember, despite all the laws, programs, and promises, is that whites will not concede anything to blacks unless blacks demand and struggle for their fair share, and do not give in or give up.

A POSTSCRIPT

Although the bulk of the research for this study was carried out during 1971–1972, as mentioned in the Preface, the findings, unfortunately, still hold today in 1975. In the years since the research was completed, I have had continuing contact and consultation with the managers in the firms participating in the study and have been able to observe the racial climate in these and other firms. I have also been active in the corporate world in analyzing and trying to deal with the provision of equal opportunities for all managers.

Negative racist attitudes are far from softening; they are becoming more solidified. There seems less likelihood than ever of true interracial harmony. Whites are becoming more angry and defensive and blacks more proud, impatient, and militant. What the final outcome will be cannot be predicted, but at least, as this study has attempted to show, the tools for harmony are there, if the principals want to use them.

APPENDIX A

The Survey Instrument

The primary survey instrument was an administered questionnaire. There were several reasons for this choice of instrument, and there were several steps taken to assure that the responses would be as valid as possible and the interview quality as high as possible.

It was felt that a personally administered questionnaire would produce the most extensive and reliable data. This was because, first, mailed questionnaires were unlikely to be returned in large numbers. Second, the length of the questionnaire might deter participants from completing it or giving careful, reliable, and thorough responses. An administered questionnaire would insure more precise, unambiguous answers to the open-end questions. And third, the interviewer would be able to make an appraisal of the interest, openness, sincerity, and honesty of each of the managers. Although I was aware that some managers might be more open if allowed to fill out the questionnaire on their own, I nevertheless felt that the advantages of an administered questionnaire outweighed those of a mailed or nonadministered questionnaire.

The questionnaire included both open-end and closed-end questions, in order to elicit as much information in as many ways as possible. An exclusively open-end questionnaire would allow the interviewers more latitude to include their personal biases in recording the responses. But an exclusively closed-end questionnaire would not permit the managers to express their more personal views, attitudes, and feelings.

STEPS TAKEN TO ASSURE HONEST RESPONSES

Five steps were taken to assure that the managers' responses would be as frank and open as possible. The first was to use both black and white interviewers. Two white interviewers were employed, Gerald Bradshaw and Caroline Kerr, and they conducted about half of both the black and white interviews. I, as the black interviewer, conducted the other half of all the interviews. I was aware that several studies have indicated that interviewees are inclined to be more honest with an interviewer of the same race than with one of a different race (Marx, 1967; Ferman, 1968). The interviews were analyzed for this possibility, and after careful analysis and a review of tables that used the interviewers as a control variable, no significant differences were found in the aggregate responses of the managers, regardless of the interviewer's racial background.

There are several ways to explain the lack of variance between the responses of the managers interviewed by a member of their own race and the responses of those who were not. The black managers may have felt comfortable dealing with whites because most of the black managers live rather integrated lives and have been conditioned or accustomed to white interviewers. With regard to white managers, several of those in charge of personnel or their companies' Affirmative Action Programs told me that many whites are willing to express their negative racial views than in the past. One middle level white manager from Ace Public Utility said that many whites will admit to harboring certain negative racial attitudes about blacks because they rationalize that since American society is racist, all its members must be: "Certainly I have racist attitudes—all people, black or white, are racist." And finally, the lack of apparent response bias may be due to the skills of the interviewers; they were able to provide an atmosphere conducive to candid and open answers.

Although there were no significant differences between the responses of managers interviewed by someone of their own race and those who were not, several black managers requested that they be interviewed by a black, and their requests were honored. These managers indicated that they wanted to be interviewed by the black project director because, they said, they wanted their responses interpreted and presented properly. They felt that a white interviewer would consciously or unconsciously distort their responses.

Several of the other black managers at first refused to participate when they found that their interviewer was Caroline Kerr, the white female interviewer, and confronted her about her participation in a study primarily concerned with blacks. After she explained the purpose of cross-race interviews, those who had objected decided to participate. In fact several of Ms. Kerr's best interviews were with those blacks who had first complained about her race.

The second step taken to assure honesty was to conduct all the interviews in private. The only people present at the interview session were the interviewer and the interviewee.

Another step was to guarantee the interviewees complete anonymity. This was accomplished in two ways. The participants were assured that their names would not appear on any part of the questionnaire or be mentioned in the study. They were also assured that none of the information in the interview schedule would be released to their company in any manner that would enable the company to identify a particular manager as the source of the information.

The fourth step was to interview only those managers who voluntarily agreed to participate in the study.

The final step was to include many differently worded questions and statements that were designed to measure the same basic concept throughout various sections of the interview schedule. For example, there were numerous questions at different points that attempted to find out how equal and fair the managers believed their companies' employment policies were toward blacks and other numerous questions that were designed to measure the managers' overall job satisfaction.

QUALITY OF THE INTERVIEW

To ascertain the quality of each interview, immediately after completion, the interviewers were to indicate on the questionnaire how much rapport they had with the interviewee, how they rated the quality of the interview, to what degree the interviewee seemed interested in the study, and whether the length of the interview had affected the subject in any way.

Because I could not conduct all of the interviews myself, nor was it desirable for me to do so, the other interviewers' evaluations were extremely helpful in determining the validity of the interviewees' responses and in giving me additional insight as to why a particular interview might not have been of high quality. It might have been because of a lack of rapport between the interviewer and interviewee, or because a manager was not really interested, was evasive, suspicious, did not understand the questions, or for other reasons.

For example, an interview was rated questionable when one of the older, less educated black managers just promoted to management from a nonmangement job was told "jokingly" by his superior that "he better not give away any company secrets." During the interview this black manager was very careful to make sure that he responded "properly." He seemed to say only what he thought his boss expected him to say—everything was fine, there were no problems, the company was more than fair, and he was completely satisfied. In another case a white manager did not like many of the questions because of their "personal" character. In addition he was quite upset about the length of the interview. His answers, although probably honest, were short and not very detailed because he wanted to finish the interview as quickly as possible.

On the whole there were not many occurrences like this. As can be seen from Table A-1, the interviewers believed that a substantial majority of the black interviews and a majority of the white interviews were of high quality, that is, the managers were not generally evasive, suspicious, or confused.

The quality of the interviews and the interest of the interviewees were directly related, as would be expected. Table A-2 shows the degree of interest on the part of the interviewees as perceived and noted by the interviewers.

On the question of rapport all three interviewers believed they had excellent rapport with more of the black managers than the white: 22 percent more. This difference is shown in Table A-3.

TABLE A–1   QUALITY OF THE INTERVIEWS (in %)

Quality	Black Managers[a] (N = 114)	White Managers[b] (N = 153)
Questionable	3	5
Generally Adequate	23	44
High quality	74	51
Total	100	100

[a] There were missing data on two cases.
[b] There were missing data on three cases.

TABLE A–2   INTEREST OF THE INTERVIEWEES (in %)

Interest	Black Managers[a] (N = 114)	White Managers[b] (N = 155)
High	75	50
Average	22	37
Low	3	13
Total	100	100

[a] There were missing data on two cases.
[b] There were missing data on one case.

The 20 to 24 percent differences in the evaluations of the questionnaires of the black and white managers in the three tables may be attributed to several things. One is that because the priority of equal employment opportunities is much greater in the minds of the black managers, they were more interested in the study and more concerned about the quality of their answers than the white managers. Many of the white managers believe the need for equal employment opportunities for blacks has been overemphasized, as we have seen at various points in this study. The whites therefore were not as interested as the blacks in this type of inquiry, and their lack of interest is reflected in their responses.

Furthermore the major emphasis of this study is on black managers and their career patterns and not on white managers. Thus the differences that occur in the

TABLE A–3   INTERVIEWERS' RAPPORT WITH THE INTERVIEWEES (in %)

Rapport	Black Managers[a] (N = 114)	White Managers[b] (N = 153)
Excellent throughout	78	56
Average	20	39
Poor throughout	2	3
Started good, became poor	0	1
Started poor, became good	0	1
Total	100	100

[a] There were missing data on two cases.
[b] There were missing data on three cases.

white and black managers' degree of interest, quality of interviews, and rapport with interviewers were not totally surprising and were even to be expected. And last, the white managers' responses about opportunities that exist for blacks in their companies were influenced by company loyalty much more than the black managers' responses. The whites, after all, have served a much longer time and the most loyal managers would therefore be most tempted to present a favorable image of their companies' employment policies. Such outlooks would, of course, result in less than candid responses.

INTERVIEW SCHEDULE*

Introduction

All information reported in this interview schedule will be held in strict confidence. No information from these sources will be published in such a manner that data relating to the interviewee or to his/her company can be identified. In addition no information reported in this interview schedule will be released to the interviewee's firm in a manner that would allow his/her firm to identify him/her as the source of information.

Firm Name _____

Interviewee's Code Number

PART I. (QUESTIONS ABOUT JOB EXPERIENCES)

First, we would like to ask you several questions about your promotional opportunities, goals, and career pattern.

1. Which, if any, of the following factors helped you attain your present position? (SHOW CARD 1) (CAN SELECT MORE THAN ONE)
   0. ____ Experience within the company
   1. ____ Experience in another company
   2. ____ Experience in the government
   3. ____ Experience in the military
   4. ____ Experience in social agencies
   5. ____ Experience in the academic world
   6. ____ Investment in the company
   7. ____ Inheritance or family influence
   8. ____ Initiative in organizing the company
   9. _____ Other (PLEASE SPECIFY)

2. Have you progressed as rapidly as you think you should in this company?
   0. ____ yes   1. ____ no

2a. Why do you say this? _____
   _____
   _____
   _____

* The writer used many comments from the 1969–1972 issues of *MBA* to develop questions for this study. He also borrowed many questions from Quinn et al., 1968.

3. Approximately how many years or months do you think it will be before you are advanced to a position at a higher level?

    a. ____ years   b. ____ months

    c. ____ never   d. ____ don't know

4. Approximately when would you like to be advanced to a position at a higher level?

    a. ____ years   b. ____ months

5. If things go according to your greatest expectations, will you stay with this company?

    0. ____ yes   1. ____ no

    (IF YES)

5a. What position in this company would you like to end up with? _____

    _____ Name of Position

    (IF NO)

5b. What position would you like to end up with? _____

    _____ Name of Position

6. How would you rate your chances of getting this position?

    0. ____ Excellent

    1. ____ Good

    2. ____ Fair

    3. ____ Poor

7. Are there any major obstacles that are preventing you from achieving this position?

    0. ____ yes   1. ____ no

    (IF YES)

7a. What are the major obstacles? _____

    _____

    _____

8. If you had the power to make any improvements you wished to make, what changes would you institute in the promotion policy of your firm? _____

    _____

    _____

9. On this card are different reasons people may have for choosing a certain job. (SHOW CARD 2) Just supposing you were going to choose a new job, which one of the things on this card would be *most important* to you?

    0. ____ High income

    1. ____ No danger of being fired; security

    2. ____ Lots of free time

    3. ____ Chances for advancement

    4. ____ The work is important and gives a sense of accomplishment

    5. ____ The work is interesting

    6. ____ The work gives lots of chances to meet people

    7. _____ Other (PLEASE SPECIFY)

9a. Which of the remaining things on the card is *second* in importance?

0 1 2 3 4 5 6 7 (CIRCLE ONE)

9b. Which of the things listed here would be of *least* importance to you?

0 1 2 3 4 5 6 7 (CIRCLE ONE)

10. If you wanted to leave your position with this company, how difficult do you believe it would be to obtain a comparable position somewhere else with similar income and fringe benefits? (SHOW CARD 3)

0. _____ Very difficult

1. _____ Fairly difficult

2. _____ Not very difficult

3. _____ Not difficult at all

10a. Why do you believe this? _____

_____

_____

_____

All of us occasionally feel bothered by certain kinds of things in our work. Listed below are a number of examples of things that sometimes bother people. We would like you to respond to each example in terms of how frequently you feel bothered by each of them. (SHOW CARD 4) Please do not bother to take much time with each statement; your first impression is perfectly all right.

11. Feeling that you have too little authority to carry out the responsibilities assigned to you.

0. _____ Never

1. _____ Rarely

2. _____ Rather often

3. _____ Nearly all the time

12. Being unclear on just what the scope and responsibilities of your job are.

0. _____ Never

1. _____ Rarely

2. _____ Rather often

3. _____ Nearly all the time

13. The possibility of losing your job.

0. _____ Never

1. _____ Rarely

2. _____ Rather often

3. _____ Nearly all the time

14. Thinking that you'll not be able to satisfy the conflicting demands of various people over you.

0. _____ Never

1. _____ Rarely

2. _____ Rather often

3. _____ Nearly all the time

15. Not knowing what your superior thinks of you, how he evaluates your performance.
    0. _____ Never
    1. _____ Rarely
    2. _____ Rather often
    3. _____ Nearly all the time

16. The fact that you can't get information needed to carry out your job.
    0. _____ Never
    1. _____ Rarely
    2. _____ Rather often
    3. _____ Nearly all the time

17. Feeling that you may not be liked and accepted by the people you work with.
    0. _____ Never
    1. _____ Rarely
    2. _____ Rather often
    3. _____ Nearly all the time

18. Feeling unable to influence your immediate superior's decisions and actions that affect you.
    0. _____ Never
    1. _____ Rarely
    2. _____ Rather often
    3. _____ Nearly all the time

19. Thinking that the *amount* of work you have to do may interfere with how *well* it gets done.
    0. _____ Never
    1. _____ Rarely
    2. _____ Rather often
    3. _____ Nearly all the time

20. Feeling that you have to do things on the job that are against your better judgment.
    0. _____ Never
    1. _____ Rarely
    2. _____ Rather often
    3. _____ Nearly all the time

The following questions deal with things your immediate superior might or might not do. Please indicate the one alternative that best describes the person who supervises you. (CONTINUE SHOWING CARD 4)

21. Lets those he supervises set their own work pace.
    0. _____ Never
    1. _____ Rarely
    2. _____ Rather often
    3. _____ Nearly all the time

22. Checks on the work of his/her subordinates.
     0. ___ Never
     1. ___ Rarely
     2. ___ Rather often
     3. ___ Nearly all the time

Please answer the following questions in terms of *how satisfied* you are with each.
(SHOW CARD 5)

23. With the group you work with.
     0. ___ Completely satisfied
     1. ___ Very satisfied
     2. ___ Not very satisfied
     3. ___ Not at all satisfied

24. With the type of work you do.
     0. ___ Completely satisfied
     1. ___ Very satisfied
     2. ___ Not very satisfied
     3. ___ Not at all satisfied

25. With your salary.
     0. ___ Completely satisfied
     1. ___ Very satisfied
     2. ___ Not very satisfied
     3. ___ Not at all satisfied

26. With your company in general.
     0. ___ Completely satisfied
     1. ___ Very satisfied
     2. ___ Not very satisfied
     3. ___ Not at all satisfied

27. What type of work would you try to get into if you could start all over again?
     _____
     _____

(IF DIFFERENT FROM PRESENT TYPE OF WORK)

28. Why would you prefer this to the work you are doing now? _____
     _____

29. If you could begin working over again, would you choose this company as a
     place to work?
     0. ___ yes   1. ___ no

Next we would like to find out about the jobs you've had. Let's start with the
earliest.

30. What was/is your job title (before this)? (RECORD COL. I)

31. For what company are/were you working? (RECORD COL. II)

32. Would you please indicate in a word or two how you found your position, i.e., recruited by a company, employment agencies, friends, etc? (RECORD COL. III)

33. When did you first get this job and when did you leave it? (RECORD COL. IV)

	I Job Title	II Company	III How Found Job	IV Duration of Job
1				
2				
3				
4				
5				
6				
7				
8				
9				

34. What kind of work do/did you do at this job? (RECORD COL. V)

35. Did you take any test for this position? If so, what type of test, i.e., skills, achievement, psychological? (RECORD COL. VI)

36. What is the size of the budget you directly control? (RECORD COL. VII)

37. How many people are directly under your supervision? (RECORD COL. VIII)

38. Approximately what was your hourly wage, weekly or monthly salary when you started and left your position? (IF CAN'T GET SALARY, GET SALARY SCALE) (RECORD COL. IX)

(REPEAT Q30-38 FOR ALL JOBS LISTED)

	V Type of Work	VI Test Taken	VII Size of Budget	VIII Number of Subordinates	IX Salary
1					
2					
3					
4					
5					
6					
7					
8					
9					

PART II. (MANAGER'S RELATIONSHIP TO THE COMPANY'S HIRING AND PROMOTING POLICIES IN THE AREAS OF INFLUENCE, UNDERSTANDING, AND PRACTICE)

This next section is about your relationship to your company's hiring and promoting policies.

39. How much influence do you feel you have over the hiring and promoting policies of this company? (SHOW CARD 6)
  0. _____ A very great deal
  1. _____ A great deal
  2. _____ A little
  3. _____ No influence

40. How much influence do you feel you have over the hiring and promoting policies that affect this department and/or division?
  0. _____ A very great deal
  1. _____ A great deal
  2. _____ A little
  3. _____ No influence

41. To what extent is *your* understanding of this company's hiring and promoting policies based on memos, job descriptions, or other kinds of written communications? (SHOW CARD 7)
  0. _____ A very great extent
  1. _____ A great extent
  2. _____ A little
  3. _____ Not at all

42. To what extent is your understanding of these policies based on your own personal observations?
  0. _____ A very great extent
  1. _____ A great extent
  2. _____ A little
  3. _____ Not at all

43. Are you in agreement with the hiring and promoting policies of this company?
  0. _____ yes   1. _____ no

43a. Why is this?_____
_____
_____

44. What are the kinds of things about a management candidate that might make you hesitate to hire or promote him/her, other than his/her lack of experience and job knowledge?
_____
_____
_____
_____
_____

45. In making a decision to hire or promote someone to a management position, how free do you feel to deviate from the formal policies of this company? (SHOW CARD 8)
    0. ____ Very free
    1. ____ Fairly free
    2. ____ Not very free
    3. ____ Not at all free

46. How often would you say you have actually deviated from the hiring or promoting policies? (SHOW CARD 9)
    0. ____ Very often
    1. ____ Fairly often
    2. ____ Not very often
    3. ____ Never
    (IF NEVER SKIP TO QUESTION 47)

46a. Would you give some examples of how your decisions tend to deviate from these policies? _____
    _____
    _____
    _____
    _____

47. In general, what are some important policies that are not written into the formal company policy, i.e., practices that may not be written or discussed but that realistically affect decisions? _____
    _____
    _____

48. Would you please discuss specific cases where black managers were hired and/or not hired, promoted and/or not promoted? (PROBE TO GET AT WHAT WENT INTO EACH DECISION) _____
    _____
    _____
    _____
    _____

49. Now we would like to get your views as to how several groups might feel about the hiring or promoting of black people into management positions in the company. (SHOW CARD 10) First . . .
    A. . . . would (READ "a" BELOW) feel in any way uncomfortable if you hired or promoted someone who was black? (REPEAT FOR GROUPS "b" THROUGH "e")

	0 YES	1 NO
a. . . . any of your (CUSTOMERS OR DISTRIBUTORS)	____	____
b. . . . any (MANAGEMENT PERSONS FROM OTHER COMPANIES)	____	____
c. . . . any (PEOPLE AT OR BELOW YOUR LEVEL IN THE COMPANY)	____	____

d.   ... your (IMMEDIATE SUPERIOR) ....   ____   ____
e.   ... any of the (PERSONS ABOVE YOUR IMMEDIATE
       SUPERIOR) ....   ____   ____
       (IF YES TO ANY OF QUESTION 49)

50. In making a hiring or promotional decision, to what extent must you take
     into account the feelings of these/this (READ "a" BELOW). Must you take
     account of their feelings to a very great extent, a great extent, some extent, a
     little extent, or not at all? (SHOW CARD 11) (REPEAT FOR GROUPS
     "b" THROUGH "e")

	0	1	2	3	4
	VERY GREAT EXTENT	GREAT EXTENT	SOME EXTENT	LITTLE EXTENT	NOT AT ALL
a. Customers or distributors	____	____	____	____	____
b. Management from other companies	____	____	____	____	____
c. People at or below your level	____	____	____	____	____
d. Immediate superior	____	____	____	____	____
e. Persons above immediate superior	____	____	____	____	____

51. Would you have answered any of the previous questions differently ten years
     ago?
     0. ____ yes   1. ____ no

51a. Why would you have done so? _____
     _____
     _____
     _____

PART III. (BLACK AND WHITE MANAGERS' VIEWS AND ATTITUDES)

Now we would like to get your views about black managers and their position in
business.

52. How do you account for a seeming underutilization of blacks in industry?____
     _____
     _____
     _____

53. How do you explain the incidence of black managers in your company?   ____
     _____
     _____
     _____

54. At what managerial level (lower, middle, or upper) do you believe your company's Equal Employment Opportunity Program meets the most resistance? (PROBE)_____

_____

_____

55. Do you believe your firm is more careful in promoting black employees than white employees because it wants to be certain that blacks will succeed before promoting them?

0. ____ yes   1. ____ no

55a. What is the evidence?_____

_____

_____

56. In your company how far up the executive ladder do you believe a black can go? _____

_____

56a. Why is this?_____

_____

_____

57. Many companies indicate that they want to do "the right thing" about hiring and promoting black managers. But what does doing "the right thing" involve? (SHOW CARD 11) (CAN SELECT MORE THAN ONE IF NECESSARY. IF SELECTS MORE THAN ONE, INDICATE BY 0–4 WHICH IS MOST IMPORTANT, 0 BEING MOST IMPORTANT)

0. ____ Hire strictly on the basis of qualification for the job

1. ____ Make special recruiting and training efforts among blacks

2. ____ Practice positive (reverse) discrimination

3. ____ Give careful attention to the promotion of qualified blacks

4. ____ Do nothing

5. _____Other (PROBE)

58. Are there any reasons why blacks can't make it in the corporate world?

0. ____ yes   1. ____ no

58a. What are some of the reasons? _____

_____

_____

59. How do you believe the ghetto riots of the 1960's affected your company's employment policies for blacks? _____

_____

_____

60. Do you believe that blacks today are pressing their case too hard?

0. ____ yes   1. ____ no

60a. Why do you believe this? _____

_____

_____

_____

61. Are you aware of any carryover into the work situation of negative white attitudes toward blacks?
0. ____ yes   1. ____ no
(IF YES)

61a. What personal experiences have you had to become aware of this situation? __

_____

_____

_____

62. Do you have any suggestions to further reduce barriers to black managerial
employment? _____

_____

_____

_____

PART IV. (WHITE MANAGERS' ATTITUDES TOWARD BLACKS)

Now I am going to read a series of statements you sometimes hear people make.
For each statement please tell me your degree of agreement. Please do not bother to
take much time with each statement; your first impression is perfectly all right.
(SHOW CARD 12)

63. A black, once promoted, could not be demoted, even if inadequate in his/her
new role, without undeserved charges of discrimination.
0. ____ Strongly disagree
1. ____ Disagree
2. ____ Agree
3. ____ Strongly agree

64. A black would be accepted by white subordinates only after he/she had been
given unusually difficult challenges in order to prove himself/herself.
0. ____ Strongly disagree
1. ____ Disagree
2. ____ Agree
3. ____ Strongly agree

65. There may be a few exceptions, but in general blacks are pretty much alike.
0. ____ Strongly disagree
1. ____ Disagree
2. ____ Agree
3. ____ Strongly agree

66. I can hardly imagine myself marrying a black.
    0. ___ Strongly disagree
    1. ___ Disagree
    2. ___ Agree
    3. ___ Strongly agree

67. Even though there are some exceptions, most blacks have annoying and offensive faults.
    0. ___ Strongly disagree
    1. ___ Disagree
    2. ___ Agree
    3. ___ Strongly agree

68. Blacks should be hired and promoted on the same basis as everyone else.
    0. ___ Strongly disagree
    1. ___ Disagree
    2. ___ Agree
    3. ___ Strongly agree

69. I probably would not choose a black person for promotion if an equally qualified nonblack were available.
    0. ___ Strongly disagree
    1. ___ Disagree
    2. ___ Agree
    3. ___ Strongly agree

70. In general I am reluctant to hire and promote blacks into important management positions.
    0. ___ Strongly disagree
    1. ___ Disagree
    2. ___ Agree
    3. ___ Strongly agree

71. Most blacks who aspire to become managers in the business world do not have the personal characteristics needed to become successful management persons in this company.
    0. ___ Strongly disagree
    1. ___ Disagree
    2. ___ Agree
    3. ___ Strongly agree

72. A black person usually has to be a little better than others to get ahead in this company.
    0. ___ Strongly disagree
    1. ___ Disagree
    2. ___ Agree
    3. ___ Strongly agree

73. In general this company is only paying lip service to the idea of equal opportunity employment for blacks.
    0. ____ Strongly disagree
    1. ____ Disagree
    2. ____ Agree
    3. ____ Strongly agree

79. Management should not be asked to influence social attitudes; its responsibility does not extend into taking public positions regarding civil rights.
    0. ____ Strongly disagree
    1. ____ Disagree
    2. ____ Agree
    3. ____ Strongly agree

75. In general blacks have low I.Q.s and less technical and analytical competence.
    0. ____ Strongly disagree
    1. ____ Disagree
    2. ____ Agree
    3. ____ Strongly agree

76. In general, blacks are pushy, loud, argumentative, arrogant, obnoxious, and aggressive.
    0. ____ Strongly disagree
    1. ____ Disagree
    2. ____ Agree
    3. ____ Strongly agree

Now we would like to ask more general questions about your attitude towards blacks.

77. What are some of the good and bad characteristics you have observed about black managers? _____
    _____
    _____
    _____
    _____

78. Do you hear derogatory remarks about blacks in your company?
    0. ____ yes   1. ____ no
    (IF YES)
    What has been your response to such remarks:

78a. With your subordinates? _____
    _____
    _____

78b. With your peers? _____
    _____
    _____

78c. With your superiors? _____
    _____
    _____

(ASK NEXT QUESTION ONLY IF YOU DO NOT HAVE A CLEAR OR DEFINITE PICTURE OF THE MANAGER'S ATTITUDES ABOUT BLACKS)

79.   In talking to various persons, we've found that some report less favorable feelings toward black people than do others. Drawing from your own personal feelings, what is *your* general impression of black people? _____

_____

_____

_____

Now we would like to ask you several questions about your personal contacts with blacks. (SHOW CARD 13)

80.   How frequently do you have contact with blacks on your job?

0. _____ Very frequently

1. _____ Fairly frequently

2. _____ Not very frequently

3. _____ Never

(IF NEVER, SKIP TO QUESTION 81)

80a.   Would you please elaborate on the type and recency of your contacts? _____

_____

_____

81.   How frequently do you have contact with blacks at social functions not related to work?

0. _____ Very frequently

1. _____ Fairly frequently

2. _____ Not very frequently

3. _____ Never

(IF NEVER SKIP TO SECTION 5)

81a.   Again, would you please elaborate on the type and recency of these social contacts? _____

_____

_____

PART IVB. (BLACK MANAGERS' ATTITUDES ABOUT THE BUSINESS WORLD AND THEIR PERSONAL EXPERIENCES)

Now we are going to ask you more specific questions about your attitudes about black managers and questions about your own personal experiences. (SHOW CARD 12)

82.   Blacks should be hired and promoted on the same basis as everyone else.

0. _____ Strongly disagree

1. _____ Disagree

2. _____ Agree

3. _____ Strongly agree

83. A black person usually has to be a little better than others to get ahead in this company.
    0. _____ Strongly disagree
    1. _____ Disagree
    2. _____ Agree
    3. _____ Strongly agree

84. In general this company is only paying lip service to the idea of equal opportunity employment for blacks.
    0. _____ Strongly disagree
    1. _____ Disagree
    2. _____ Agree
    3. _____ Strongly agree

84a. Would you give me some reasons for your answer? _____
_____
_____

85. Management should not be asked to influence social attitudes; its responsibility does not extend into taking public positions regarding civil rights.
    0. _____ Strongly disagree
    1. _____ Disagree
    2. _____ Agree
    3. _____ Strongly agree

86. I could hardly imagine myself marrying a white person.
    0. _____ Strongly disagree
    1. _____ Disagree
    2. _____ Agree
    3. _____ Strongly agree

87. Whites are superficially evaluated for promotion whereas blacks are carefully and thoroughly evaluated.
    0. _____ Strongly disagree
    1. _____ Disagree
    2. _____ Agree
    3. _____ Strongly agree

87a. Do you have firsthand knowledge to support your answer? _____
_____
_____
_____

88. All that really has changed in the past few years is that corporations have shifted the point at which they begin to apply discriminatory practices against their black managers. They will hire a black but will not allow him/her to realize his/her full potential.
    0. _____ Strongly disagree
    1. _____ Disagree
    2. _____ Agree
    3. _____ Strongly agree

88a. What is your evidence? _____
_____
_____

89. Is governmental pressure needed to force *industry* really to practice equal employment for blacks?
0. ____ yes   1. ____ no
(IF YES)
89a. What kind of governmental pressure? _____
_____
_____

90. Is governmental pressure needed to force *your company* to really practice equal employment for blacks?
0. ____ yes   1. ____ no
(IF YES)
90a. What kind of governmental pressure? _____
_____
_____

91. What incidental pressures must a black put up with that whites do not have to put up with? (PROBE ABOUT DISCRIMINATION IN FIRM)_____
_____
_____

92. Would you accept a transfer to a plant located in a small white city or town?
0. ____ yes   1. ____ no
92a. Could you tell me more about your attitude toward a transfer of that kind? __
_____
_____

93. If you hold a position previously held by whites, do you believe you have the same power and authority as the white person had?
0. ____ yes   1. ____ no
(IF NO)
93a. Why do you believe you do not have the same power and authority? _____
_____
_____

Here is a statement written by a black executive vice-president of a white firm. (SHOW CARD 13)
"Even those blacks who are hired for jobs which are not specifically public relations oriented (for example, chemists, accountants, engineers, marketing researchers,

data processing systems analysts and lawyers) find that they are expected to spend a good deal of their time "showcasing" for their corporate masters. These black employees are required to attend numerous public relations type meetings, race relations dinners, and equal employment opportunity-urban affairs conferences, spreading the gospel of their respective companies. In effect, they perform two jobs, one for which they were hired and the other for public relations."

94.   Do you generally agree or disagree with this statement?
       0. _____ agree   1. _____ disagree

94a.   Would you please make a few comments about this statement? _____
       _____
       _____
       _____

95.   Do you generally agree or disagree with this statement? (SHOW CARD 14)

"Many black people, especially separatists or Black Nationalists, believe that black people working in corporations are undermining the black movement toward developing viable black economic institutions. They say that the corporation physically and psychologically removes black people from the community; thus black people are deprived of the knowledge, technical skill, and expertise of the black manager.

       0. _____ agree   1. _____ disagree

95a.   Why do you (AGREE OR DISAGREE)? _____
       _____
       _____
       _____

96.   Have you ever been categorized in the black community as an "Uncle Tom" or "sellout," a traitor to black people and the black movement in general because of your position in this firm?
       0. _____ yes   1. _____ no
       (IF YES)

96a.   On what occasion? _____
       _____
       _____

97.   What is the best path for blacks as a group to pursue in this country? (SHOW CARD 15)
       0. _____ Form their own separate black nations
       1. _____ Withdraw into the urban areas and form separate all-black communities
       2. _____ Form strong social, political, and economic organizations to pressure white society into assuring blacks equal opportunity and freedom in the larger society
       3. _____ Assimilate and integrate completely into white society
       4. _____
          _____ Other (PLEASE SPECIFY)

97a. Why do you believe this is the best path?_____
_____
_____
_____

98.   What advice would you give an individual black person with regard to the best possible strategy to follow in this society in order to live a prosperous, free life? _____
_____
_____
_____

99.   With what segment of the black community do you have good communications (for example, militant, moderate, revolutionary, etc.)?_____
_____

99a. Why do you have good communications with them? _____
_____
_____

100. With what segments of the black community do you have poor communications? _____
_____

100a. Why do you have poor communications with them? _____
_____
_____

101. Would you advise a young black man or woman just out of school or college to enter the business world?
      0. _____ yes   1. _____ no
      (IF NO)

101a. Why not?_____
_____
_____
_____

      (IF YES)

101b. What would you say is the best way for a young black to achieve high managerial positions? _____
_____
_____
_____

102. What advice could you give to a black manager entering your company? ____
_____
_____
_____

   Now we would like to ask you several questions about your personal contacts with whites. (SHOW CARD 16)

103. How frequently do you have contact with whites on your job?
0. ＿＿ Very frequently
1. ＿＿ Fairly frequently
2. ＿＿ Not very frequently
3. ＿＿ Never
(IF NEVER SKIP TO QUESTION 104)

103a. Would you please elaborate on the type and recency of your contacts? ＿＿＿＿＿

＿＿

＿＿

＿＿

104. How frequently do you have contact with whites at social functions not related to work?
0. ＿＿ Very frequently
1. ＿＿ Fairly frequently
2. ＿＿ Not very frequently
3. ＿＿ Never
(IF NEVER SKIP TO THE NEXT SECTION)

104a. Again, would you please elaborate on the type and recency of these social contacts? ＿＿＿＿＿＿＿＿＿＿＿＿＿＿＿＿＿＿＿＿＿＿＿＿＿＿＿＿＿＿＿

＿＿

＿＿

＿＿

PART V. (IMAGE OF A PROMOTABLE MANAGER. TO BE GIVEN TO R TO FILL OUT)

105.   We would like you to complete this chart that has questions that are related to your image of a promotable manager. What is your *ideal image* of a promotable person (COL. I) and what are your images of the person who *actually* gets ahead *in your firm* (COL. II) and *in business generally* (COL. III)?

Please grade EACH ITEM in ALL THREE COLUMNS below, thus:
0 Mark PLUS (+) for items you deem HELPFUL for promotion TO SUPERVISOR AND BEYOND
1 Mark ZERO (0) for items you deem IRRELEVANT for promotion TO SUPERVISOR AND BEYOND
2 Mark MINUS (−) for items you deem HARMFUL for promotion TO SUPERVISOR AND BEYOND

HOW ITEMS RATE IN *MY IDEA* OF
A PROMOTABLE PERSON

	ITEMS	A I. Ideally IN MY OPINION	B II. Actually IN MY FIRM	C III. Actually IN BUSINESS GENERALLY
	EDUCATION AND TRAINING			
a.	College Education			
b.	Graduate Work in Business Administration			
c.	Graduate of "Ivy League" College			
d.	Technical knowledge of specific job to be done			
e.	Seniority			
	PHYSICAL CHARAC-TERISTICS			
f.	Age: Under 30			
g.	Under 45			
h.	Over 45			
i.	Race: Negro			
j.	Oriental			
k.	White			
l.	Sex: Male			
m.	Female			

| ITEMS | HOW ITEMS RATE IN *MY IDEA* OF A PROMOTABLE PERSON | | |
	A I. Ideally IN MY OPINION	B II. Actually IN MY FIRM	C III. Actually IN BUSINESS GENERALLY
SOCIAL FACTORS			
n. Artistic, cultural interests, wide reading			
o. Community interests and activities			
p. Membership in local country club			
q. National origin: Continental USA			
r. Chicano			
s. Foreign country			
t. "Pull" with top management			
u. Regular attendance at a house of worship			
v. Religion: Catholic			
w. Jewish			
x. Protestant			
y. Spouse who is helpful to career			

PART VI. (COMPANY'S EMPLOYMENT POLICIES)

Section A. Employment Data

106. How would you describe your company's growth in the past eleven years?
    0. ＿＿＿ Phenomenal
    1. ＿＿＿ Rapid
    2. ＿＿＿ Moderate
    3. ＿＿＿ Slow
    4. ＿＿＿ Very slow
    5. ＿＿＿ Nil

107. How has your total employment changed since 1960?
    0. ＿＿＿ Has increased substantially
    1. ＿＿＿ Has increased slightly
    2. ＿＿＿ Has decreased substantially
    3. ＿＿＿ Has decreased slightly
    4. ＿＿＿ Has been relatively stable
    5. ＿＿＿ Has fluctuated, but with little net change

108. If total employment has changed appreciably in size since 1960, please indicate the main reasons. _____

_____
_____
_____
_____

109. We would like to have the position titles, area of work, and salary levels of all your black executives.

Position Title	Area (Finance, Personnel, etc.)	Salary Level
_____	_____	_____
_____	_____	_____
_____	_____	_____
_____	_____	_____
_____	_____	_____

110. When was the first time that your company hired a black for a nonmanagerial position? _____Date

111. When was the first time that your company hired or promoted blacks into management positions? _____Date

112. Which departments or divisions are without black managers?

_____
_____
_____

113. What is the main reason for the absence of black managers in those departments or divisions?_____

_____
_____
_____
_____

Section B. General Employment Questions

114. Who is in charge of your employment policies?

Name	Position Title
_____	_____
_____	_____
_____	_____

115. Does this policy vary from one part of the country to another?
0. ____ yes   1. ____ no   2. ____ not applicable
(IF YES)

115a. In what manner and in what part of the U. S. does it vary? _____

_____
_____

116. Is this policy written?
0. ____ yes   1. ____ no

117. Is this policy ever reviewed?
      0. _____ yes   1. _____ no
      (IF YES)
117a. How frequently? _____
      _____
      _____
      _____

      (IF POLICY REVIEWED)
118. Who reviews the policy?
                    Name   Position Title

      _____   _____

      _____   _____

      _____   _____

      _____   _____

119. In the administration of an employment program in your company, what is
      the usual procedure of policy enforcement? _____
      _____
      _____
      _____

Section C. Recruiting

120. In general do you recruit at colleges and universities?
      0. _____ yes   1. _____ no
121. Do you recruit at colleges and/or universities whose students are pre-
      dominantly members of minority groups?
      0. _____ yes   1. _____ no
      (IF YES)
121a. Which major universities or colleges? _____
      _____

122. When did you start recruiting at the minority colleges/universities? _____Date
123. Do you attempt to select, *as potential managers,* applicants with particular
      majors or courses of study in their educational backgrounds such as business
      administration, engineering, natural sciences, social sciences or the hu-
      manities?
      0. _____ yes   1. _____ no
      (IF YES)
123a. What majors or courses of study do you favor? _____
      _____
      _____

124. Do you use employment agencies for recruiting potential managers?
      0. _____ yes   1. _____ no
      (IF YES)
124a. What are the names of the agencies? _____
      _____
      _____

125.   What other recruiting mechanisms do you use to recruit potential managers?

_____

_____

126.   What is the most important and productive managerial recruiting source for
       your company? _____

_____

_____

_____

126a. Why is this?_____

_____

_____

127.   Do you have any other general remarks concerning your management recruit-
       ing methods? _____

_____

_____

Section D. Training Programs

128.   Does your company have training programs for managers?

       0. _____ yes   1. _____ no

       (IF YES)

128a. What type of program and what are the average number of participants?

                    Type of Program   Average No. of Participants

       _____   _____

       _____   _____

       _____   _____

       _____   _____

129.   What has been the average number of blacks in these programs? _____#

Section E. Hiring and Promoting

130.   What % of your vacancies are filled from within? _____%

131.   Does your company use tests to help determine which people are *hired* for
       managerial positions?

       0. _____ yes   1. _____ no

       (IF YES)

131a. What types of tests are used? (i.e., psychological, aptitude, etc.) _____

_____

_____

132.   Does your company use tests to help determine which managers are
       promoted?

       0. _____ yes   1. _____ no

       (IF YES)

132a. What types of tests are used? (i.e., psychological, aptitude, etc.) _____

_____

_____

133. Is a manager's racial attitude a factor in promotion?
0. ____ yes   1. ____ no
(IF YES)

133a. Why do you believe this is so? _____

_____

_____

_____

PART VII. (EQUAL EMPLOYMENT OPPORTUNITY PROGRAM)

134. Has any municipal, state, or federal agency contacted your company to review your practices with respect to minority employment?
0. ____ yes   1. ____ no
(IF YES)

134a. In what manner?_____

_____

135. Has your company been the target for any picketing, selective buying campaigns, etc., with the purpose of forcing your company to change its employment policy towards blacks?
0. ____ yes   1. ____ no
(IF YES)

135a. Could you give me more details as to the date, nature, length of time, etc.? ___

_____

_____

_____

136. Does your company have an active policy of encouraging its managers to involve themselves in black community affairs?
0. ____ yes   1. ____ no

137. Did your company participate in the Plans for Progress Program?
0. ____ yes   1. ____ no
(IF YES)

137a. When did it become a member? _____Date

138. Is your company a member of the National Alliance of Businessmen?
0. ____ yes   1. ____ no
(IF YES)

138a. When did it become a member? _____Date

139. Do you require people or firms you deal with to have an equal employment policy orientation?
0. ____ yes   1. ____ no

139a. Why is this?_____

_____

_____

_____

(IF ANSWER TO QUESTION 139 IS YES)

139b. How do you know the company or people are actually following an EEO Program?_____

_____
_____
_____

140. In January 1970, Secretary of Labor, George P. Schultz, amended Title 41 of the Code of Federal Regulations, to require each firm with fifty or more employees and a contract of $50,000 or more to submit a written Affirmative Action Compliance Program. When did your company first implement its Affirmative Action Program? (NOTE: IT COULD BE BEFORE JANUARY 1970) _____Date

141. If your program was developed before January 1970, were there any special circumstances that led to the Affirmative Action Program? _____

_____
_____

142. Who are the people in the corporate headquarters primarily responsible for the administration of your AAP?

Name	Position
_____	_____
_____	_____
_____	_____
_____	_____

143. Does the top administrator of the program report to a higher authority?
0. ____ yes   1. ____ no
(IF YES)

143a. What is the title and department of the higher authority? _____

_____

144. Does more than one department share responsibility for the program?
0. ____ yes   1. ____ no
(IF YES)

144a. Which departments? _____

_____

145. Are there any special formal procedures used to check the enforcement of your AAP?
0. ____ yes   1. ____ no
(IF YES)

145a. What are they? _____

_____

146. Are there any informal procedures used by corporate headquarters to check compliance in the divisions? (i.e., telephone conversations, informal chats, etc.)
0. ____ yes   1. ____ no
(IF YES)

146a. Would you be more specific about the informal procedures? _____

_____

_____

_____

146b. How frequently are these informal checks made? _____

_____

147. Is setting goals and timetables an essential element in an affirmative action
      program (AAP)?
      0. _____ yes   1. _____ no

147a. Would you please explain your answer? _____

_____

_____

_____

148. Have any of the procedures that you developed initially in implementing your
      AAP been modified since that time?
      0. _____ yes   1. _____ no
      (IF YES)

148a. For each change, can you indicate the type of change, the approximate date of
      change, and the major considerations that led to the change?

	Type of Change	Date
1.	_____	_____
2.	_____	_____
3.	_____	_____
4.	_____	_____
5.	_____	_____
6.	_____	_____

Major Considerations

1. _____

2. _____

3. _____

4. _____

5. _____

6. _____

149. Which one of the following would be considered a major, good, minor, or no measure of success by your company in a program of equal employment opportunity?

	0 MAJOR MEASURE	1 GOOD MEASURE	2 MINOR MEASURE	3 NO MEASURE
a. Number of black employees in relation to the number of blacks in the community	___	___	___	___
b. Distribution of blacks through job classifications	___	___	___	___
c. The income level of the blacks in the company	___	___	___	___
d. The visibility of blacks in company jobs	___	___	___	___
e. Job mobility of blacks in the company	___	___	___	___
f. The presence of black employees in the management, technical, or supervisory levels of the company	___	___	___	___
g. The number of entry jobs that have been filled by blacks	___	___	___	___
h. _____ _____ _____ ___ Other (SPECIFY)	___	___	___	___

150. What problems did you anticipate prior to the adoption of these minority group employment practices to be major, some, minor, or no problem in your firm?

	0 MAJOR PROBLEM	1 SOME PROBLEM	2 MINOR PROBLEM	3 NO PROBLEM
a. Resistance by white workers	___	___	___	___
b. Lack of qualified blacks to fill available jobs	___	___	___	___

  c. Interference with
    productivity or
    worker efficiency ____ ____ ____ ____

  d. Community opposi-
    tion ____ ____ ____ ____

  e. Poor customer rela-
    tions where blacks
    had to deal with
    whites ____ ____ ____ ____

  f. Resistance by super-
    visors ____ ____ ____ ____

  g. Resistance by execu-
    tives ____ ____ ____ ____

  h. Black dissatisfaction
    with available job
    opportunities ____ ____ ____ ____

  i. _____
    __ Other (SPECIFY) ____ ____ ____ ____

151. Looking back since the development of your AAP, which of these problems, if
   any, did occur? Again, please rate them according to major, some, minor, or no
   problem.

	0 MAJOR PROBLEM	1 SOME PROBLEM	2 MINOR PROBLEM	3 NO PROBLEM
a. Resistance by white workers	____	____	____	____

b. Lack of qualified
  blacks to fill avail-
  able jobs
	____	____	____	____

c. Interference with
  productivity or
  worker efficiency
	____	____	____	____

d. Community opposi- tion	____	____	____	____

e. Poor customer rela-
  tions where blacks
  had to deal with
  whites
	____	____	____	____

f. Resistance by super- visors	____	____	____	____
g. Resistance by execu- tives	____	____	____	____

h.   Black dissatisfaction
     with available job
     opportunities   ____   ____   ____   ____
i.   _____

     _____
     __ Other (SPECIFY) ____   ____   ____   ____

152. Looking back on your own experiences with a nondiscriminatory policy, what
      advice would you give a company that was just beginning to hire and promote
      blacks for managerial positions, especially advice in the area of employment
      and policy procedures? _____
      _____
      _____
      _____

PART VIII. (PERSONAL BACKGROUND)

Now just a few more minutes on some questions about your personal background
and we'll be through.

153. First, what is your date of birth? _____
                                          Mo.   Day   Year

154. In what state did you live most of the time you were growing up—until you
      were about eighteen years old?
                    _____ State
                    _____ Other country (SPECIFY)

155. In what state have you lived most of your adult life?
                    _____ State
                    _____ Other country (SPECIFY)

156. Would you please tell me what city or town you live in?
                    _____ Name

157. Do blacks live in your neighborhood?
      0. ____ yes   1. ____ no
      (IF YES)

157a. About what percentage of blacks live in your neighborhood? ____ %

158. What is your present marital status?
      0. ____ Single
      1. ____ Married
      2. ____ Divorced
      3. ____ Widowed
      4. ____ Separated
      (IF MARRIED)

159. Does your spouse work?
      0. ____ yes   1. ____ no
      (IF YES)

159a. What is your spouse's occupation? _____

159b. What is the name of the firm or organization that he/she is working for? ____
_____

159c. Number of hours per week? _____

160. What was the highest grade of school or college you completed? (CIRCLE ONE)

0		1	2	3	4		5	6	7	8	9
8 or less		9	10	11	12		13	14	15	16	Graduate Training
			High School					College			

(IF 4 YEARS OF COLLEGE OR MORE)

160a. What college degrees do you have? (RECORD COL. I)

160b. What was your major field? (RECORD COL. II)

160c. What was the name of the institution you received it from? (RECORD COL. III)

I	II	III
Degree(s)	Major Field	Institution(s)
_____	_____	_____
_____	_____	_____
_____	_____	_____

161. Did you ever take any special courses or formal training—things like trade school, business school, a correspondence course, or a job training program?
0. ____ yes   1. ____ no
(IF YES)

161a. What type of training? (RECORD COL. I)

161b. How long was the training? (RECORD COL. II)

161c. Where did you obtain the training? (RECORD COL. III)

I	II	III
Type of Training	Length	Place of Training
_____	_____	_____
_____	_____	_____
_____	_____	_____
_____	_____	_____

162. How necessary is your scientific, technical, or professional training in your present position?
0. ____ Not very necessary
1. ____ Very necessary
2. ____ Absolutely necessary
3. ____ I have no such training

163. Is there any formal scientific, technical, or professional training you lack which you feel would be especially helpful in your position?
0. ____ yes   1. ____ no
(IF YES)

163a. What type of training? _____
_____
_____

164. What was the highest grade of school or college your spouse completed? (CIRCLE ONE)

0	1	2	3	4	5	6	7	8	9
8 or less	9	10	11	12	13	14	15	16	Graduate Training
	High School				College				

(IF 4 YEARS OF COLLEGE OR MORE)

164a. What college degrees did she/he receive? (RECORD COL. I)

164b. What was her/his major field? (RECORD COL. II)

164c. What was the name of the institution she/he received it from? (RECORD COL. III)

I	II	III
Degree(s)	Major Field	Institution(s)
_____	_____	_____
_____	_____	_____
_____	_____	_____
_____	_____	_____

165. How many years of school did your father complete? (CIRCLE ONE)

0	1	2	3	4	5	6	7	8	9
8 or less	9	10	11	12	13	14	15	16	Graduate Training
	High School				College				

166. How many years of school did your mother complete? (CIRCLE ONE)

0	1	2	3	4	5	6	7	8	9
8 or less	9	10	11	12.	13	14	15	16	Graduate Training
	High School				College				

167. When you were a teenager what was the best job your father had? (BE SPECIFIC)_____

168. When your spouse was a teenager what was the best job his/her father had? (BE SPECIFIC)_____

169. What is your religious preference?
   0. _____ Catholic
   1. _____Protestant (SPECIFY DENOMINATION)
   2. _____ Jewish
   3. _____Other (SPECIFY)

170. Approximately how frequently do you attend religious services?
   0. _____ More than once a week
   1. _____ Once a week
   2. _____ Once or twice a month
   3. _____ A few times a year
   4. _____ Never

171. Politically do you consider yourself a:
   0. _____ Radical
   1. _____ Liberal
   2. _____ Moderate
   3. _____ Conservative
   4. _____ Right winger
   5. _____Other (SPECIFY)

172. What is your political affiliation?
     0. _____ Democrat
     1. _____ Republican
     2. _____ Independent
     3. _____Other (SPECIFY)
     4. _____ No interest in politics

173. Now here is a list of clubs and organizations that many people belong to.
     Please look at this list (SHOW CARD 17), and tell me which of these kinds
     of organizations you belong to, if any. (CHECK BELOW)
     0. _____ Church-connected groups
     1. _____ Fraternal organizations or lodges
     2. _____ Veteran's organizations
     3. _____ Business or civic groups, service clubs
     4. _____ Neighborhood clubs or community centers
     5. _____ Organizations of people of the same race and/or nationality
     6. _____ Civil rights organizations (NAACP, CORE, Urban League, Black
              Panthers, etc.)
     7. _____ Country clubs
     8. _____ Professional groups
     9. _____ Political clubs or organizations
     0. _____ Social clubs
     1. _____ Charitable and welfare organizations
     2. _____Other (SPECIFY)
     3. _____ None

(IF INTERVIEWEE BELONGS TO NO ORGANIZATIONS, THE IN-
TERVIEW IS OVER. QUESTIONS ON THE FOLLOWING PAGE ASKED
OF EACH GROUP R IS IN. REPEAT QUESTIONS FOR EACH ORGANI-
ZATION UNTIL ALL ARE COVERED.)

174. What is the name of
     (TYPE OF GROUP)?
     (IF NOT CLEAR: as
     you see it, what
     are the main things
     it does?)

175. What year did you
     join?

176. Would you say you
     are strongly inter-
     ested in this group,
     somewhat interested,
     or not very inter-
     ested in it?

177. Why do you feel
     this way?

178. (FOR WHITES ONLY)
     Are there any
     black members?

178a. (FOR BLACKS ONLY)
     Are there any
     white members?

INTERVIEWER DATA EVALUATION FORM (TO BE COMPLETED IMMEDIATELY AFTER THE INTERVIEW)

179. Racial background of interviewee:
     1. _____ Black male
     2. _____ Black female
     3. _____ White male
     4. _____ White female

180. Is this interview of questionable value, generally adequate, or high quality?
     0. _____ Questionable
     1. _____ Generally adequate
     2. _____ High quality
     (IF QUESTIONABLE)

180a. Why? (CHECK EACH WHICH APPLIES TO RESPONDENT)
     0. _____ Evasive, suspicious
     1. _____ Confused by frequent interruptions
     2. _____ Confused—didn't understand questions
     3. _____ Other (SPECIFY)

181. How was rapport with R?
  - 0. _____ Excellent throughout
  - 1. _____ Average
  - 2. _____ Poor throughout
  - 3. _____ Started good, became poor
  - 4. _____ Started poor, became good

182. What was R's interest in the interview?
  - 0. _____ High
  - 1. _____ Average
  - 2. _____ Low

183. Was there any indication that length of interview affected rapport? _____
_____

184. What was the interview setting? _____
_____

185. Who else was present during the interview, and what effect did this have?
  _____ Only R Present

Persons Present	How Long	What Effect
_____	_____	_____
_____	_____	_____
_____	_____	_____

Frequency Distributions*

1. What college degrees do you have?

	Black Managers	White Managers
Bachelor	67%	50%
Bachelor and at least One Year of Graduate Work Completed	1	6
Bachelor and Teaching Credentials	1	2
Bachelor and Master	17	20
Bachelor and MBA	7	13
Bachelor and Law	7	5
Bachelor, MBA, and Law	0	2
Bachelor, Master, and Ph.D.	0	2

2. What was your major field?

	Black Managers	White Managers
Business Administration	24%	34%
Engineering: Mechanical, Industrial, Electrical, Civil	10	21
Accounting	10	5
Sociology, Anthropology	9	6
Political Science, History	7	8
Law	6	6
Chemistry	6	1
Math	6	1
Economics	4	14
Social Sciences	4	4
Education	4	2
English, Speech, Journalism	3	6
Biology, Zoology	3	2
Philosophy	3	2
Art, Music, Drama	3	1
Home Economics	3	0
Psychology	1	7
Religion	1	1
Other	3	0

* Some of the total percentages in this appendix are over or under 100 because of rounding errors and/or due to multiple responses of interviewees.

3. What was the name of the institution you received degree(s) from?

	Black Managers	White Managers
IVY LEAGUE SCHOOLS: Harvard, Dartmouth, Columbia, Cornell, Univ. of Pennsylvania	1%	7%
SELECT PRIVATE UNIVERSITIES/COLLEGES: Univ. of Chicago, Smith, Occidental, Claremont, Stanford, MIT, New York Univ., Northwestern	13	13
SELECT PUBLIC UNIVERSITIES/COLLEGES: U.C. Berkeley, Univ. of Michigan, Univ. of Wisconsin, UCLA	8	31
SELECT BLACK UNIVERSITIES/COLLEGES: Lincoln Univ., Hampton Institute, Tuskeegee, Morehouse, Fisk, Howard, Morgan State	21	0
OTHER PRIVATE UNIVERSITIES/COLLEGES: Washington Lee, Univ. of Pacific, Purdue, Whittier, U.S.C., Suffolk Univ., Univ. of Puget Sound, Golden Gate College, Geneva College, Miami of Ohio, Williams College	21	16
OTHER PUBLIC UNIVERSITIES: Ohio Univ., Univ. of Colorado, Univ. of Okla., Univ. of Pittsburgh, Univ. of Md., Arizona Univ., Univ. of Iowa	8	20
STATE COLLEGES: Cal. State, L.A., Long Beach, Hayward, San Jose, San Francisco State, Sacramento State, Penn State, Weber State, Arizona State, Washington State, Oregon State, Florida State	28	22

OTHER BLACK UNIVERSITIES/COLLEGES: Prairie View College, Wiley College, Grambling, Southern Univ., Toogaloo College, Texas Southern Univ.	14	0
PRIVATE RELIGIOUS COLLEGES: Loyola of Chicago, U.S.F., Providence College, S.F. College for Women, St. Mary's, Boston College, St. Peter's College	7	14
OTHER UNIVERSITIES/ COLLEGES: Pasadena School of the Playhouse, Univ. of Hiedelberg	0	2
JUNIOR COLLEGES: Compton Jr. College, Santa Rosa, City College of S.F.	3	2

4. What is your present marital status?

	Black Managers	White Managers
Single	11%	11%
Married	74	82
Divorced	13	5
Widowed	0	1
Separated	2	1

5. What was the highest grade of school or college your spouse completed?

	Black Managers	White Managers
8 Years or Less	0%	1%
9 Years	0	0
10 Years	1	0
11 Years	1	2
12 Years	31	38
13 Years	17	10
14 Years	21	18
15 Years	5	8
16 Years	24	24
16 + Years	0	0

6.   When your spouse was a teenager what was the best job his/her father
     had?

	Black Managers	White Managers
Unskilled Laborer	18%	10%
Skilled Laborer	17	18
Small Business Owner	6	15
Medium Business Owner	2	2
Low Level Supervisor/Manager	0	4
Middle Level Supervisor/Manager	1	6
Upper Level Supervisor/Manager	0	2
Professional: Engineers, Real Estate, Accountant, Publisher/ Editor, Statistician	2	14
Lawyer or Doctor	0	4
Clergyman	1	0
School Principal or Professor	6	2
School Teacher or Counselor	3	2
Governmental Service	13	8
Large Farm Owner	2	1
Small Farm Owner	1	2
Doesn't know	21	3
Didn't Have a Father	6	2
Other	1	2

7.   Which one of the following would be considered a major, good, minor,
     or no measure of success by your company in a program of equal
     employment opportunity?

	MAJOR MEASURE		GOOD MEASURE		MINOR MEASURE		NO MEASURE	
	Black Mgrs.	White Mgrs.	Black Mgrs.	White Mgrs.	Black Mgrs.	White Mgrs.	Black Mgrs.	White Mgrs.
Number of black employees in relation to the number of blacks in the community	4	4	1	3	1	1	0	0
Distribution of blacks through job classifications	5	5	1	2	0	1	0	0
Income level of the blacks in the company	4	1	2	3	0	4	0	0
Visibility of blacks in company jobs	1	0	1	2	3	5	1	1

	MAJOR MEASURE		GOOD MEASURE		MINOR MEASURE		NO MEASURE	
	Black Mgrs.	White Mgrs.	Black Mgrs.	White Mgrs.	Black Mgrs.	White Mgrs.	Black Mgrs.	White Mgrs.
Job mobility of blacks in company	3	3	3	2	0	3	0	0
Presence of black employees in the management, technical, or supervisory levels of company	5	3	1	3	0	2	0	0
Number of entry level jobs that have been filled by blacks	1	4	1	3	2	1	2	0

8. What problems did you anticipate prior to the adoption of these minority group employment practices to be major, some, minor, or no problem in your firm?

	MAJOR PROBLEM		SOME PROBLEM		MINOR PROBLEM		NO PROBLEM	
	Black Mgrs.	White Mgrs.	Black Mgrs.	White Mgrs.	Black Mgrs.	White Mgrs.	Black Mgrs.	White Mgrs.
Resistance by white workers	2	3	4	3	0	1	0	1
Lack of qualified blacks to fill available jobs	2	1	4	7	0	0	0	0
Interference with productivity or worker efficiency	0	0	2	0	3	4	1	4
Community opposition	1	0	1	0	2	1	2	7
Poor customer relations where blacks had to deal with whites	2	0	1	1	2	1	1	6
Resistance by supervisors	2	1	4	3	0	3	0	1
Resistance by executives	1	0	5	1	0	4	0	3
Black dissatisfaction with available job opportunities	0	0	6	4	0	4	0	0

9. Looking back since the development of your AAP, which of these problems, if any, did occur? Again, please rate them according to major, some, minor, or no problem.

	MAJOR PROBLEM		SOME PROBLEM		MINOR PROBLEM		NO PROBLEM	
	Black Mgrs.	White Mgrs.	Black Mgrs.	White Mgrs.	Black Mgrs.	White Mgrs.	Black Mgrs.	White Mgrs.
Resistance by white workers	0	1	4	4	2	1	0	2
Lack of qualified blacks to fill available jobs	1	1	2	5	2	1	1	1
Interference with productivity or worker efficiency	0	0	0	1	3	2	3	5
Community opposition	0	0	0	0	4	1	2	7
Poor customer relations where blacks had to deal with whites	0	0	0	0	4	2	2	6
Resistance by supervisors	1	1	3	3	2	2	0	2
Resistance by executives	0	0	4	1	1	2	1	5
Black dissatisfaction with available job opportunities	0	1	3	3	2	4	1	0

10. At what managerial level (lower, middle, or upper) do you believe your company's AAP meets the most resistance?

	Black Managers	White Managers
Lower Management	25%	36%
Middle Management	37	19
Upper Management	42	18
No Resistance	2	22
All Levels	5	3
Resistance is Individual	0	3
Don't know	1	5

10a. Why is resistance most at lower level?

There are many more blacks competing with whites at the lower level; therefore, the whites	67	59

feel more threatened, fear blacks
more, and become more
antagonistic toward blacks than
middle and upper level white
managers.

Because of the relatively low level of education of the individuals lower management is the least enlightened management level, which leads to greater racial hatreds.	23	32
It is hard to communicate and obtain the acceptance of the AAP by the lower level of management.	7	18
The middle and upper levels of management are not threatened because there are few, if any, black managers at those levels; however, they will begin to resist the AAP when blacks begin to compete with them.	7	7

10b.   Why is resistance most at middle level?

	Black Managers	White Managers
Middle management is the most prejudiced managerial level because most of the white managers have leveled off in their careers; thus they are concerned with protecting their positions from black managers who could displace them; there are relatively fewer middle management positions; thus this level fears black competition more than the other levels.	35%	17%
The paucity of black managers in the middle level indicates that it is at this level that blacks meet the most resistance.	30	13
Middle management is older, more conservative, and has more rigid attitudes than other levels; therefore, they are least likely to accept change in the area of equal employment opportunities.	21	53

	Black Managers	White Managers
Middle management distorts the company's AAP because upper management does not insure that it is being properly carried out.	9	7
Individuals in the upper level of management are alert, receptive, and innovative and the individuals in the lower level of management are younger and feel less threatened; therefore, the middle level of management is the level at which blacks meet the most resistance.	5	10

10c.   Why is resistance most at upper level?

	Black Managers	White Managers
Blacks are at a disadvantage because subjective criteria and politics play a greater role for the few upper management positions; blacks are not acceptable at this level because social intercourse and interaction play a very important role.	29%	24%
Upper management does not want blacks to have real power to make policy decisions.	24	14
Upper management is really not committed to a nondiscriminatory employment policy.	12	14
The fact that there are no blacks in upper management suggests that it is at this level where blacks meet the most resistance.	10	14
Upper management is generally older, more conservative, and more rigid in their attitudes than lower and middle management; thus, they are more racist.	8	10
There are extremely few upper management positions; thus the great competition for these positions brings out the white racist attitudes.	6	7
Other	10	17

11. Length of total service with present company.

	Black Managers	White Managers
0–2 years	17%	4%
2(+)–4 years	28	5
4(+)–6 years	16	6
6(+)–8 years	15	5
8(+)–10 years	8	7
10(+)–12 years	3	11
12(+)–14 years	5	7
14(+)–16 years	6	11
16(+)–18 years	2	6
18(+)–20 years	1	5
20(+)–22 years	1	7
22(+)–24 years	0	4
24(+)–26 years	0	10
26(+)–28 years	0	5
28(+)–30 years	0	3
30(+)–32 years	0	2
32(+)–34 years	0	1
Over 34 years	0	4

12. How many people are directly under your supervision?

	Black Managers	White Managers
0	31%	13%
1–5	33	19
6–30	24	28
31–80	8	13
81–180	3	9
181–380	1	7
381–780	0	5
781–1580	0	3
Over 1580	0	4

13. All that really has changed in the past few years is that corporations have shifted the point at which they begin to apply discriminatory practices against their black managers. They will hire a black but will not allow him/her to realize his/her full potentials.

	Black Managers
Strongly disagree	3%
Disagree	28
Agree	48
Strongly agree	22
Other	1

13a.   What is your evidence? (Strongly disagree; Disagree)

	Black Managers
Respondent's personal experiences.	24%
This company has a firm commitment to an AAP.	15
Respondent cannot really agree with the statement because most companies are only in the first stages of an Affirmative Action Program; the progress of blacks cannot be measured yet.	15
There has been some change, but not a substantial change; corporations need to make greater efforts.	12
Respondent knows of blacks above him/her at the present time and/or blacks who have been promoted.	9
Most corporations only want blacks as show pieces or "token niggers," but there are a few who are not.	9
Most corporations have a firm commitment to equal employment opportunities.	6
Other	12

13b.   What is your evidence? (Agree; Strongly agree)

	Black Managers
Respondents personally know of blacks in the company who are qualified to be at higher levels, but are not promoted.	21%
Respondent's personal experiences.	15
Most corporations still practice discrimination.	12
No evidence; just a general feeling.	10
Most corporations put limits on blacks by keeping them in a black "bag" and limiting their power.	7
Respondents believe that the company shoud have blacks at higher levels.	7
Respondents know of cases where blacks were promoted only to a certain level but not higher, even	6

though they were qualified,
because the company felt it was
not the "right" time.

Tokenism; companies promote only   5
a few blacks for show.

Corporations are not ready to   4
employ blacks at high levels of
management.

Other   6

14. If you hold a position previously held by whites, do you believe you
have the same power and authority as the white person had?

	Black Managers
Yes	68%
No	32

14a. Why do you believe you do not have the same power and authority?

	Black Managers
Respondents are always being checked on; they are not given the same power, authority, and latitude that whites are given.	46%
Respondents feel they have to prove themselves before they are given the power and authority, whereas whites are given them immediately.	41
Whites do not accept blacks' mental reasoning ability; they feel blacks are mentally inferior.	14
Whites are unable to relate to blacks; they bypass them and go to their superiors.	11
Respondents have not had many opportunities to exercise their power and authority so they can't answer the question specifically.	5
Respondents' hiring power has been limited; they feel they should have more authority to say who is going to work for them.	3
White customers won't accept blacks with a great deal of power.	3
Respondents feel they might have the same power, but just being black makes them paranoid.	3

15. "Even those blacks who are hired for jobs that are not specifically public relations oriented (for example, chemists, accountants, engineers, marketing researchers, data processing systems analysts, and lawyers) find that they are expected to spend a good deal of their time showcasing for their corporate masters. These black employees are required to attend numerous public relations type meetings, race relations dinners, and equal employment opportunity–urban affairs conferences, spreading the gospel of their respective companies. In effect, they perform two jobs, one for which they were hired and the other for public relations."

Do you generally agree or disagree with this statement?

	Black Managers
Agree	78%
Disagree	22
Doesn't know	0

15a. Would you please make a few comments about this statement? (Agree responses)

	Black Managers
Respondents' personal experiences where they have done what the firms asked such as attend meetings, dinners and conferences, give speeches, and have their pictures taken.	24%
Companies need to improve their image with the public so they encourage blacks to showcase.	21
Respondents have not been asked to perform public relations functions, but they do know of people in the firm who do perform these functions.	16
Respondents have been asked to attend conferences, give speeches to black groups, and so on, but they would not do it.	13
Firms showcase their blacks because of governmental pressures.	12
Respondents know that it does not happen in their firms, but know of cases in other firms.	6
All management positions are in effect public relations positions.	6

	Black Managers
It is a good thing if it is actually showing what the company is doing, but it is bad if the company isn't doing anything.	4
Other	7

15b. Would you please make a few comments about this statement? (Disagree responses)

	Black Managers
Respondents have not experienced that kind of a situation in their companies.	57%
It is not required, but the company would like blacks to go along with their requests to attend conferences, make speeches, and so on.	11
For the most part companies are interested in work efficiency; if they wanted a public relations person, they would hire a black to perform the functions.	7
Respondents think it is good to let people know what's happening on a voluntary basis.	7
Other	18

16. What advice could you give to a black manager entering your company?

	Black Managers
Blacks should stand up for what they believe is right; be their own men; blacks should be themselves.	38%
Blacks should be wary of corporate politics and play along with them.	26
Blacks should always work hard at whatever they are doing and do it well.	24
Blacks should pursue an education; they should get the best education available.	24
Respondent would give no advice.	16
Blacks should promote themselves, i.e., they should get to know their supervisors and let them know	12

their goals, aspirations, and
feelings about their job situation;
they should use their personal
initiative; they should be
aggressive.

Blacks should watch their backs, be skeptical and careful.	8
Blacks should stay abreast of corporate and business happenings and developments.	7
Blacks should be aware that they have to do their jobs better than the white man.	6
Blacks should forget about their color; they should not be color conscious.	2
Other	12

17. Do you believe your firm is more careful in promoting black employees than white employees because it wants to be certain that blacks will succeed before promoting?

	Black Managers	White Managers
Yes	67%	26%
No	33	74

17a. What is the evidence? (Yes responses)

	Black Managers	White Managers
Respondent believes the blacks are screened and investigated much more carefully than whites; blacks are given more tests (written or on-the-job) and are observed more than whites.	22%	7%
Black managers' personal experiences.	20	0
Respondent's knowledge of qualified and deserving blacks being held back while less qualified and less deserving whites are promoted over them.	19	2
No evidence; just a feeling.	15	12
There are only a few blacks above low level managerial positions.	9	2
Respondent believes that only the "right" type of black is promoted,	4	0

i.e., blacks who do not speak out,
who are not too militant, and not
too aggressive.

Blacks have a much higher success record than whites.	3	29
The firm is more careful in promoting blacks because it would be a big disservice to blacks and to the company to promote a black who could not do the job.	1	15
White managers' personal involvements or first hand knowledge that the company is more careful with black employees than with white employees.	0	20
Other	8	18

17b.   What is the evidence? (No responses)

	Black Managers	White Managers
No evidence; just a feeling.	28%	17%
Everyone is promoted on the same basis.	19	39
Blacks are promoted as a matter of convenience to governmental and outside social pressures.	14	6
The company had such a practice several years ago, but now it does not.	8	2
Blacks are given the advantage over whites; the company's policy is just the opposite—it is less careful in promoting blacks than whites.	6	30
Respondent's personal experiences.	5	0
Other	19	7

18.   Which of the remaining things on the card is *second* in importance?

	Black Managers	White Managers
The work is important and gives a sense of accomplishment	26%	17%
High income	23	14
The work is interesting	21	37
Chances for advancement	19	21
The work gives lots of chances to meet people	6	6
No danger of being fired; security	3	3
Lots of free time	3	3

18a.   Which of the remaining things on the card would be of *least* importance
        to you?

	Black Managers	White Managers
Lots of free time	53%	55%
No danger of being fired; security	28	30
The work gives lots of chances to meet people	11	11
High income	6	3
Chances for advancement	3	2
Other	0	1

19.   In your company, how far up the executive ladder do you believe a
        black can go?

	Black Managers	White Managers
Lower Management Level	17%	3%
Middle Management Level	44	17
Upper Management Level	26	30
Top; President; All the way; No limit	10	47
Doesn't know	2	3

19a.   Why is this? (Lower Management Level)

	Black Managers	White Managers
The company is not committed to an AAP; therefore, its employment policies are still discriminatory.	45%	80%
There aren't any blacks above the lower level because the firm is only practicing tokenism because of governmental pressures and laws.	28	0
The lack of blacks above the lower level indicates that blacks can go only this far.	14	0
Whites do not want blacks to have a great deal of power; thus they will not promote blacks above the lower managerial level.	9	20
Other	14	0

19b.   Why is this? (Middle Management Level)

	Black Managers	White Managers
The company has unfair employment policies for blacks;	32%	4%

thus middle management is the
limit; the company will promote a
few blacks to middle management
as a token gesture because of
governmental and social
pressures.

The company is not ready to accept blacks socially and to give blacks a great deal of power; thus middle management is the limit.	32	26
Blacks have been with the company for only a short period of time; therefore, they don't have the qualifications needed for higher managerial positions.	16	37
Respondent has not seen blacks above this level and those at this level are few.	10	7
The company has an effective AAP, i.e., fair hiring and promotional policies for all managers.	2	15
Other	2	2

19c.   Why is this? (Upper Management Level)

	Black Managers	White Managers
Blacks can make it to the lower level of upper management because of an acceptance of the gradual change, but they can't make it to senior upper level positions where attitudes haven't changed that much.	33%	20%
The "right" black (not militant, outspoken or aggressive, but a "supernigger") can make it to upper management; a few blacks can make it to the upper level of management so that the firm can say, "Look what we did," i.e., tokenism and showcasing.	27	13
The company has an effective AAP, i.e., fair hiring and promotional policies for all managers.	20	39
Blacks can make it to the upper level of management, but not to extremely senior positions	7	11

because of the few number of
positions available at that level
that require proven loyalty,
experience, and dedication to the
firm.

Because blacks are not considered social equals they can't make it to extremely senior positions where social intercourse becomes very important at this level.	7	11
Blacks can make it to the upper level of management, but not to the Presidency because of opposition from the stockholders, or Board of Directors, or some customers with large accounts, or any combination.	3	13
Blacks can make it to the upper level of management because they have the ability, intelligence, and knowledge to do so.	3	4

19d.   Why is this? (President)

	Black Managers	White Managers
The company has an effective AAP, i.e., fair hiring and promotional policies for all managers.	39%	93%
Blacks can go to the top, even the Presidency, because they have the ability, intelligence and knowledge.	39	3
Blacks can make it if they are superniggers; blacks must be much better than whites.	15	1
Social and governmental pressures combined with the success of blacks makes it possible for blacks to reach the top level; the present trend in social pressures is toward having blacks; therefore, they have unlimited opportunities.	8	3
Other	8	0

20. Many companies indicate that they want to do the "right thing" about hiring and promoting black managers. But what does doing "the right thing" involve? (First right thing)

	Black Managers	White Managers
Hire and promote strictly on the basis of qualification for the job	22%	41%
Make special recruiting and training efforts among blacks	50	44
Practice positive (reverse) discrimination	9	1
Give careful attention to the promotion of qualified blacks	12	11
Do nothing	0	0
Other	7	4

20a. Many companies indicate that they want to do "the right thing" about hiring and promoting black managers. But what does doing "the right thing" involve? (Second right thing)

	Black Managers	White Managers
Hire and promote strictly on the basis of qualification for the job	13%	10%
Make special recruiting and training efforts among blacks	22	20
Practice positive (reverse) discrimination	6	5
Give careful attention to the promotion of qualified blacks	32	22

20b. Many companies indicate that they want to do "the right thing" about hiring and promoting black managers. But what does doing "the right thing" involve? (Third right thing)

	Black Managers	White Managers
Hire and promote strictly on the basis of qualification for the job	10%	6%
Make special recruiting and training efforts among blacks	9	5
Practice positive (reverse) discrimination	9	8
Give careful attention to the promotion of qualified blacks	14	11

21. Would you advise a young black man or woman just out of school or college to enter the business world?

	Black Managers
Yes	96%
No	4

21a. What would you say is the *best way for young blacks to achieve high managerial positions*?

	Black Managers
Blacks should always work hard at whatever they are doing and do it well; blacks must be better than whites.	38%
Blacks should set priorities and goals, then vigorously pursue them; blacks should always strive for more and not be complacent and satisfied—they should use their personal initiative and be aggressive.	22
Blacks should obtain degrees in business, law, and the like.	18
Blacks should become well educated and develop their skills.	18
Blacks should not allow whites to deal unfairly with them; blacks should realize what is expected of them without losing their identity.	11
Learn the rules of the game and play them.	11
Blacks should select large, progressive, liberal companies.	7
Blacks should know and stay abreast of their business.	5
Blacks should set up their own companies—they should be self-employed.	4
Blacks should learn their limits and abilities.	2
Doesn't know	6
Other	10

APPENDIX D

Supplementary Tables

TABLE D-1   MOTHERS' AND FATHERS' EDUCATIONAL LEVELS (in %)

	Mothers		Fathers	
Educational Level	Black[a] Managers' (N = 115)	White Managers' (N = 155)	Black Managers' (N = 113)	White Managers' (N = 152)
Grade school	14	28	35	40
9th grade	4	1	3	2
10th grade	5	6	4	6
11th grade	8	2	5	1
12th grade	43	35	29	18
1 year of college	1	3	0	2
2 years of college	7	9	4	7
3 years of college	0	3	4	4
4 years or more of college	19	13	15	21
Total	101[b]	100	99	101

[a] The cases (N) do not equal the number of managers participating in the study because of missing data.

[b] The total percentages are over or under 100 because of rounding errors.

TABLE D-2   BEST OCCUPATION OF FATHERS WHEN MANAGERS WERE
TEENAGERS (in %)

Occupations	Black Managers'[a] Fathers (N = 115)	White Managers' Fathers (N = 154)
Unskilled laborer	20	8
Skilled laborer	21	14
Small business owner	10	10
Medium business owner	1	4
Large business owner	0	1
Low level supervisor/manager	5	12
Middle level supervisor/manager	3	9
Upper level supervisor/manager	0	6
Lawyer or doctor	2	4
Clergyman	3	0
School principal or professor	2	2
School teacher or counselor	1	1
Other professional: engineers, real estate broker, accountant, publisher/editor, statistician	5	11
Governmental service	11	5
Large farm Owner	0	3
Small farm Owner	6	5
Dining room waiter or porter for the railroad	8	0
Didn't have a father	3	5
Doesn't know	4	1
Other	2	1
Total[b]	106	102

[a] The cases (N) do not equal the number of managers participating in the study because of missing data.

[b] The total percentages are over or under 100 because of rounding errors.

TABLE D-3   LENGTH OF SERVICE OF *ALL* THE BLACK MANAGERS IN THE
COMPANIES (in %)

Companies	Number of Black Managers	Years in Service[a]			
		Mean Year(s)	Median Year(s)	Mode Year(s)	Range Year(s)
Ace Public Utility	508	13	11	1 (54)	1–36
Triple C Bank	111	7	4	2 (21)	1–20
Aunts Manufacturing	76	7	5	4 (12)	1–25
Ajax Manufacturing	3	7	6	0	6–12
Century Manufacturing	2	7	0	0	6–7
Deuce Public Utility	37	4	3	2 (11)	1–20
Triple A Bank	47	3	2	1 (11)	1–8
Cousins Manufacturing[b]	13	3	3	3 (6)	1–10

[a] All figures are rounded to the nearest year.
[b] Data are for only the managers who participated in this study.

TABLE D–4   WHY THE MANAGERS AGREE WITH THEIR COMPANIES
EMPLOYMENT POLICIES (in %)

Reasons	Black Managers ($N = 42$)	White Managers ($N = 128$)
Policies are fair	41	84
Agrees with AAP	29	10
Respondent's experiences, i.e., he/she has been treated fairly	12	0
Agrees with affirmative action for women	10	2
Agrees with policies but they need better implementation	7	2
Agrees with policies in general but does not agree with AAP	0	2
Other	14	5
Total[a]	113	105

[a] The total percentages are over 100 because several managers gave more than one reason and also because of rounding errors.

TABLE D–5   HOW THE MANAGERS' EMPLOYMENT DECISIONS DEVIATED FROM
COMPANIES' EMPLOYMENT POLICIES (in %)

Types of Deviations	Black Managers ($N = 32$)	White Managers ($N = 69$)
Overlooked seniority if the individual had a good education, potential, drive and initiative	45	13
Hired and promoted individuals when others recommended against it	33	11
Overlooked work experience (seniority), if the individual had the educational background	21	6
Overlooked educational requirements if the individual had seniority, drive and initiative	9	17
Gave higher salaries than policies indicated	9	8
Promoted equally qualified blacks before whites	9	0
Did not rely on tests as much as the company policy indicated they should	6	8
Gave people a second chance	6	3
Really can't say deviated because the policies are so broad and general	3	34
Other	0	6
Total[a]	141	106

[a] The total percentages are over 100 because some managers gave more than
one reason and also because of rounding errors.

TABLE D–6   WHY CORPORATIONS DO NOT REMOVE BLACKS
FROM THE COMMUNITY (in %)

Reasons	Black Managers ($N = 101$)
Before blacks can help the black community they need to work in white corporations to get the skills, training, and money needed.	35
It is not the case with the black people these respondents know; they have goals and objectives to help the black people and they do live in black areas.	20
Respondents do not believe in separatism.	17
The only way blacks can really make it in this society is through the corporate world.	10
Only those blacks who are "Toms" or who are showcasing will leave the community.	5
Blacks have to work and the jobs that are available are mostly in white firms.	4
The problem is that many times people are with or against and nothing in the middle.	3
Other.	13
Total[a]	107

[a] The total percentage is over 100 because several managers gave more than one reason.

TABLE D–7   ADVICE FOR LIVING A FREE AND PROSPEROUS
LIFE IN THIS SOCIETY (in %)

Advice	Black Managers ($N = 116$)
Blacks should become well-educated and develop their skills.	50
Blacks should be independent, believe in themselves, stand up for their rights, and have pride in themselves.	25
Blacks should set goals and standards, then vigorously pursue them.	16
Blacks should work hard at whatever they are doing or want to do; they should always do the job well.	15
Blacks cannot lead a free, prosperous life in this country at this time.	10
Blacks should find something they will be happy doing.	9
Blacks should have flexible attitudes in order to be able to function in different situations.	6
Blacks should be self-employed.	4
Blacks should learn as much as they can about their company, i.e., the goals, organization, policies, and so on.	3
Blacks should be highly critical of themselves; they should learn their abilities and limits.	3
Blacks should join large, progressive firms.	1
Blacks should use their color; black is beautiful now, but it might not be later.	1
Total[a]	143

[a] The total percentage is over 100 because many managers had several things they would advise blacks to do and also because of rounding errors.

TABLE D–8   WHY FORMING STRONG SOCIAL, POLITICAL, AND
ECONOMIC ORGANIZATIONS IS THE BEST PATH FOR BLACKS
TO PURSUE (in %)

Reasons	Black Managers ($N = 88$)
Statements that suggest that this is the most effective way to bring about social change in the U. S.; whites understand social, economic, and political pressures.	51
Blacks must be in a position of strength; the only way they can be accepted as equals is through unity.	26
For the present this is the best path; blacks must start from a power position, but believe that assimilation into white society would be the ultimate.	13
There are no advantages in a separate black nation; the ghetto is already an all-black community with little improvements; blacks don't want to lose their identity, which would happen if we assimilated completely into white society; thus, forming strong organizations is the best path.	11
Blacks do not have the money or resources to form their own separate black nations or to withdraw into the urban areas and form separate all-black communities.	6
Blacks just want a chance; they do not want separatism.	1
Respondents are not certain that this is the best path, but they think so.	1
Total[a]	109

[a] The total percentage is over 100 because some of the managers gave more than one reason.

APPENDIX E

Questions for Tables 5-3 and 5-4, Chapter 5

Questions for Table 5-3: the responses that would give the managers a score of 1 are shown in parentheses.

How do you explain the seeming underutilization of blacks in industry? (Responses related to Racial Discrimination)

Are there any reasons why blacks can't make it in the corporate world? (Yes—Responses related to Racial Discrimination)

Is being black a harmful, helpful, or irrelevant factor for promotion in business in general? (Harmful)

Is being white a harmful, helpful, or irrelevant factor for promotion in business in general? (Helpful)

Questions for Table 5-4: the responses that would give the managers a score of 1 are shown in parentheses.

How do you explain the incidence of black managers in your company? (Responses related to Racial Discrimination)

Do you believe your firm is more careful in promoting black employees than white employees because they want to be sure the blacks will succeed before promoting them? (Yes)

At the present time, how far up the executive ladder do you believe a qualified black can go in your company? (Negative comments about company policy)

Blacks must be a little better than others to get ahead in this company. (Agree or Strongly Agree)

In general, this company is only paying lip service to the idea of equal employment opportunities for blacks. (Agree or Strongly Agree)

Is being black a helpful, harmful, or irrelevant factor for promotion to supervisor and beyond in your firm? (Harmful)

Is being white a helpful, harmful, or irrelevant factor for promotion to supervisor and beyond in your firm? (Helpful)

Discrimination: Statistical Explanations

MULTIPLE REGRESSION ANALYSIS

Nine factors were originally used in the basic regression analysis formula. These were:

> Race (R)
> Job Duration (JD)
> Outside Job Experience and Duration (OJD)
> Age (A)
> Education (ED)
> Special Training (ST)
> Mothers' Educational Achievement (MED)
> Fathers' Educational Achievement (FED)
> Fathers' Occupational Achievement (FO)

The relationship of these factors to salary would be:

$$\text{Salary} = f(R, JD, OJD, A, ED, ST, MED, FED, FO)$$

With the expected additive effect, the regression formula would then be:

$$\text{Salary} = B_1 + B_2R + B_3JD + B_4OJD + B_5A + B_6ED + B_7ST + B_8MED + B_9FED + B_{10}FO$$

After running several regressions using the above variables, it became apparent that race, job duration at present firm, work experience at other firms related to present jobs, and educational levels were the only significant factors in the general regression equations. These factors were found significant using the T-score for each of the regression coefficients. The T-score is the ratio of the regression coefficient to its standard deviation. Using a one-tailed test at the .01 level of significance, the estimate coefficient will be significantly different from zero if the T-score exceeds 2.326. All the factors dropped out of the equation were not significant at the .10 level, and those remaining were significant at the .01 level. It should be noted that age was significant when job duration in present firm and work experience in other firms directly related to present job were removed from the equation but was not when they were included. Therefore, age was removed from the equation.

Separate equations are used for the black and white managers as individual groups. Once again, using a one-tailed test at the .01 level for whites and at the .01 level for blacks, the estimate coefficient will be significantly different from zero if the T-score exceeds 2.326. For white managers R^2 (amount of explained variance) was 34 percent and for blacks 37 percent. The F-scores for both equations were significant at the .001 (P) level. The two equations follow:

$$\text{Salary (blacks only)} = -1.2 + .36JD + .48ED + .090JD$$
$$\text{Salary (whites only)} = -4.9 + .52JD + 1.0ED + .310JD$$

A quick glance at the partial regression coefficients clearly shows that a unit change in any of the independent variables means a greater increase in salary for whites than for blacks—a clear sign of racial discrimination.

APPENDIX G

Questions for Table 8, Chapter 6

These 14 questions form the basis for the index on the white managers' racial attitudes, Table 6-8 in Chapter 6. The managers received a score of 1 for each of the responses in parentheses.

In general, I am reluctant to hire and promote blacks into important management positions. (Agree or Strongly Agree)

Most blacks who aspire to become managers in the business world do not have the personal characteristics needed to become successful management persons in this company. (Agree or Strongly Agree)

In general, blacks have low IQs and less technical and analytical competence. (Agree or Strongly Agree)

In general, blacks are pushy, loud, argumentative, arrogant, obnoxious, and aggressive. (Agree or Strongly Agree)

What are some of the bad characteristics you have observed about black managers? (Negative Stereotyped Responses)

How do you explain the seeming underutilization of blacks in industry? (Negative Stereotyped Responses)

How do you explain the incidence of black managers in your company? (Negative Stereotyped Responses)

Why blacks can or cannot make it in the corporate world today. (Negative Stereotyped Responses)

Why blacks are pressing too hard. (Negative Stereotyped Responses)

A black, once promoted, could not be demoted, even if inadequate in his new role, without undeserved charges of discrimination. (Agree or Strongly Agree)

There may be a few exceptions, but in general blacks are pretty much alike. (Agree or Strongly Agree)

I can hardly imagine myself marrying a black. (Agree or Strongly Agree)

Even though there are some exceptions, most blacks have annoying and offensive faults. (Agree or Strongly Agree)

I probably would not choose a black person for promotion if an equally qualified nonblack were available. (Agree or Strongly Agree)

References

Albrook, Robert J. "Why It's Harder to Keep Good Executives." *Fortune,* November, 1968, pp. 137–180.

Alexander, Clifford. "Jobs, the Heart of the Problem." *MBA,* **5** (1971), 6–16.

Anderson, Bernard E. *The Negro in the Public Utility Industries.* Philadelphia: University of Pennsylvania Press, 1970.

Anderson, Charles H. *White Protestant Americans: From National Origins to Religious Groups.* Englewood Cliffs: Prentice-Hall, 1970.

Argyris, Chris. "T-Groups for Organizational Effectiveness." *Harvard Business Review,* **42** (1964), 60–74.

———. "A Few Words in Advance." In Alfred J. Morrow, ed., *The Failure of Success.* New York: American Management Association, 1972.

Barnard, Chester I. *The Functions of the Executive.* Cambridge: Harvard University Press, 1948.

Baron, Harold M. "The Web of Urban Racism." In Louis L. Knowles and Kenneth Prewitts, eds., *Institutional Racism in America.* Englewood Cliffs: Prentice-Hall, 1969.

Beattie, C. F. "Minority Men in a Majority Setting: Middle Level Francophones at Mid-Career in the Anglophone Public Service of Canada." Unpublished doctoral dissertation. Berkeley: University of California, 1970.

Bendix, Reinhard. *Work and Authority in Industry.* New York: Wiley, 1956.

———, and Seymour M. Lipset. *Class, Status, and Power.* Glencoe: Free Press, 1953.

———, and Seymour M. Lipset. *Social Mobility in an Industrial Society.* Berkeley and Los Angeles: University of California Press, 1962.

Blake, Robert R., and Jane S. Mouton. *The Managerial Grid.* Houston: Gulf Publishing Company, 1964.

Blauner, Robert. *Alienation and Freedom: The Factory Worker and His Industry.* Chicago: University of Chicago Press, 1964.

———. *Racial Oppression in America.* New York: Harper & Row, 1972.

Bowman, Garda W. "The Image of a Promotable Person in Business Enterprise." Unpublished doctoral dissertation. New York: New York University, 1962.

———. "What Helps or Harms Promotability?" *Harvard Business Review,* **42** (1964), 6–26, 184–196.

Bray, Douglas W.   "The Assessment Center Method of Appraising Management Potential." In J. W. Blood, ed., *The Personnel Job in a Changing World.* New York: American Management Association, 1964.

―――.   "The Assessment Center: Opportunities for Women." *Personnel,* 48 (1971), 30–34.

―――, and Richard J. Campbell.   "Assessment Centers: An Aid in Management Selection." *Personnel Administration,* 30 (1967), 6–13.

―――, and Richard J. Campbell.   "Selection of Salesmen by Means of an Assessment Center." *Journal of Applied Psychology,* 52 (1968), 36–41.

―――, and Donald L. Grant.   "The Assessment Center in the Measurement of Potential for Business Management." *Psychological Monographs,* 80 (1966), 17.

―――, and Donald L. Grant.   "Contributions of the Interview to Assessment of Management Potential." *Journal of Applied Psychology,* 53 (1969), 24–34.

―――, Richard J. Campbell, and Donald L. Grant.   *The Management Recruit: Formative Years in Business.* New York: Wiley-Interscience, 1974.

Brewer, Weldon M.   *Behind the Promises: Equal Employment Opportunity in the Federal Government.* Washington, D. C.: Public Interest Group, 1972.

Brown, William H.   "The EEOC's Chairman Comments on the Persistence of Racism." *MBA,* 6 (1972), 12–16, 104.

Bullock, Paul.   *Equal Opportunity in Employment.* Los Angeles: University of California, Institute of Industrial Relations, 1966.

Byham, William C.   "Assessment Centers for Spotting Future Managers." *Harvard Business Review,* 48 (1970), 150–160.

―――, and G. C. Thornton.   "Assessment Centers: A New Aid in Management Selection." *Studies in Personnel Psychology,* 2 (1970), 21–35.

Campbell, Angus.   *White Attitudes Towards Black People.* Ann Arbor: University of Michigan Institute for Social Research, 1971.

Campbell, John P., Marvin D. Dunnette, Edward E. Lawler, and Karl E. Weich. *Managerial Behavior, Performance, and Effectiveness.* New York: McGraw-Hill, 1970.

Campbell, R. J.   "Attitudes, Expectations, and Career Mobility." Unpublished article. New York: AT&T, 1973.

Caplan, Robert D., and John R. P. French, Jr.   "Organizational Stress and Industrial Strain." In Alfred J. Morrow, ed., *The Failure of Success.* New York: American Management Association, 1972.

Caplow, Theodore.   *The Sociology of Work.* New York: McGraw-Hill, 1954.

Clark, Kenneth B.   "A Psychologist Looks at Discrimination Patterns." *MBA,* 6 (1972), 33–34.

Coates, Charles H., and Roland J. Pellegrin.   "Executives and Supervisors: A Situational Theory of Differential Mobility." *Social Forces,* 35 (1956), 121–126.

Collins, Randall.   "Employment and Education: A Study in the Dynamics of Stratification." Unpublished doctoral dissertation. Berkeley: University of California, 1968.

Crochett, Harry J., Jr. "Psychological Origins of Mobility." In Neil J. Smelser and Seymour M. Lipset, eds., *Social Structure, Social Mobility and Economic Development.* Chicago: Aldine, 1965.

Dalton, Melville. "Informal Factors in Career Achievement." *American Journal of Sociology,* 56 (1951), 407–415.

Dodd, W. E. "Summary of IBM Assessment Validations." Paper presented as part of the symposium, "Validity of Assessment Centers," at the 79th Annual Convention of the American Psychological Association, 1971.

Douglass, Frederick. Quoted in *Black Scholar*, October, 1970, p. 15.

Drake, St. Clair. "The Ghettoization of Negro Life." *Daedelus* (Fall, 1965), 119.

Drucker, Peter F. *The Practice of Management.* New York: Harper & Row, 1954.

———. *Managing for Results.* New York: Harper & Row, 1964.

Duster, Troy. "Aims and Control of the Universities: A Comparative Study of Sweden and the U.S." Unpublished paper. Berkeley: University of California, 1971.

Ferman, Louis A. *The Negro and Equal Employment Opportunities.* New York: Praeger, 1968.

———, et al. *Negroes and Jobs.* Ann Arbor: University of Michigan Press, 1968.

Fletcher, Linda P. *The Negro in the Insurance Industry.* Philadelphia: University of Pennsylvania Press, 1970.

Fogel, Walter A. *Labor Market Obstacles to Minority Job Gains.* Los Angeles: University of California, Institute of Industrial Relations, 1968.

———. *The Negro in the Meat Industry.* Philadelphia: University of Pennsylvania Press, 1970.

Ford, Robert N. *Motivation Through the Work Itself.* New York: American Management Association, 1969.

———. "Job Enrichment Lessons from AT&T." *Harvard Business Review,* 51 (1973), 96–106.

Foulkes, Fred K. *Creating More Meaningful Work.* New York: American Management Association, 1969.

Friedlander, Frank, and Eugene Walton. "Positive and Negative Motivations Toward Work." *Administrative Science Quarterly,* 9 (1964), 194–207.

Frazier, E. Franklin. *Black Bourgeoisie.* New York: Free Press, 1957.

Freeman, Evelyn S., and Charles L. Fields. *A Study of Black Male Professionals in Industry.* Washington, D.C.: U.S. Labor Dept., 1972.

———, and Charles L. Fields. "Black Professionals: The Gap is Not Closing." *MBA,* 6 (1972), 73–84 (a).

Ginzberg, Eli, et al. *Occupational Choice.* New York: Columbia University Press, 1951.

Goodwin, Leonard. *Do the Poor Want to Work?* Washington, D.C.: Brookings Institution, 1972.

Gordon, Robert A., and James E. Howell. *Higher Education for Business.* New York: Columbia University Press, 1959.

Gourlay, Jack G. *The Negro Salaried Worker*. New York: American Management Association, 1965.

Gurin, G., J. Veroff, and S. Field. *Americans View Their Mental Health*. New York: Basic Books, 1960.

Havemen, Ernest, and Patricia S. West. *They Went to College*. New York: Harcourt Brace, 1952.

Herzberg, Frederick. *Work and the Nature of Man*. Cleveland: World, 1966.

Hughes, Charles L. *Goal Setting*. New York: American Management Association, 1965.

Hughes, E. C. *Men and Their Work*. New York: Free Press, 1958.

Jackson, W. Kirk. "Placement Director." *MBA*, 3 (1969), 6.

Jennings, Eugene. *The Mobile Manager*. Ann Arbor: University of Michigan Press, 1967.

Jet. Gallup Poll. December 7, 1972, p. 30.

Keller, Suzanne. *Beyond the Ruling Class: Strategic Elites in Modern Society*. New York: Random House, 1953.

Kidder, David E., et al. *Negro and White Perceptions of Company Employment Policy in the South*. Springfield, Va.: National Technical Information Service, 1971.

Krislov, Samuel. *The Negro in Federal Employment*. Minneapolis: University of Minnesota Press, 1967.

Likert, Rensis. *New Patterns of Management*. New York: McGraw-Hill, 1961.

———. *The Human Organization: Its Management and Value*. New York: McGraw-Hill, 1967.

Lynd, Robert S., and Helen M. Lynd. *Middletown*. New York: Harcourt Brace, 1929.

Marx, Gary. *Protest and Prejudice*. New York: Harper & Row, 1967.

McGregor, Douglas. *The Human Side of Enterprise*. New York: McGraw-Hill, 1960.

Miller, William, Ed. *Men in Business*. Cambridge: Harvard University Press, 1952.

Mills, C. Wright. *The New Men of Power*. New York: Harcourt Brace, 1963.

Molotch, Harvey, and Linda Wolf. "Racism in Dominant Organizations: Scheme for Instituting Change." Unpublished paper. Santa Barbara: University of California, 1972.

Morgan, John S., and Richard L. Van Dyke. *White Collar Blacks: A Breakthrough?* New York: American Management Association, 1970.

Morrow, Alfred J., ed. *The Failure of Success*. New York: American Management Association, 1972.

Moses, Joel L. "Assessment Center Performance and Management Progress." Paper presented as part of the symposium, "Validity of Assessment Centers," at the 79th Annual Convention of the American Psychological Association, 1971.

Newcomer, Mable. *The Big Business Executive: The Factors that Made Him.* New York: Columbia University Press, 1955.

Northrup, Herbert R. *The Negro in the Aerospace Industry.* Philadelphia: University of Pennsylvania Press, 1968.

————. *The Negro in the Automobile Industry.* Philadelphia: University of Pennsylvania Press, 1968. (a)

———— et. al., *Negro Employment in Basic Industry.* Philadelphia: University of Pennsylvania Press, 1970.

————. *The Negro in the Tobacco Industry.* Philadelphia: University of Pennsylvania Press, 1970. (a)

Odiorne, George S. *Management Decisions by Objectives.* Engelwood Cliffs: Prentice-Hall, 1969.

Packard, Vance. *The Pyramid Climbers.* New York: McGraw-Hill, 1962.

Peterson, R. E. "American College and University Enrollment Trends in 1971." A Technical Report Sponsored by the Carnegie Commission on Higher Education, June, 1972.

Porter, Lyman W. "A Study of Perceived Need Satisfactions in Bottom and Middle Management Jobs." *Journal of Applied Psychology,* **45** (1961), 1–10.

————. "Job Attitudes in Management. I. Perceived Deficiencies in Need Fulfillment as a Function of Job Level." *Journal of Applied Psychology,* **46** (1962), 375–384.

Poussaint, Alvin F. "The Negro American: His Self-Image and Integration." In Floyd B. Barbour, ed., *The Black Power Revolt.* Boston: Sargent, 1968.

Quay, William H. *The Negro in the Chemical Industry.* Philadelphia: University of Pennsylvania Press, 1969.

Quinn, R. P., L. K. Gordon, and J. M. Tabor. *The Decision to Discriminate: A Study of Executive Selection.* Ann Arbor: Institute for Social Research, 1968.

Rosenbloom, David H. "Equal Employment Opportunity: Another Strategy." *Personnel Administration and Public Personnel Review,* **1** (1972), 39–41.

Rowan, Carl. "A Defense of Job Quotas." *San Francisco Chronicle,* September 6, 1972, p. 9.

Rowan, Richard L. *The Negro in the Steel Industry.* Philadelphia: University of Pennsylvania Press, 1968.

Sayles, Leonard R., and George Strauss. *Human Behavior in Organizations.* Englewood Cliffs: Prentice-Hall, 1960.

Sexton, Patricia C. *Education and Income.* New York: Viking, 1961.

Silberman, Charles E. *Crisis in Black and White.* New York: Random House, 1964.

Smelser, Neil J., and Seymour M. Lipset, eds. *Social Structure, Social Mobility and Economic Development.* Chicago: Aldine, 1965.

Taussig, Frank W., and Carl S. Joslyn. *American Business Leaders.* New York: Macmillan, 1932.

Thieblot, Armand J., Jr. *The Negro in the Banking Industry*. Philadelphia: University of Pennsylvania Press, 1970.

U.S. Equal Employment Opportunity Commission. "Hearing Before U.S.E.E.O.C. on Discrimination in White Collar Employment." New York, January 15–18, 1968; Los Angeles, March, 1969.

————. "Second Annual Report, June 1, 1968."

————. "Third Annual Report, April 22, 1969."

U.S. Labor Department. "The Negro Job Situation: Has It Improved?" Special Labor Report No. 102.

Valentine, Charles A. *Black Studies and Anthropology: Scholarly and Political Interests in Afro-American Culture*. Reading: Addison-Wesley, 1972.

Vroom, Victor H. *Work and Motivation*. New York: Wiley, 1964.

————. *Motivation in Management*. New York: American Foundation for Management Research, 1965.

Warner, William L., and James C. Abeggelen. *Occupational Mobility in American Business and Industry*. Minneapolis: University of Minnesota Press, 1955.

————, and James C. Abeggelen. *Big Business Leaders in America*. New York: Harper & Row, 1963.

Wernimont, P. F., and J. P. Campbell. "Signs, Samples, and Criteria." *Journal of Applied Psychology,* **52** (1968), 372–376.

Wilensky, Harold L. "Measures and Effects of Social Mobility." In Neil J. Smelser and Seymour M. Lipset, eds., *Social Structure, Social Mobility and Economic Development*. Chicago: Aldine, 1966.

————. "Careers, Counseling, and the Curriculum." *Journal of Human Resources,* **2** (1967), 19–40.

————, and Charles N. Lebeaux. *Industrial Society and Social Welfare*. New York: Free Press, 1965.

————, and Jack Ladinsky. "From Religious Community to Occupational Group: Structural Assimilation Among Professors, Lawyers, and Engineers." *American Sociological Review,* **32** (1967), 541–561.

Work in America. Report of a Special Task Force to the Secretary of Health, Education, and Welfare. Cambridge: MIT Press, 1973.

Index